I0099665

Migration diplomacy in the Middle East and North Africa

Manchester University Press

Migration diplomacy in the Middle East and North Africa

Power, mobility, and the state

Gerasimos Tsourapas

MANCHESTER UNIVERSITY PRESS

Copyright © Gerasimos Tsourapas 2021

The right of Gerasimos Tsourapas to be identified as
the author of this work has been asserted by them in
accordance with the Copyright, Designs and Patents
Act 1988.

Published by Manchester University Press
Oxford Road, Manchester M13 9PL

www.manchesteruniversitypress.co.uk

British Library Cataloguing-in-Publication Data
A catalogue record for this book is available from the
British Library

ISBN   978 1 5261 3209 3   hardback
ISBN   978 1 5261 7902 9   paperback

First published 2021

The publisher has no responsibility for the persistence or
accuracy of URLs for any external or third-party internet
websites referred to in this book, and does not guarantee
that any content on such websites is, or will remain,
accurate or appropriate.

Typeset
by New Best-set Typesetters Ltd

'Thus the inhabitants of a more populous city are more prosperous than their counterparts in a less populous one: the judge in the former being better off than the judge in the latter; the trader, than the trader; the craftsman, than the craftsman; the man in the street, than the man in the street; the prince, than the prince; and the policeman, than the policeman.'

Ibn Khaldun, *Muqaddimah* (1377)

Contents

Figures and tables

Figures

Tables

Preface

The rise of varied forms of cross-border mobility into, out of, and across the Middle East and North Africa has generated both tensions and opportunities for states within the region. Not surprisingly, Arab and non-Arab states alike have developed complex policies that engage with labour emigration and immigration, forced displacement, as well as diasporic mobilisation. One dimension of the politics of migrants, refugees, and diasporas in the Middle East that has received less academic attention concerns the interplay between states' migration and foreign policymaking. How does cross-border mobility feature in Middle East states' diplomatic strategies? This book aims to enhance existing scholarly work, which has yet to engage in a sustained manner with the international politics of migration in the Global South, by exploring four dimensions of *migration diplomacy* in the contemporary Middle East. It examines how emigration-related processes become embedded in governmental practices of establishing and maintaining power; how states engage with migrant and diasporic communities residing in the West; how oil-rich Arab monarchies have extended their support for a number of sending-states' ruling regimes via cooperation on labour migration; and, finally, how labour and forced migrants may serve as instruments of political leverage. Drawing on multi-sited fieldwork and data collection and employing a range of case studies across the Middle East and North Africa, the book adds to existing understandings of regional migration governance in the Global South. It identifies how the management of cross-border mobility in the Middle East is not primarily driven by legal, moral, or human rights considerations but dictated by state actors' key concern – political power.

Acknowledgements

A number of friends and colleagues contributed to this research project as it evolved since my time at SOAS, University of London into this monograph. Work on migration diplomacy has grown exponentially over the last few years, with a number of scholars building on the pioneering work of Hélène Thiollet, Ahmet İçduygu, and Kelly M. Greenhill, all outstanding and supportive colleagues who graciously helped me find my own voice in the field. I am grateful to the numerous discussions with Fiona B. Adamson, with whom I worked together to develop this concept further across a range of publications. Since my early days as a graduate student, Fiona has generously offered her time to discussing my work and has been instrumental in the development of the arguments presented in this monograph. I hope to continue learning from her passion for research on migration, her support for early career scholars, and her respect for the discipline.

The monograph itself has been fortunate to be read by a range of scholars, all of whom offered constructive feedback that improved the final product considerably. A workshop at the University of Birmingham brought together an impressive group of colleagues – Fiona Adamson, May Darwich, Irene Fernández-Molina, Saipira Furstenberg, Katharina Natter, and Adam Quinn – who offered their time reading and reviewing the monograph. Ibrahim Awad, James F. Hollifield, Maria Koinova, and Covadonga Meseguer also provided key advice that allowed me to improve the monograph's argumentation and framing. I have been lucky to become part of supportive communities across both institutions that I have been affiliated with – SOAS, University of London and the University of Birmingham – and to benefit tremendously from generous opportunities they offered to fund additional fieldwork as I collected material for this project.

I would be remiss to not acknowledge the support of numerous fellowships by the British Academy and the Council for British Research in the Levant, without which I would not have been able to finish this project. Partner institutions across the Middle East – particularly the American University in Cairo – have been instrumental in allowing me to engage in fieldwork across a number of different countries amidst challenging contexts. The monograph brings together past writings that have been presented or published at a range of venues – thus, I remain immensely grateful to countless anonymous reviewers, conference organisers, discussants, and participants, as well as to journal editorial teams for believing in this research agenda and supporting it over the past few years. The main drafting of the book itself occurred in the welcoming context of the Center for European Studies at Harvard University, which provided a wonderful home for me during the 2019–20 academic year.

Needless to say, the arguments presented here have been raised across a range of academic conference workshops, panels, and roundtables in Europe, North America, and the Middle East. I am grateful to participants for their comments and their help in improving this work. The book would not have been possible without the support and unending patience of the dedicated Manchester University Press team. I was very lucky to work with Rob Byron, in particular, who has been a wonderful editor that believed in the project from the very beginning, as well as a number of supportive anonymous reviewers whose careful reading of the manuscript and astute comments improved it significantly. Caroline McPherson has done an outstanding job working through the multiple iterations of the text, which is now much better for it. Finally, I owe a debt of gratitude to my family, particularly Fergus Reoch, for putting up with many discussions on the logistics of migration politics in the Middle East and the countless evenings and weekends that I dedicated to research and writing.

Introduction

In June 1965, alarmed by frequent reports of Egyptian teachers inciting political activism among Libyan students, King Idris, the country's first post-independence ruler, decided it was time to act: he arranged for secret police to be dispatched to secondary schools across the country. Since the mid-1950s, Egyptian professionals dispatched throughout the Arab world were frequently accused of acting as political agents of the Egyptian regime, but never had a host country gone through such an extreme step to verify these claims. Placed among young secondary school students, members of the Libyan secret police quickly reported back that the Egyptians were, indeed, engaged in disseminating revolutionary ideas through their teachings. Across Libyan schools, they had been discussing ideas of anti-colonialism and Arab unity, inspired by Egyptian President Gamal Abdel Nasser's own regional political agenda. By early July 1965, eighty Egyptian teachers seconded to Libya were deported, their contracts duly terminated. Yet Cairo remained nonchalant: despite harsh warnings from British diplomats in Benghazi, over six hundred Egyptians continued to be employed across Libya, while more teachers were later recruited from Cairo. The Libyan case was far from an exception, with Egyptian migrants engaging in political activism across the Arab world, from North Africa to the Gulf. In fact, for much of the twentieth century, migration and foreign policy were intricately intertwined across the Middle East.

As the international politics of migration become more complex, there appears a growing need to understand how citizens' cross-border mobility features in states' domestic and foreign policymaking, particularly within non-democratic contexts. This is a pressing matter for understanding the politics of migration across the Global South, where most of the world's durable authoritarian regimes are situated. For many states in the Middle East and North Africa (which, in this book, will be referred to as the Middle East for ease of reading) in particular, migration continues to be an intrinsically political act, and the regulation of cross-border mobility remains tied to ruling regimes' policy priorities. On 19 November 2016, for instance, Azza Soliman, the Egyptian founder of the Centre for Egyptian Women's Legal Assistance, made her way to Cairo International Airport. She was planning to take a flight to Jordan in order to participate in a workshop on human rights, but it was not meant to be; Soliman was informed by authorities that she had been banned from travelling outside Egypt, together with hundreds of Egyptian citizens (Michaelson 2016). A few months earlier, in a similar attempt at a clampdown on political dissent in Turkey, the Erdoğan regime banned thousands of academics from travelling abroad (Cockburn 2016) – replicating Arab states' strategies of emigration restriction that span back decades.

But even citizens of autocracies that are living abroad find it exceedingly difficult to 'exit' the grip of their homelands: for instance, the October 2018 assassination of Jamal Khashoggi, a Saudi journalist who had emigrated to the United States, inside Saudi Arabia's Istanbul consulate served as a brutal demonstration of how migrants and diaspora groups remain within reach of the long arm of authoritarian states. Similar processes were not uncommon across most North African post-independent states of the twentieth century, as Libya, Tunisia, Morocco, and Algeria developed intricate mechanisms of monitoring, intimidating, and punishing citizens abroad. Even today, autocracies' attempts to control their citizens abroad are widespread – from Central Asian republics' targeting of political exiles, to African states' close monitoring of diaspora activities. In the Middle East, most cases do not make international headlines – such as Kuwait's extradition of eight migrants who belonged to the Muslim Brotherhood to Egypt in July 2019, where they are currently awaiting long prison sentences.

At the same time, the regulation of mobility between countries of origin, transit, and destination is often beholden to the shifting nature of inter-regime relations: amicable relations between sending- and host-states have contributed to inter-state cooperation that increased migrant stock and bilateral migration flows between numerous Middle East states: for instance, Syrians have historically been able to engage in short-term labour emigration into Lebanon and the Gulf Cooperation Council states, while hundreds of thousands of Yemenis have secured employment in Saudi Arabia for much of the second half of twentieth century. At the same time, however, the breakdown of inter-regime relations has also had repercussions on host-states' treatment of migrant workers: the cooling of Saudi–Yemeni relations in 1990, for example, led to the immediate expulsion of the entire Yemeni migrant community living and working inside the Kingdom. Finally, migrant and refugee communities are often employed as bargaining chips in numerous diplomatic processes – the Gaddafi regime often used Libya's migrant and refugee communities as an instrument of leverage against Arab and European states; similarly, Lebanese workers across the Gulf have often been victims of the Arab monarchies' strategies against Hezbollah.

Taking note of historic and recent examples of migration politics across the broader Middle East, there exists a pressing need for a deeper understanding of how cross-border mobility features in regional competition for political power and, more particularly, in the diplomatic strategies of migrant and refugee sending, transit-, and host-states. Yet, the field currently lacks an adequate comparative framework for comprehending how Middle East autocracies adapt to migration in response to shifting domestic and foreign policy exigencies. Ultimately, the management of cross-border mobility becomes emmeshed into questions of nation-building, subject-making processes, or authoritarian regime durability that affect elites' decision-making processes; at the same time, matters of state–diaspora relations, the shifting nature of alliances within the broader Middle East, as well as the position of states within the broader international order similarly shape patterns of international migration. This points to an intriguing yet under-researched phenomenon within the literature on international relations and the politics of cross-border mobility: how does cross-border mobility feature in Middle East states' diplomatic strategies?

Cross-border mobility in world politics

Within the broader literature on international relations and cross-border mobility, researchers have yet to fully identify how such movements feature into states' foreign policymaking. Arguably, this can be attributed to two main factors: firstly, an inadequate attention to the need for developing a framework that takes sending-, transit-, and host-state diplomatic strategies into account and, secondly, a largely artificial division of the relevant literature into the study of labour and forced migration as separate and distinct phenomena. In terms of the former, research has identified how international relations scholarship on migration chooses 'to focus on the consequences of immigration in wealthy, migrant-receiving societies, and to ignore the causes and consequences of migration in origin countries' (Castles, Miller, and De Haas 2014, 26). Boucher and Gest have identified that 'the most glaring shortcoming of contemporary migration policy regime typologies is a general reluctance to include non-OECD countries' (Boucher and Gest 2014, 7). In one sense, this is indicative of a broader trend within international relations that has only recently begun to examine the interplay between migration and inter-state politics as a separate field of inquiry (Hollifield 2012, 351–2). The realist and neorealist tradition, in particular, approached labour migration more as a 'low' politics issue, which was expected to have commonalities with other domestic economic and social issues, rather than a 'high' politics issue of national and international security.

That said, early scholars of dependency theory focused on migration's importance for the 'development of underdevelopment' (Frank 1966), and examined the contribution of cross-border mobility to uneven trade relations between 'developed (migration receiving) and less-developed (migration sending) countries' (Hollifield 2012, 366; cf. Sassen 1988). Similarly, Wallerstein and other world-systems theorists identified that labour migration sustains 'relations of domination' between core and periphery nations confirming the expectations of mainstream international relations' theory regarding stronger powers exerting pressure on weaker ones (Castles, Miller, and De Haas 2014, 33). Yet these approaches do not examine the role of individual states or governments: structuralist scholars, as well as theorists rooted in Marxist political economy, conceptualise international migration flows more as resulting from economic interests operating across the domestic and international systems, rather than driven by sovereign states' policies. Migration scholars have also historically tended to marginalise the role of the state altogether: 'the most striking weakness in migration theories drawn from the social sciences,' wrote Teitelbaum in 2001, 'is their failure to deal in a serious way with government action in initiating, selecting, restraining, and ending international migration movements' (Teitelbaum 2001, 26).

This is not to undermine a line of international politics scholars that critically examine the use of immigration and refugee policy within the evolving Cold War context, and beyond. A number of researchers have identified the foreign policy underpinnings of the United States' policy, with Washington considering refugees 'a weapon in the cold war' (Loescher and Scanlan 1986; Zolberg 1988, 661; Munz and Weiner 1997; Adamson 2006, 190). Beyond their aiding of 'lone individuals crossing borders to seek political freedom in the West' (Stedman and Tanner 2004, 5), host-states have also used refugees instrumentally in military conflicts. In the Middle East, the status of Palestinian refugees served as a strategic asset for Arab states' ongoing struggle against Israel (Hinnebusch 2003, 157); in the Rwandan and Pakistani contexts, humanitarian aid to refugee camps fuelled violence by providing legitimacy and support to militants (Lischer 2003). In fact, research has demonstrated the wide impact of refugees in the diffusion and exacerbation of conflict (Lischer 2015), with Kaldor including displacement as a form of post-1989 'new wars' in the Balkans, sub-Saharan Africa, and elsewhere (Kaldor 2013). Beyond refugee movements, scholars of the development of the European project have long established the importance of states' immigration policy within a broader context of inter-state cooperative relations (cf. Moravcsik 1998).

Within the literature on the securitisation of immigration and refugee policy, two research agendas have developed that may also shed some light on the importance of migration as a foreign policy instrument. Firstly, a small group of researchers on refugees examines issue-linkage strategies and suggests that 'win-win' strategies may convince Global North states to continue providing support for protecting refugees in the South. As Betts argues, 'in the absence of altruistic commitment by Northern states to support refugees in the South, issue-linkage has been integral in achieving international cooperation on refugees' (Betts and Loescher 2011, 20; Betts 2017). Secondly, work on leverage suggests that sending-states are also able to proceed unilaterally, aiming at extracting resources from target-states that fear being overwhelmed by migrants or refugees. As Greenhill demonstrates, host-states may employ deportation in order to create targeted migrant or refugee 'crises' in liberal democracies of the Global North that, through fear of being 'capacity-swamped', are likely to comply with these states' demands (Greenhill 2003; 2010). As a result, states such as Libya have been able to pursue issue-linkage strategies that link the management of cross-border population mobility to extracting foreign policy and economic benefits (Paoletti 2010; Tsourapas 2017a).

Yet, both research agendas examine host-states' refugee foreign policymaking from the point of view of the Global North (cf. Hollifield 2012), via largely Eurocentric interpretations of security and international relations as it relates to North American or European states. The extent of scholarly engagement with the foreign policy importance of immigration and refugee policy is not reflected in the study of emigration politics. This is partly to due to the fact that many sending-states were authoritarian and were expected to restrict – rather than encourage – population mobility. This was a predominantly Cold War perspective, formed at a time when 'communist countries rightly feared a mass exodus of dissatisfied citizens, while many people living under communist rule secretly hoped for an opportunity to leave' (Munz and Weiner 1997, vii; cf. Dowty 1989). While this perspective accurately described a number of non-democratic states' emigration policies at the time, including Cuba, China, and the Soviet bloc countries, it also obscured the intricacies of many communist regimes' emigration practices: Tito's Yugoslavia, for instance, was a Marxist–Leninist regime that had also adopted a liberal emigration policy since the 1960s (Kosinski 1978). Communist regimes' cross-border mobility management and, in particular, short-term high-skilled migration across states of the 'Iron Curtain' remains an under-studied phenomenon (cf. Babiracki 2015). More importantly, however, this perspective also disregarded non-communist authoritarian regimes, such as Turkey or Morocco, which developed intricate labour emigration policies from the 1950s onwards. Until today, states in the Global South were seen as more likely to restrict citizens' emigration than either established liberal states (Messina and Lahav 2006, 24–30), or emerging democracies (Massey 1999). The binary between liberal democracies that keep their borders open to emigration and autocracies that are expected to exclude such opportunities to their citizens became more prominent with the dramatic events of the fall of the Berlin Wall:

> Democratisation and political liberalisation of authoritarian regimes have enabled people to leave who previously were denied the right to exit. An entire region of the world, ranging from Central Europe to the Chinese border, had imprisoned those who sought to emigrate. Similar restrictions continue to operate for several of the remaining communist regimes [in 1992]. If and when the regimes of North Korea and China liberalise, another large region of the world will allow its citizens to leave. (Weiner 1992, 92)

Research on emigration was gradually introduced into international relations scholarship via pioneering post-Cold War social sciences work on transnationalism and belonging (Basch, Schiller, and Szanton Blanc 1994; Schiller, Basch, and Blanc 1995), which inspired a long line of scholars working on the politics of diaspora communities (Adamson and Demetriou 2007; Shain 2007; Varadarajan 2010). The literature on diaspora politics identified how migrant communities abroad may constitute developmental or political assets for sending-states (Østergaard-Nielsen 2003c; Kapur 2010). Scholars also identify their particular foreign policy importance along two lines: a first group of scholars employs diasporas as their unit of analysis, and theorises on diasporas' foreign policy repercussions for the sending-state and its international relations (King and Melvin 2006; Koinova 2012); a second group of scholars focuses on the sending-state, and how it is able to employ diaspora groups as lobbying instruments (Mearsheimer and Walt 2008; cf. Shain and Barth 2003). Yet, despite an evolving social sciences literature on 'emigration states' (Gamlen 2008; Fitzgerald 2009; Collyer 2013), foreign policy is almost exclusively examined via the diasporic lens. How may labour migration, or economically driven cross-state mobility, itself constitute an instrument of foreign policy?

Even so, the politics of labour migration have yet to be fully examined within the field of international relations, a gap that is starkly evident when one considers the extensive relevant literature within political economy and comparative politics. Discussions within these subfields involve the macroeconomic and developmental importance of migration, primarily through remittances, as well as its domestic political effects (Meseguer and Burgess 2014; Escribà-Folch, Meseguer, and Wright 2015). Emigration also constitutes an important outlet for political dissidents that aim to 'exit' an autocracy (Brubaker 1990; Ahmadov and Sasse 2016), a phenomenon which leads a number of emigration states to develop complex extraterritorial policies aimed at silencing its emigrant population abroad (Moss 2016b; Dalmasso et al. 2017). That said, a number of questions remain unanswered with regard to emigration states' foreign polices: can we also identify emigration of regime loyalists, rather than merely dissenters, and how may that affect a state's standing abroad? If an emigration state is able to fulfil specific countries' needs in foreign labour, how may that feature in its foreign policy? Finally, are countries of destination able to accrue foreign policy gains from an emigration state's reliance on remittances? A number of questions on the interplay between foreign and emigration policy have yet to be clearly addressed.

Moving to work on refugees, how does forced migration affect the politics of transit- and host-states and, in particular, how do the latter employ the presence of refugees in their foreign policy decision-making? A number of international relations scholars has attempted to address these questions, albeit not systematically. As Betts and Loescher argue, 'only relatively isolated pockets of theoretically informed literature have emerged on the international politics of forced migration', while the study of refugee politics has yet to form part of mainstream international relations (Betts and Loescher 2011, 12–13). As previously discussed, scholars pioneered empirical work on the politics of forced migration (Gordenker 1987; Zolberg 1989), primarily within the context of inter-state conflict. Within the Cold War context in particular, research identified how superpower rivalry resulted in forced displacement across developing countries of the Third World (Zolberg, Suhrke, and Aguayo 1989).

At the same time, the socio-economic and political risks perceived to be associated with hosting large numbers of refugees have led to states' lukewarm response in tackling the problem of forced migration (Zolberg 1989, 415; Loescher 1996, 8). This also highlights some of the main problems behind the development of a functional global refugee regime (Betts 2011), as 'states have a legal obligation to support refugees on their own territory, [but] they have no legal obligation to support refugees on the territory of other states' (Betts and Loescher 2011, 19). Tackling this dichotomy lies at the heart of host-states' political engagement with forced migration. For historical and structural reasons, states across the Global South feature the large majority of refugee populations, which creates a power asymmetry with seemingly unaffected Global North states. Yet, Global North states continue to provide economic support for the governments of refugee host-states in the Global South in an act of 'calculated kindness' (Loescher and Scanlan 1986; cf. Arar 2017b). From a security perspective, they do so aiming to prevent the diffusion of forced displacement into their own territory, be it North America (Weiner 1992, 101), or Europe (Huysmans 2000; Greenhill 2016). In attempting to examine how the North–South asymmetry may be perceived from the point of view of refugee host-states, forcibly displaced populations arguably become a source of revenue, particularly given Western states' tendency to offer 'charity' in order to outsource refugee problems to the Global South (cf. Loescher 1996). Empirical examples attest to this: for instance, the influx of Afghani refugees into Pakistan paved the way for a five-year $3.2 billion aid package by the Reagan administration in 1981 (Loescher 1992). More recently, between 2001 and 2007, Nauru received $30 million from the Australian government in order to host refugees and asylum seekers within the Nauru Regional Processing Centre, in addition to Australia covering its operating costs, at $72 million for 2001–2 alone (Oxfam 2002). This is not to suggest that host-states consciously encourage inflows of forcibly displaced populations; rather, that an inflow of refugees may also constitute a strategic resource for these states' governments.

Migration Diplomacy in the Middle East

In order to conceptualise how cross-border population mobility features in the conduct of states' diplomacy, this book adopts the framework of *migration diplomacy*, namely the use of diplomatic tools, processes, and procedures to manage cross-border population mobility as well as the strategic use of migration as a means to obtain other aims (Tsourapas 2017a, 4; Adamson and Tsourapas 2019). In other words, migration diplomacy addresses both the effects of cross-border mobility upon a state's foreign policy, as well as the impact of a state's foreign policy upon its migration and refugee policies. While this phenomenon is not new, as mentioned earlier, it has yet to constitute a separate field of inquiry within international relations, which has restricted theorisation on the importance of cross-border mobility for inter-state relations. In fact, only recently has work on this particular interplay between migration and foreign policy taken off in the literature (see, for instance: Fernandez-Molina 2020; Frowd 2020; Geddes and Mehari 2020; Norman 2020; Seeberg and Volkel 2020; Malit and Tsourapas 2021). This book aims to expand the utility of the concept by developing existing work on processes of migration diplomacy (Thiollet 2011; İçduygu and Aksel 2014; Oyen 2015; Tsourapas 2017a; Adamson and Tsourapas 2019) further via in-depth, empirically grounded case studies drawn from the Arab world and the broader Middle East, from 1952 until today.

As Fiona Adamson and myself discussed in a separate piece (Adamson and Tsourapas 2019), three main scope conditions apply to this approach to migration diplomacy. Firstly, migration diplomacy refers to state actions and investigates how cross-border population mobility is linked to state diplomatic aims – as such, it does not investigate the internal workings of international organisations, the media, or social actors, such as non-governmental organisations – although it is possible to apply the framework to state-like international actors, such as the European Union or even the United Nations High Commissioner for Refugees. Indeed, states often engage in migration diplomacy vis-à-vis international organisations; for example, states such as Tanzania have made exaggerated public appeals to the United Nations High Commissioner for Refugees and other actors as a way of securing resources (Whitaker 2002). Kenya may have used threats to close the Dadaab camps as a type of diplomatic bargaining chip, and countries such as Denmark sometimes engage in direct public diplomacy as a means of deterring unwanted migration. While globalisation has diminished the monopoly of the sovereign state in world politics, the state is still the main actor in the regulation of cross-border population mobility and is likely to continue to be so, especially with the recent rise in populist nationalism and the renewed significance of borders. As Torpey (1998) has noted, a key feature of modern nation-states is that they not only have a monopoly over the legitimate means of violence, but also the legitimate means of movement. Their territorial logic means that they have an interest in maintaining and controlling their national borders as an aspect of their domestic, Westphalian, and interdependence sovereignty (Krasner 1999; Adamson 2006).

Secondly, a state's migration diplomacy is not synonymous with its overall migration policy – migration policies may range from completely restrictive to allowing free migration (Messina and Lahav 2006; Hollifield et al. 2014), but these are only relevant when states include them as part of their foreign relations and diplomacy. For example, standard elements of migration policy – such as the issuing of visas, the control of borders, or a state's refugee and asylum policy – are not in and of themselves elements of migration diplomacy. Typically, US visa policy is not shaped by diplomatic priorities in the United States; that said, in some instances it has also been used as a migration diplomacy tool during inter-state bargaining processes – as for example occurred in the October 2017 dispute between Turkey and the United States when there was a tit-for-tat imposition of travel and visa restrictions (Shaheen 2017). Diplomacy is often about negotiation, and migration diplomacy centres on how states employ cross-border population mobility management in their international relations, or how they use diplomatic means to obtain goals relating to migration. In other words, migration diplomacy can include both the strategic use of migration flows as a means to obtain other aims or the use of diplomatic methods to achieve goals related to migration. Finally, migration diplomacy highlights the importance of the management of cross-border mobility as an international issue; thus, it needs to be analytically disassociated from a wealth of migration matters that, however political, do not have a direct impact upon inter-state relations; internal displacement, the regulation of immigrants' citizenship status or access to rights, tariff rules determining which goods migrants are able to transport, diaspora politics, and the welfare of refugees are only relevant to migration diplomacy insofar as they impact on inter-state interactions. For instance, a state may in some cases institutionalise diaspora engagement policies – such as preferential investment conditions for diaspora members – largely for reasons of promoting domestic economic development. Internal displacement is a major global migration issue – with millions displaced annually due to conflict, violence, and natural disasters – yet it may often be wholly unrelated to issues of inter-state diplomacy.

This book focuses on four distinct processes of migration diplomacy in the Middle East via empirically driven analyses of select case studies. In its first section, a discussion of Egypt in the 1952–2011 period demonstrates how management of cross-border mobility has been instrumental in the state's construction of the migrant as a subject of power within an archetypical sending-state, under both the Nasserite regime (1954–70) as well as under Sadat and Mubarak (1970–2011). A focus on Egypt demonstrates how processes related to migration are embedded in both governmental practices and social norms of interaction, and how these processes affect the subject. In this reading, migration is deeply entrenched within different structures of power; the act of migration arguably signifies less an act that affirms agency, or the subject's sovereignty, than a deeper entrenchment of the subject within social norms and practices, as well as within the governmental techniques of power that govern and delineate conduct. This is evident in Egypt's migration diplomacy in these two periods, in which the Egyptian subject abroad becomes embedded in an effort to extend revolutionary ideas across the Arab world or, under Sadat and Mubarak, instrumental in the gradual empowerment of de-politicised neoliberalism. Under Nasser, the ruling regime encouraged the emigration of high-skilled Egyptian professionals as an instrument of cultural diplomacy to spread revolutionary ideals of Arab unity and anti-imperialism across the Middle East, as well as a tool for disseminating developmental aid, particularly in Yemen and sub-Saharan Africa. From 1970 onwards, Egypt sought to pursue a *status quo* position in the region, and to develop closer relations with the oil-producing Arab states; its migration diplomacy focused on satisfying host-states' demand for labour via the dispatch of low- and medium-skilled migrants with a lack of any ideological project. In examining population movements in the empirical case of the post-1952 modern Egyptian state, the first part of the book traces how migration supported the Egyptian regime, both under

Nasser and under Sadat and Mubarak, in distinct discursive and material manners.

Having established how the migrant constitutes a subject of state power in the Middle East, the book's second part shifts focus from states' management of emigration processes to their engagement with migrant and diaspora groups abroad, and how state–diaspora relations are tied to matters of regime security. In the Middle East, the workings of the long arm of the state have yet to be examined. Ruling regimes arguably face a distinct trade-off in their management of citizens abroad: on the one hand, they wish to reap the economic benefits associated with large emigrant populations – primarily an influx of remittances, but also the diaspora's investment in the home country, skills acquisition and training, a reduction in unemployment, and so on; on the other hand, authoritarian states also face the political need to maintain control of emigration flows, to monitor the movements of political dissenters, and to contain diasporas' activism abroad. In the book's second part, I detail how this trade-off manifests itself as Arab states across North Africa have vacillated between courting and controlling their migrant populations abroad. On the one hand, Algeria, Tunisia, Morocco, and Libya have all engaged in varied processes of securitising their diaspora populations in Europe; on the other hand, Egyptian diaspora policymaking towards citizens in Europe and North America has approached diaspora populations abroad as part of the country's developmental potential.

In its third section, the book shifts its attention to processes beyond the state–citizen relationship discussed in its first two sections. It proceeds to examine patterns of inter-state cooperation, focusing on how labour migration to Arab oil-producing countries in the post-1970 era contributed to strengthening regime security in the countries of origin. It details how short-term Jordanian and Egyptian emigration into Iraq and the Gulf Cooperation Council states resulted in inter-state cooperation, via processes of bilateral policy coordination between the sending- and host-states. With regard to Jordan, regional labour migration has constituted part of the regime's 'rent-seeking' strategies, as it has sought economic support from its Arab allies from the 1960s onwards. The chapter also pays particular attention to how regional Egyptian migration allowed the regime to overcome one of its most difficult challenges, namely the 1978 Egyptian–Israeli peace treaty.

The book's final section examines how migrant and refugee populations may constitute bargaining chips, particularly with regard to host-states' issue-linkage strategies. The chapter focuses on two types of mobility as leverage – labour and forced migration. In terms of the former, the chapter examines how Egypt was faced with numerous attempts by Arab host-states to target Egyptian migrant communities within their borders, predominantly unskilled or low-skilled, as instruments of *coercion*. The chapter's second half focuses on forced migration and issue-linkage strategies, examining how host-states of first asylum responded to the influx of Syrian refugees in the post-2011 era. The chapter's findings point to the emergence of a new type of state, a *refugee rentier state*, in which elites adopt policies aimed at extracting revenue from other state or non-state actors in exchange for maintaining refugee groups within its borders.

Methodology and data collection

The choice of focus on the Middle East is based on the region's rich history in both labour and forced migration flows, be it into, across, or out of the Middle East, which here includes Iran, Israel, Turkey, and the twenty-two members states of the League of Arab States, namely: Algeria, Bahrain, Comoros, Djibouti, Egypt, Iraq, Jordan, Kuwait, Lebanon, Libya, Mauritania, Morocco, Oman, Palestine, Qatar, Saudi Arabia, Somalia, Sudan, Tunisia, United Arab Emirates, Yemen, and Syria (currently suspended). The choice of the Middle East is also part of a conscious effort to steer research away from essentialist claims of exceptionalism ascribed to Arab, Muslim, or Middle East culture. While each region is endowed with its own socio-political specificities, there are multiple parallels that can be drawn between the Middle East and other areas, such as Latin America or Southeast Asia, in terms of the centrality of migration in the countries of origin's political structures, as will be discussed across the book. At the same time, the book aims to add to the small, albeit growing, literature on research discussing the intricacies of labour and forced migration within the Global South, in an attempt to move beyond Eurocentric accounts of the political importance of cross-border mobility.

Although the relevant literature identifies the importance of sending-, transit-, and host-states, there also exists a debate on how accurately such categorisations describe the phenomenon of migration: Egypt, for instance, is a sending-state of labour migrants to Libya and the Gulf, but also a transit-state for sub-Saharan African migrants, as well as a host-state of small numbers of immigrant workers from Arab states. Listing Jordan as a 'sending-state' would omit Jordanian policymaking towards its large Egyptian immigrant community (where Jordan constitutes a 'host-state') or its post-2003 policymaking towards Iraqi refugees that sought to cross Jordanian territory in order to reach Lebanon (where Jordan constitutes a 'transit-state'). That said, attention has been paid to select cases that will achieve maximum analytical leverage, in order to demonstrate four dimensions of migration diplomacy in the contemporary Middle East: the importance of migration as a subject-making process; the varied manners through which states reach out to their migrant and diaspora populations abroad; the use of migration as an instrument of cooperation; and, finally, the importance of migrants and refugees as instruments of political leverage. These four dimensions of migration diplomacy are not meant to be exhaustive, but rather are used to indicate how the management of cross-border mobility and foreign policymaking are intertwined across different contexts in the broader Middle East.

In terms of data, the book draws on multi-sited data collection that has occurred in the 2013–18 period across Egypt, Lebanon, and Jordan. The decision to pursue multi-sited fieldwork is linked to the fact that fieldwork in authoritarian contexts presents unique challenges (Kapiszewski, MacLean, and Read 2015, 218), particularly in light of the fact that regional migration is traditionally considered a security issue for Arab elites (Kapiszewski 2001; Tsourapas 2014). At the same time, research is plagued by a lack of detailed, publicly available statistical data on intra-Arab flows (Fargues 2014), as well as by the fact that migration management is handled at the highest levels of the executive (Feiler 2003). As Brand (2013, 8) wrote on seeking statistical data on the Jordanian political economy, 'one works under the assumption that such documents will probably never be released or may never have existed in the first place'. In particular, I rely upon a meticulous collection of the coverage of regional labour migration issues in the 2012–13 period across the three main Egyptian newspapers (*al-Ahram*, *al-Akhbar*, *al-Gomhuriya*), as well as North African media sources. Finally, for the purposes of triangulation, I employ semi-structured expert and elite interviews conducted in Cairo between July 2013 and June 2014, as well as Amman and Beirut in 2017 and 2018. This includes former Prime Minister Abdel Aziz Hegazy, current and former ministers, and high-ranking Egyptian government officials. For the purposes of triangulation, I also employ elite interviews, reports, briefs, and communications by international organisations and non-governmental organisations (NGOs) with regard to migrant and refugee politics across the three states.

This book presents an initial attempt to place a number of arguments that have developed over time and been presented in different venues in conversation with each other. This process necessarily implies that the book does not seek to offer the authoritative work on migration diplomacy, but to sketch a range of processes in which mobility and diplomacy appear to be interlinked. Much of this work has been put forth and discussed across various conferences, most notably Annual Meetings of the International Studies Association, the American Political Science Association, the International Studies Association, the British International Studies Association, and the Middle East Studies Association, as well as a number of smaller workshops held in the United Kingdom and abroad. The nature of the book's argument also points to the need for an interdisciplinary approach. In fact, the majority of the work contained in this book has also appeared in major journals across different disciplines – these include the *British Journal of Middle Eastern Studies, International Political Science Review, Ethnic and Racial Studies, International Studies Quarterly, International Studies Review*, and the *Journal of Global Security Studies*. I remain grateful to journal editors and reviewers for their invaluable help in developing this research agenda over time, as well as to publishers' permissions to compile this work into a more useful, monograph-long format.

What lies ahead

The book initially takes the reader through a sustained discussion of the basic tenets of its theoretical framework by examining its development as a specific research agenda within international relations and migration studies, and provides a detailed discussion of the theoretical underpinnings of migration diplomacy while also identifying potential avenues for further scholarly work (Chapter 1, Analysing mobility in the Middle East from the perspective of migration diplomacy). The chapter also identifies the main key challenges faced by international relations researchers of migration, namely the need to problematise and unpack the terminology employed in the study of migration politics; the desire to move beyond the study of archetypical cases, and shift attention to non-traditional cases; as well as the difficulties involved in data collection methods and methodological approaches that need to take the realities of Middle East migration politics into account. Chapter 2 provides a historical contextualisation of migration diplomacy in the Middle East by examining the regional politics of migration within four broad periods – the colonial, the postcolonial, the oil boom, and the de-Arabisation period.

Chapters 3, 4, 5, and 6 examine four distinct dimensions of migration diplomacy in the contemporary Middle East. Chapter 3, Constructing the migrant as a subject of power in Egypt, examines how emigration-related processes became embedded in governmental practices of establishing and maintaining power via a focus on Egyptian policymaking from 1952 until 2011. The Egyptian subject was constructed, and expected to act, in certain ways both at home and abroad, corresponding to the domestic and foreign policy priorities of the ruling regime. By identifying how migration supported the ruling Egyptian regime both materially and discursively over a seventy-year period, this discussion sets the stage for the remainder of the book. Chapter 4, State–diaspora relations and regime security in North Africa, examines how Egypt and the Maghreb countries (Algeria, Libya, Morocco, Tunisia) have approached their migrant and diaspora groups residing beyond the Middle East. It explores how authoritarian sending-states vacillate between courting and control, as they seek to profit materially from these communities while minimising any political threat they may pose. Chapter 5, Inter-state cooperation and labour migration to the Gulf, identifies how the oil-rich Arab monarchies have extended their support for a number of sending-states' ruling regimes – notably Egypt and Jordan – via cooperation on labour migration. It examines, in particular, the importance of labour migration flows for resolving sending-states' perennial problems of unemployment and over-population, as well as the historic centrality of migrant remittances in their economies. Chapter 6, Managing mobility as a host-state issue-linkage strategy, shifts focus to the use of labour and forced migrants as political leverage by host-states in the Middle East. It identifies how Libya, Iraq, and Jordan have attempted to coerce Egypt by targeting the Egyptian migrant communities within their borders, from the early 1970s until today. Shifting to more recent events, the chapter's second part details how Jordan, Lebanon, and Turkey have attempted to employ their positions as host-states of Syrian refugees for international economic aid. The book's Conclusion offers a discussion on the applicability of its theorisation to explain processes of cross-border mobility across the Middle East and, more broadly, across the Global South, while also identifying potential further avenues for future research.

1

Analysing mobility in the Middle East from the perspective of migration diplomacy

'International migration has traditionally been visualized as under the control (in both legal and practical terms) of the receiving country, with the role of the sending country a passive one. It now appears, however, that sending countries may have more control over outmigration than was previously thought and indeed may visualize it as a kind of "national resource," to be managed like any other.'

Myron Weiner (quoted in Teitelbaum 1984, 447)

International relations scholars of the politics of migration outside the Global North are arguably confronted with three main challenges in terms of further study on the topic of migration diplomacy. Firstly, there exists a need to systematically unpack the types of mobility that are encompassed within the terminology employed, and to attempt more nuanced explanations of the variables under study. In many ways, this refers to a broader issue that scholars of migration politics are faced with, regarding commonly acceptable definitions of phenomena under study, from 'diasporas' or 'emigration', to 'sending-states'. Secondly, a key challenge concerns the need to move beyond the study of archetypical cases in the field of emigration politics, and to shift our attention to non-traditional cases or, more ambitiously, engage in comparative work – either via within-case analysis across time periods or via cross-case research. Finally, scholars need to pay more attention to the adoption of data collection methods and methodological approaches that take the empirical realities of emigration politics into account – conducting fieldwork in many sending- or host-states of the Global South is extremely difficult, for instance, while accurate data on migration flows and stocks is either impossible to retrieve or unavailable.[1]

The analytical confusion on the concepts employed constitutes a main issue that affects political science research into questions of population mobility and, in particular, emigration states. From an international relations perspective, there exists a considerable degree of difficulty in the proper classification and theorisation of states' rationale behind emigration and diaspora policies, which translates into the need to unpack core concepts into their key parameters. Within the emerging literature in political science, the term 'diaspora' has developed from one rarely used to one currently suffering from conceptual stretching and conflation – often encompassing not merely a state's citizens who have emigrated, but also those emigrants' descendants, as well as other co-ethnics. As Brubaker argued in his critique, 'emigrant groups have been conceptualised as diasporas, even when they have been largely assimilated. The Italian diaspora is a case in point' (Brubaker 2005, 3). Gamlen's key study of the 'emigration state', for instance, equates diasporas with 'extra-territorial populations', including:

> temporary or transnational migrants who spread their time between their sending state and elsewhere and fall more or less arbitrarily into one or other policy category of the origin state. They also include longer-term but still first-generation emigrants settled in another country, and descendants of emigrants who – in certain places at certain times – identify as diasporic or even as members of a fully fledged diaspora 'community'. (Gamlen 2008, 842–3)

Over the past few years, a growing literature has successfully eschewed such problems of conflation by explicitly centring on states' emigration, rather than diaspora, policies. By avoiding discussion of co-ethnics, this body of research focuses exclusively on policies towards those who have emigrated with the intention of living abroad. The reasons behind states' engagement with emigrants correspond to the findings of the state–diaspora relations literature, traditionally viewing 'emigrants as a resource that can be mobilised in support of the political or economic interests of the sending state' (Collyer 2013, 5; cf. Østergaard-Nielsen 2003a). However, while accurately differentiating between states' emigration and diaspora policies, this strand of literature assumes migration is unidirectional, and does not take into account the importance of emigrants' potential return as a shaping factor of state policy. As states develop new institutional mechanisms that target emigrant populations (Fitzgerald 2009; Naujoks 2013), they frequently build ties not solely with emigrants, but also with prospective emigrants (Rodriguez and Schwenken 2013) as well as with return migrants (Markowitz and Stefansson 2004; Tsuda 2009). This points to an important, albeit un-problematised, aspect of states' policies towards its emigrants, namely the interconnectedness of emigration and return (Tsourapas 2015b). 'Return movements across time and space have largely been ignored in anthropology and migration research', Markowitz and Stefansson (2004, 3) argued. While sociologists and historians have addressed this gap (Levitt 1998; Khater 2001), Stefansson's argument remains true within political science. The literature on diaspora acknowledges that diaspora policies often aim to attract groups of co-ethnics back to the homeland, but the research on states' emigration policy has not taken that into account. Put differently, a state's policy of encouraging or discouraging its citizens' emigration is connected to its respective discouragement, or encouragement, of its citizens' return migration.

Similarly, as I have shown elsewhere (Tsourapas 2015b), the question of how and why states target different external populations has not been sufficiently problematised. This is not to say that researchers have disregarded differentiated state policies – see, for instance, Naujok's (2013) work on India or Nyíri's (2013) work on China. Yet they have yet to theorise their political rationale and purposes. Schmitter Heisler's work on sending-state policies, for instance, acknowledges that states differentiate between 'long-term-temporary', 'short-term-temporary', and 'permanent' migration, but employs this to argue that a state 'benefits [from migration] only if emigrants remain abroad for an extended period without settling permanently' (Heisler 1985, 475). Levitt and de la Dehesa provide an extensive analysis of sending-states' various engagement policies but do not account for within-state variation (Levitt and De la Dehesa 2003), an argument that can be made with regard to Collyer's edited volume on the subject (Collyer 2013). Koinova's work on diaspora 'positionality' and Gamlen's research on 'tapping', 'embracing', and 'governing' further enhance our understanding of sending-states' strategies, yet without explicitly theorising on the rationale behind multiple engagement policies (Koinova 2012; Gamlen 2014). Despite the fact that the line between 'temporary' or 'short-term' and 'long-term' or 'permanent' (or, indeed, between 'voluntary' and 'forced' migration) is necessarily blurred, research on emigration politics needs to critically reflect on these categorisations, as well as make a renewed effort towards unpacking these core concepts.

The second challenge facing international relations scholars' work on emigration politics is the need to move beyond a small universe of archetypical cases that have attracted the bulk of researchers' attention in the last few decades. These cases primarily include Mexico (Fitzgerald 2006; Délano 2011) and India (Kapur 2010, Varadarajan 2010; Naujoks 2013), as well as the Philippines (Guevarra 2009; Rodriguez 2010). As Burgess and Meseguer recognise in an edited issue of *Studies of Comparative International Development* on 'International Migration and Home Country Politics', there exists an 'over-representation of Mexico in current research' (Meseguer and Burgess 2014, 7). While these three cases feature a wealth of empirical observations that may undeniably shed light on emigration politics across the Global South, there exists a number of analytical risks in extrapolating solely based on findings from these cases. For one, the study of emigration politics outside democratic contexts continues to constitute a major gap in the literature (cf. Dalmasso et al. 2017), save from notable exceptions in the state-diaspora literature (Brand 2006; Moss 2016b). Autocracies are examined either in terms of their immigration policies (Cooley and Heathershaw 2017; Shin 2017), or, with regard to emigration and diasporas, in terms of transitions to democracy (Koinova 2009; Brand 2014b).

In particular, emigration scholars' focus on democratic contexts has side-lined two distinct aspects of autocracies' migration politics. Firstly, autocracies aim to exert, by definition, a greater degree of control throughout citizens' migration trajectory, and are better equipped at managing short-term versus long-term migration. 'Inclusive' policies developed by democracies do not travel as easily in autocratic contexts that do not share liberal understandings of citizenship, membership, or rights. Article 13b of the United Nations Declaration of Human Rights ('Everyone has the right to leave any country, including his own, and to return to his country') has been challenged by many non-democracies that do not regard cross-border mobility as a right (cf. Dowty 1989). Beyond policies that exclusively target those citizens and co-ethnics already residing outside its borders, non-democracies develop two additional sets of policies in order to control the size and make-up of their diasporas: firstly, they regulate emigration processes. For citizens aiming to emigrate from Uzbekistan or North Korea, for example, exit visas continue to remain a strict requirement. Particularly in previous decades, the prominent phenomenon of 'black lists' included citizens, usually political dissenters, who were specifically prohibited from emigrating. Secondly, they regulate return migration processes. Autocracies may also complicate the process of return migration by not allowing dual citizenship or by unilaterally stripping political dissenters of their nationality. This is particularly popular across the Gulf states (*The Economist* 2016). In even more extreme cases, a number of autocracies have also not hesitated to diminish such 'opposition in exile' through forced extraditions, as in Central Asia (Cooley and Heathershaw 2017) or, even, to engage in political assassinations, as in the case of Russia under Putin.

A second characteristic of autocracies' migration politics is the use of migration management as an element of cross-regime relations between migrant-sending and migrant-host states. For instance, there is evidence that autocratic leaders rely on each other for material and immaterial support (von Soest 2015, 628). They provide vetoes in the United Nations Security Council, offer bilateral and multilateral aid in military and security issues, they exchange ideas on developmental strategies, or they engage in ideational and material support (Erdmann et al. 2013, 5). The extent to which migration features in these processes remains unexamined; Brand identifies that 'it may make sense to think of [...] Jordanian expatriate labor in Kuwait' as a form of 'economic statecraft', but she does not carry this argument any further (Brand 2013, 148). On the other hand, migration flows are also affected when these cross-regime personalistic relations deteriorate or break down (Tsourapas 2017a). This is a common occurrence in intra-Arab migration flows, for instance, as well as in Central Asian states' migration into Russia (Schenk 2016). While this phenomenon may also exist – albeit to a less prominent degree – within democratic contexts, it has yet to be adequately explored in the relevant literature.

A final challenge that international relations scholars of migration politics face has to do with the development and adoption of appropriate data collection methods and methodological approaches that take the empirical realities of emigration politics into account. This is, perhaps, most evident with regard to collecting statistical information on migration. A number of states in the Global South lack the infrastructural ability to collect reliable data on migration stocks and flows, either as a result of weak state structures or porous borders, as in sub-Saharan Africa (Beling 1968); some states may intentionally manipulate this data in order to grossly over-estimate their population and under-estimate the number of foreign workers, as in the case of the Gulf Cooperation States (Kapiszewski 2001); others tend to treat migration as a national security issue, refusing to divulge any cross-border mobility data to researchers (Birks and Sinclair 1980, 44; Feiler 1986). These issues complicate analyses of South–South or South–North migration politics for social scientists as a whole. As a key textbook on Middle East political economy argues:

> Severe issues with the accuracy of data plague all estimates of the magnitude of migration. For labor migration, the data typically count inflows, not outflows. They usually enumerate work permits rather than persons, making no allowance for multiple entries. They also suffer from a variety of other difficulties, including the underreporting of unauthorized migration, which all analysts agree is substantial. Moreover, different countries use different definitions for 'visitor,' 'short-term migrant' and 'long-term resident foreigners.' The distinction between 'temporary' and 'permanent' migrants is contentious, as is that between 'economic migrant' and 'refugee.' Although some of these problems bedevil EU statistics on MENA immigrant labor, they are especially severe in the data on labor migration to the major oil-exporting countries of the Persian Gulf. In that area, where some of the problems are due to imprecise definitions, labor force numbers are lower than total migrant population numbers. (Cammett et al. 2015, 500)

A related issue refers to the specific difficulties involved in the planning and conducting of fieldwork on emigration politics. It could be argued that this is a necessity for those working with mobile populations, as well as the need to conduct multi-sited fieldwork, sometimes encompassing different countries of origin, transit, and destination. But additional issues arise for those researching emigration politics in the Global South – the unstable socio-political situation in some of these states prevents fieldwork activity altogether; in other contexts, a researcher may be able to conduct elite or expert interviews, but find it logistically impossible to conduct ethnographic work if states prevent access to certain migrant communities – thus, certain types of information are prioritised over others; finally, triangulation of findings becomes extremely difficult, particularly with regard to South–South migration.

It is not easy to provide solutions to these issues, which are likely to become more pressing in the future, as sending-, transit-, and host-states outside the Global North become more adept at both manipulating data and withholding access to researchers working on cross-border mobility. The identification of alternative sources of statistical data – from United Nations or the Word Bank repositories to regional organisations' reports, such as those issued by the League of Arab States or the Association of Southeast Asian Nations – would be one potential avenue; the creation of public-access depositories might be another; researchers might even explore the possibility of collaboration on multi-sited research. Yet, it is important to first identify and discuss the particularities of methodology and data collection challenges within the scholarly community, in order to foster a common approach to resolving these issues.

Four dimensions of migration diplomacy in the Middle East

Migrants, diasporas, and the rise of transnational authoritarianism

Although, as seen earlier, much of the existing scholarship on migration and diaspora studies focuses on Western host-states, this is not to say that there has been no attention to migration and diaspora policymaking in non-democratic contexts. Working from a political economy perspective, one group of scholars examines the importance of migrants in sustaining authoritarian rule via the inflow of remittances and the tackling of structural problems such as unemployment and overpopulation (Choucri 2002; Escribà-Folch, Meseguer, and Wright 2018; Tsourapas 2019b). A range of scholars also examine autocracies' immigration policymaking processes (Shin 2017; Miller and Peters 2018), their refugee and asylum strategies (Arar 2017b; Norman 2018), as well as their migration diplomacy practices (Greenhill 2002; Paoletti 2011; Tsourapas 2018). A growing line of research examines patterns of cooperation between authoritarian countries of origin or transit and liberal democratic countries of destination (Ippolito and Trevisanut

2015; Collyer 2016). Finally, a key strand of the literature that emerged out of the study of transnationalism theorises on how cross-border mobility affects sending-states and country-of origin politics (Heisler 1985; Østergaard-Nielsen 2003b; Kapur 2010; Margheritis 2015; Betts and Jones 2016), or how autocracies manage migrant and diaspora groups abroad (Brinkerhoff 2005; Brand 2006; Natter 2014). Yet, despite the growing scholarly interest around the international politics of migration in authoritarian contexts, we still lack a systematic understanding of autocracies' management of emigration and diaspora.

This section introduces Hollifield's (2004) concept of the 'liberal paradox' as a starting point. It argues that its expansion to illiberal contexts would make it more suitable for cross-regional comparisons that depart from Western liberal democratic norms. By placing Hollifield's work into conversation with Hirschman's seminal work on 'exit' and 'voice' (1970), it offers a useful framework in order to understand migration policymaking in authoritarianism. Almost twenty years ago, James F. Hollifield (2004) established that contemporary states are 'migration states', for which the management of cross-border mobility constitutes a key policy component. According to Hollifield, a fundamental characteristic of states' policymaking on migration is the 'liberal paradox': on the one hand, migration states today wish to encourage the free flow of migrant labour for economic reasons; on the other hand, states seek to maintain immigration restrictions for political and security purposes. Thus, migration states remain trapped in their need to balance economic and political exigencies: '[I]n order to maintain a competitive advantage, governments must keep their economies and societies open to trade, investment, and migration. But unlike goods, capital, and services, the movement of people involves greater political risks' (Hollifield 2004, 886–7).

The concept of the 'liberal paradox' has been a fruitful contribution to the literature on the international politics of migration, pointing to the contradictions that are inherent in states' management of migration. At the same time, its focus on liberal democratic countries of destination hinders its portability outside Europe and North America (Natter 2018; Adamson and Tsourapas 2020). Could countries of origin – frequently authoritarian – feature a similar dilemma between maximising economic gains and minimising political and security risks from cross-border mobility? Arguably, a similar dynamic occurs in authoritarian countries of origin, where emigration also intensifies the tensions between markets and rights. On the one hand, autocratic governments seek to control their borders and restrict emigration because of domestic political and security reasons – citizens' right to travel abroad comes into conflict with autocracies' wish to maintain order and eliminate dissent (Dowty 1989; Alemán and Woods 2014). Autocracies have long understood that allowing potential political dissenters the freedom to travel abroad risks encouraging opposition activism that remains outside state control. On the other hand, autocracies wish to encourage emigration under an economic rationale that expects cross-border mobility to increase migrant remittances, lower unemployment, and address the pressures of over-population (Brand 2006; Mosley and Singer 2015) – fully closed autocracies are economically unsustainable. How do autocracies attempt to escape this 'illiberal paradox' (Tsourapas 2020b)?

Traditionally, authoritarian states have addressed the illiberal paradox by prioritising politics over economics and securitising emigration at the border: the freedom to travel abroad was a privilege, rather than a right, for citizens of mercantilist regimes or, more recently, communist regimes. This took a number of forms, from the creation of 'black lists' of political dissenters not permitted to travel abroad, to the denaturalisation of nationals who emigrated without authorisation – measures prevalent in the Soviet Union and China (Messina 1994; Peretz 2015). For most of the twentieth century, a broad number of non-Western countries implemented emigration restrictions to varying degrees. Mozambique introduced an 'exit visa' policy that forced applicants to justify their case for wishing to leave. Egypt did not hesitate to strip the citizenship of those who emigrated without permission (Tsourapas 2019b). Often, such policies are tied to nationalist economic measures: the construction of the Berlin Wall, for instance, was both an attempt to cut off 'brain drain' as well as a physical manifestation of the impossibility of East Germans' exit to the West (Pfaff 2006). In Syria, all engineering graduates are forbidden from emigrating until after they have been employed in the public sector for at least five years; similar measures existed in Haiti, Pakistan, Ethiopia, and elsewhere (Dowty 1989).

Autocracies continue to seek control of citizens' movement today, albeit to a lesser extent. Uzbekistan, for instance, abolished exit visas only in early 2019. North Korea considers unauthorised emigration a form of defection and has adopted a shoot-to-kill policy for citizens attempting to cross its borders (Byman and Lind 2010). Those who survive an escape attempt face torture and forced labour in re-education camps. In Cuba, up until 2013, citizens faced a six-month prison sentence for even talking about unauthorised travel abroad. Following a failed attempted military coup in Turkey in July 2016, Recep Tayyip Erdoğan's increasingly authoritarian government cracked down on individuals suspected of being affiliated with the Gülen movement, including through revoking or confiscating passports.[2] In post-Arab Spring Egypt, the military's return to power in 2013 was followed by an extensive use of 'terrorism lists' that prevented travel abroad, but also included political activists. Mozn Hassan, head of Nazra for Feminist Studies, and Azza

Soliman, head of the Center for Egyptian Women's Legal Assistance, have been unable to leave Egypt.

Arguably, the main reason why the securitisation of emigration is becoming less prevalent today is the rise of economic interdependence and globalisation. Increasingly, a number of authoritarian regimes liberalised their emigration policies over time, granting citizens greater freedom to travel abroad: in the late 1970s, Deng Xiaoping's economic reforms afforded Chinese people the opportunity to travel and study abroad for the first time in the history of the People's Republic of China. Egypt famously adopted an 'open-door' policy in the early 1970s that saw hundreds of thousands of Egyptian workers emigrate to the oil-producing Arab states (Ibrahim 1982). Beyond functioning as a 'safety valve' against existing or potential political unrest, emigration affords these regimes multiple economic benefits, primarily via migrant remittances (Meseguer and Burgess 2014; Mosley and Singer 2015). For instance, monetary transfers from the diaspora amounted to 37% of Eritrea's GDP in 2004 (Hirt and Mohammad 2017). Emigration also offers other developmental benefits, usually described as 'brain gain': Libya under Muammar Gaddafi, for example, encouraged its citizens to pursue educational opportunities abroad, eager to develop a native bureaucratic apparatus and lessen its dependence on foreign labour – a strategy that is still employed by Saudi Arabia and other Gulf states.

At the same time, social scientists have identified another reason behind the shift away from emigration restrictions: cross-border mobility restrictions may frequently produce the exact opposite effects that an authoritarian regime intends. This has been identified by Albert Hirschman (1970), who has argued for the mutually exclusive processes of 'exit' versus 'voice' – briefly, in the context of migration politics, citizens that are dissatisfied in an existing polity can either protest against it – i.e. exercise 'voice' – or emigrate abroad – i.e. engage in 'exit' (cf. Dowding et al. 2000).[3] A fundamental aspect of this binary is that 'the presence of the exit alternative can ... atrophy the development of the art of voice' (Hirschman 1993, 199). One's freedom to leave can function as a 'safety valve' against domestic political unrest: the influential 'Turner thesis' suggests that the possibility of 'going West' undermined a strong workers' movement in the United States (Turner 1920). In sharp contrast, the inability to escape often serves as a stimulant for further political discontent, as in the case of the German Democratic Republic (Brubaker 1990).

However, the liberalisation of emigration does not resolve the tensions inherent within the 'illiberal paradox'. In fact, as the well-established literature on transnationalism and diaspora activism demonstrates (Østergaard-Nielsen 2003b; Tarrow 2005; Adamson 2015), emigrants have often been able to exercise their 'voice' once abroad (Ahmadov and Sasse 2016). There are vocal diaspora communities that closely follow the politics of their country of origin, and do not hesitate to protest against authoritarian rule from afar: in the United States, Cuban-Americans have participated in American domestic politics, formed interest groups, and act as powerful lobbyists for causes related to Cuban politics (Adamson 2016). Rwandan and Zimbabwean exiles have engaged in sustained mobilisation against autocratic rule back home (Betts and Jones 2016). Arab diaspora communities across Europe and North America have featured prominently in the development of the 2011 Arab Uprisings from afar (Moss 2016a; Müller-Funk 2016).

How do autocracies respond to the political and security risks generated by citizens' exercise of 'voice' while abroad? One possibility would be to return to the mercantilist and communist tradition of restricting mass emigration, but that would come with severe economic and political drawbacks in an era of globalisation and interconnectedness, as the illiberal paradox suggests. In fact, recent trends suggest that autocracies are attempting to bypass the illiberal paradox altogether – to both reap the material benefits of free movement while ensuring that migrant and diaspora groups pose little political or security threat to their survival.

Migration, cooperation, and regime security

Can the management of migration serve as a tool of cooperation? To understand the process of cooperation, Keohane provides a classic definition:

> Cooperation occurs when actors adjust their behavior to the actual or anticipated preferences of others, through a process of policy coordination. To summarize more formally, intergovernmental cooperation takes place when the policies actually followed by one government are regarded by its partners as facilitating realization of their own objectives, as the result of a process of policy coordination. (Keohane 1984, 51)

Keohane's work has led to a voluminous literature on processes of cooperation among advanced capitalist countries, under the liberal institutionalist framework, but very little work has been conducted on its effects upon sending host-state relations (cf. Hollifield 2012). Instead, the study of migration through the prism of cooperation has featured in analyses of international organisations and international regimes (Hansen, Koehler, and Money 2011), or in the study of immigration controls (Ellermann 2009). Most often, it is the literature on European integration that looks at how migration may feature into processes of inter-state cooperation either in terms of internal mobility (Hollifield 1992), or external controls (Andreas and Snyder 2000; Huysmans 2000). Yet, empirical studies have frequently highlighted how short-term unskilled or low-skilled migration between labour-rich sending-states and labour-poor host-states has facilitated bilateral cooperation and issue-linkage strategies. The ILO recently recognised that an increasing number of bilateral agreements and memoranda of understanding on migration focus on circular or temporary low-skilled, rather than high-skilled, migration (Wickramasekara 2015, 18). More specifically, studies have highlighted how bilateral Mexico–US migration flows, as per the Bracero programme, resulted in closer coordination of the two states' security and border control policies (Fitzgerald 2009; Délano 2011). In the Pacific, the New Zealand 'Recognized Seasonal Employee' programme, launched in 2007 to fill seasonal positions via recruitment from seven Pacific countries, has allowed closer bilateral cooperation in areas of transport, regional integration, and development (Stahl and Appleyard 2007). In the European context, the German state coordinates a number of policies with its sending-state counterparts in the context of the guestworker (*Gastarbeiter*) programmes – initially with sending-states of the Southern Europe and, since the mid-1950s, with Turkey – including double taxation agreements, provisions on pensions, and so on (Martin 1991; Akgündüz 2008). The reasons behind inter-state cooperation in terms of temporary low-skilled migration are clear: this form of mobility caters to the short-term economic needs of the host-state by alleviating labour shortages until a more permanent solution can be identified; at the same time, it provides a short-term economic boost to the sending-state, in the form of migrant remittances and the lowering of unemployment.

The underlying assumption in researching the effects of emigration upon cross-regime cooperation and competition is that the Middle East constitutes a regional sub-system of international relations. The broader discussion on this, ongoing for decades, is beyond the scope of this book (see key works: Binder 1958; Gerges 1994; Gause 1999). Suffice it to say that the existence of such a sub-system can be defended on the basis of common attributes and frequent interactions between the Arab and non-Arab states of the Middle East (Turkey, Iran, Israel – the latter particularly following the Camp David accords) as well as the proximity of these actors. The degree of geographical continuity, the regionally interconnected structures, and a certain degree of density in their interaction further corroborates the approach of the Middle East as a sub-system (Tibi 1998).

Processes of cross-regime cooperation on issues of migration management have been left unexamined, disregarding multiple empirical examples in which migration management could facilitate *rapprochement* between non-democratic regimes. The small literature on alliances between non-democratic regimes seems to disregard the issue of migration. Beyond work in comparative politics, a nascent research agenda approaches the issue of authoritarianism from an international relations prism, examining the effect of intra-state cooperation upon ruling authoritarian regimes. The importance of such factors in explaining the durability of authoritarian regimes becomes particularly prominent when we examine, for instance, the controversy on a 'reverse wave' of democratisation (Merkel 2010), or regimes' 'backlash against democracy promotion and democracy more generally' (Carothers 2009, 6), which should indicate the relevance of this dimension in the politics of authoritarian rule. The historical development of the literature on democratisation – which transitioned from a comparative politics perspective to one examining the importance of international factors, such as diffusion, democracy promotion strategies, and so on (Whitehead 1996) – paves the way for the literature on authoritarianism to move towards similar agendas (von Soest 2015, 628).

This strand of research relies on a growing literature on authoritarian regimes' reactions to the diffusion of democratisation, particularly within the European context. Researchers have identified that processes of democratisation across twentieth-century Europe led to efforts by many regimes that aimed to prevent its diffusion beyond the origin state's borders. Mann's work identifies the transformative processes that fascist regimes embraced in order to thwart democratisation pressures (Mann 2004). Weyland argued that:

> conservative authoritarian regimes sought to maintain traditional elite rule and cement it through corporatist institutions. They deliberately wanted to avoid and suppress the plebeian, populist tendencies embodied in fascism and national socialism. Therefore, authoritarian regimes in Eastern, Central, and Southern Europe often cracked down on fascist or proto-fascist movements or stifled their advance. (Weyland 2010, 1168)

Taking this train of thought a step further, researchers begin to identify how authoritarian regimes act in unison in order to prevent democratisation. Various methods of cross-regime cooperation have, so far, been identified. Employing Elinks and Simmons' framework, Ambrosio's (2010) work attempted to conceptualise the process of 'authoritarian diffusion' as an unintentional process that does not involve 'any collaboration, imposition, or otherwise programmed effort on the part of any of the actors' (Simmons and Elkins 2005, 6). For some scholars, this constitutes a process of 'authoritarian learning' – as in Heydemann's and Leenders' research (2011), which examined such processes of policy adaptation among Arab non-democratic regimes in the process of the post-2011 Arab Uprisings. This constitutes 'change of beliefs, skills or procedures based on the observation and interpretation of experience' (von Soest 2015, 628). Empirical evidence supports such research agendas, given that many authoritarian regimes also rely on each other for material and immaterial support. They provide vetoes in the United Nations Security Council, offer bilateral and multilateral aid in military and security issues, they exchange ideas on developmental strategies, or they engage in ideational and material support (Erdmann et al. 2013, 5). Von Soest's 2015 article approaches cross-regime cooperation as 'bilateral engagements between authoritarian regimes', which he differentiates in 'unintentional' engagement (essentially policy diffusion), and 'intentional' engagement (in term of learning, cooperation, and support).

There is little doubt of the empirical proof that shows how authoritarian regimes do engage in various forms of cooperation. Yet, this literature continues to be 'highly fragmented' and its empirical and conceptual bases are found to be lacking (Erdmann et al. 2013, 27). The international cooperation of authoritarian regimes remains an under-theorised field of study, Von Soest admits (2015, 628): 'testimony to this incoherence is the fact that scholars use widely different concepts to analyse authoritarian regimes' international relationships with each other.' At the same time, research has been hindered by applying this framework to empirical research: given the opacity of authoritarian regimes, and the difficulty in approaching elites and other key actors within them, the concept of 'learning', albeit useful in shifting focus to the agency of such actors, is hard-pressed to properly analyse the processes at play, while the specifics of such cooperation remain obscure.

Migration and issue-linkage strategies

Existing empirical and analytical work also suggests that migration diplomacy cannot be separated from states' pursuit of other goals, which may be economic, political, security-centred, and so on. To comprehend such processes, this book draws on work from the literature on issue-linkage diplomacy, or the simultaneous negotiations on two or more issues aiming for joint settlement (Haas 1980; Davis 2009). The majority of work on linkage and leverage suggests that it constitutes a mechanism for stronger states, particularly those situated within the Global North, to impose their will upon weaker states. Levitsky and Way's 2011 analysis of these mechanisms, for instance (without taking into account migratory flows), demonstrates how the United States and the EU have been able to exert pressure on weaker states through such mechanisms (Levitsky and Way 2011). Other authors have looked at 'suasion games' to identify hegemonic powers' strategies over other actors in the international system (Martin 1992). The Global South rarely engages in issue-linkage diplomacy in these analyses, save from discussions on military conflict or counter-insurgency (Mack 1975; Paul 1994; Arreguin-Toft 2005).[4] By introducing the issue-linkage literature into the discussion of migration diplomacy, I aim to put forth a more convincing account for how cross-border population mobility affects states' diplomatic practices across the Middle East.

The analysis in this monograph focuses on two types of issue-linkage migration diplomacy, focusing on labour migration and forced migration, respectively. In terms of labour migration, a first line of work that ties migration to coercive inter-state relations sees cross-border mobility in terms of existing power imbalances between sending- and host-states. Early scholars of dependency theory, as well as recent critics of globalisation, focus on migration's contribution to the 'development of underdevelopment' (Frank 1966). Rooted in Marxist political economy, such research examines migration flows as part of broader patterns of uneven trade between 'developed (migration receiving) and less-developed (migration sending) countries' (Hollifield 2012, 366; see for comparison Sassen 1988). Wallerstein and other world-systems theorists identify that labour migration sustains 'relations of domination' between these two groups of nations, confirming the expectations of mainstream international relations theory regarding stronger powers exerting pressure on weaker ones (Castles et al. 2014, 33). For instance, Mexican migration into the United States features as a main dimension in the power imbalances between the two states (FitzGerald 2009, 55, 167–9). The presence of 15–20 million Bangladeshi immigrants across India is indicative of the unequal distribution of economic power between the two states (Sadiq 2009). Although such work affirms the importance of labour migration in inter-state relations, it approaches economically driven cross-border population mobility not as an instrument of foreign policy or coercion, but as part and parcel of global power imbalances. How might a host-state leverage its position against a sending-state for specific policy goals?

Working broadly within the field of global power politics (Berenskoetter 2007; Goddard and Nexon 2016), three separate research agendas allow us to identify potential leverage mechanisms: firstly, work on economic remittances long established the importance of such capital inflows for sending-states (Orrenius and Zavodny 2012; Hollifield et al. 2014, 7; Escribà-Folch et al 2015; Mosley and Singer 2015, 293–7). Economic remittances constitute a valuable source of foreign exchange and produce multiplier effects on the aggregate economy (Kapur 2010). They enhance access to public services (Adida and Girod 2011) and decrease demand for social spending (Doyle 2015). The importance of migrant remittances is frequently identified in the extensive literature on state–diaspora relations (Delano and Gamlen 2014; Koinova 2014; Koinova and Tsourapas 2018). An extensive political economy literature also highlights how remittances may additionally constitute a form of rent distribution, particularly in the Middle East, suggesting that it may contribute to the stability of sending-states' political regimes

(Korany 1986; Soliman 2011). Warnings regarding the risks of over-reliance on remittances, of Dutch disease effects, or of associated inflationary risks notwithstanding (Chami et al. 2008), sending-states habitually place significant value upon the ability to attract economic remittances (Castles et al. 2014, 75–83).

Consequently, host-states attempting to exercise leverage against sending-states may target the latter's reliance on remittances, mainly via disrupting migrants' ability to send earnings home. The rationale behind such a strategy of restricting remittances is similar to states' adoption of negative economic sanctions (Lindsay 1986; Hufbauer et al. 1990), as both mechanisms aim to force target states' compliance on a range of issues via disrupting capital inflows. 'Because economic sanctions can impose costs … without carrying the degree of risk attached to military actions,' Martin (1993, 3) argues, 'governments use them to signal resolve and exert pressure for policy changes.' In a similar fashion, a host-state may curtail migrants' financial transfers as leverage. There is a wealth of empirical examples of host-states' targeting the outflow of economic remittances for political purposes. For example, the United States' embargo against Cuba prohibited migrants from dispatching remittances, while Cubans had to use third countries to transfer funds back home (Vanderbush and Haney 2005). Or when Japanese–North Korean relations deteriorated in March 1999 as Pyongyang prepared to test-fire a new long-range ballistic missile, Japan threatened to ban all migrant remittances to North Korea, estimated at $600 million to $1 billion per year (Miyashita 2003, 163).

Beyond migrant remittances, cross-border mobility serves a second political economy purpose for sending-states. Comparative political scientists and political economists identify that economically driven migration allows for an outflow of domestic labour, constituting what Turner described as a 'safety valve' (1920), or the reduction of labour surpluses and the easing of accompanying socio-political and economic pressures. Drawing on Hirschman's thesis on 'voice' versus 'exit', research demonstrates that sending-states find it preferable to encourage the 'exit' of disenfranchised social actors rather than allow them to 'voice' their grievances (Hirschman 1970, 15–43; for comparison, Dowding et al. 2000, 478–80). Sending-states often attempt to curb over-population or unemployment, in particular, by aiming to 'export' citizens abroad. Such policies are evident in India, Bangladesh, Pakistan, and Sri Lanka, as well as poorer Middle East states, which traditionally promote labour migration to the oil-producing Arab states (Weiner 1985, 445). The 1942–64 Bracero programme allowed for the outflow of Mexican labour into the US (FitzGerald 2009, 48–50). In the second half of the twentieth century, Tunisia and Morocco began fostering emigration to Europe for similar political economy reasons (Brand 2006, 17), while Western European countries, notably Germany, engaged in recruitment of labour from Turkey and other Mediterranean states (Martin 1991).[5]

By extension, I expect host-states aiming to leverage their position against a sending-state to also attempt to restrict the outflow of its citizens abroad. An extensive literature exists on various methods of immigration control: a host-state may decide to curb immigration flows from a specific sending-state through the tightening of border controls, an increase in security and policing, the introduction of new visa requirements or the strengthening of existing ones, the criminalisation of irregular migration, and so on (Andreas and Snyder 2000). Following Turkey's shooting down of a Russian Su-24M military aircraft on the Turkish–Syrian border on 24 November 2015, for instance, President Putin responded by suspending visa-free travel for Turkish citizens (Schenk 2016, 481–6). The strengthening of immigration controls, when employed within a coercive inter-state context, is similar to a potential disruption of remittances' outflows: by restricting sending-states' access to its labour market, a host-state aims to elicit their compliance.

Finally, beyond a strategy of restriction – disrupting the outflow of migrant remittances, strengthening immigration controls, or both – a host-state may adopt a second strategy, namely the expulsion of a sending-state's migrant population, either in part or in its entirety. This occurs either through the deportation of a sending-state's migrant community or through the implementation of policies that render a migrant group susceptible to deportation. Such policies may involve novel provisions on required documentation or on immigrants' family history (on the politics of deportation, see Ellermann 2009; De Genova and Peutz 2010; Oyen 2015, 99–127). Security studies scholars approach such policies of 'demographic engineering' as extreme measures (Weiner and Teitelbaum 2001, 55–6, 65–74), for they are able to target both a state's reliance on migrant remittances and its ability to allow the outflow of domestic labour at the same time, effectively 'capacity-swamping' it (Greenhill 2010, 39). Russia's 2008 law *On the Legal Status of Foreign Citizens* includes the option to declare certain foreigners 'undesirable' (*nezhelatel'nyi*). Only in 2015 it was estimated that it deported 117,493 foreigners, particularly citizens of Central Asian and Western states (MVD Rossii – Grazhdanskoe Sodeistvie). Similarly, foreign policy analysts highlight how Saudi Arabia, Libya, and other Arab states do not hesitate to deport certain states' migrants, when bilateral relations deteriorate (Kapiszewski 2001; Thiollet 2011; Tsourapas 2015a; 2016).[6]

How do refugee flows feature into the politics of host states, and, in particular, how might they shape their diplomatic strategies? As discussed in the Introduction, there has yet to be a systematic approach to understanding the role that forced migration might play in international relations. Significant work within the bipolar context of the Cold War remained fixed on understanding, and arguably shaping, the American policymaking thereby prioritising Western viewpoints. This tendency shifts significantly in the post-Cold War context, albeit without leading to major theorisation of the interplay between forced migration and international politics. Most often, research on the international politics of refugees across the Global South has tended to to examine their role through the prism of violence and conflict, as discussed earlier.

At the same time, the socio-economic and political risks perceived to be associated with hosting large numbers of refugees has led to states' lukewarm response in tackling the problem of forced migration (Zolberg 1989, 415; Loescher 1996, 8). This also highlights some of the main problems behind the development of a functional global refugee regime (Betts 2011), as 'states have a legal obligation to support refugees on their own territory, [but] they have no legal obligation to support refugees on the territory of other states' (Betts and Loescher 2011, 19). Tackling this dichotomy lies at the heart of host-states' political engagement with forced migration. For historical and structural reasons, states across the Global South feature the large majority of refugee populations, which creates a power asymmetry with seemingly unaffected Global North states. Yet, Global North states continue to provide economic support for the governments of refugee host-states in the Global South in an act of 'calculated kindness' (Loescher and Scanlan 1986; cf. Arar 2017b). From a security perspective, they do so aiming to prevent the diffusion of forced displacement into their own territory, be it North America (Weiner 1992, 101), or Europe (Greenhill 2016; Huysmans 2000). In attempting to examine how the North–South asymmetry may be perceived from the point of view of refugee host-states, forcibly displaced populations arguably become a source of revenue, particularly given Western states' tendency to offer 'charity' in order to outsource refugee problems to the Global South (cf. Loescher 1996). Empirical examples attest to this: for instance, the influx of Afghani refugees into Pakistan paved the way for a five-year $3.2 billion aid package by the Reagan administration in 1981 (Loescher 1992). More recently, between 2001 and 2007, Nauru received $30 million from the Australian government in order to host refugees and asylum seekers within the Nauru Regional Processing Centre, in addition to Australia covering its operating costs, at $72 million for 2001–2 alone (Oxfam 2002).[7] This is not to suggest that host-states consciously encourage inflows of forcibly displaced populations; rather, that an inflow of refugees may also constitute a strategic resource for these states' governments.

How does the strategic importance of these forcibly displaced populations affect refugee host-states' foreign policy decision-making? Two research agendas are relevant in this regard: firstly, a small group of researchers examines issue-linkage processes, suggesting that 'win-win' strategies may convince Global North states to continue providing support for protecting refugees in the South (cf. Hollifield 2012). As Betts argues, 'in the absence of altruistic commitment by Northern states to support refugees in the South, issue-linkage has been integral in achieving international cooperation on refugees' (Betts and Loescher 2011, 20; Betts 2017). Secondly, work on leverage suggests that host-states are also able to proceed unilaterally, aiming at extracting resources from target states that fear being overwhelmed by migrants or refugees: Greenhill demonstrates that host-states may employ deportation in order to create targeted migrant or refugee 'crises' in target states that, through fear of being 'capacity-swamped', are likely to comply with these states' demands (Greenhill 2003; 2010). As a result, states such as Libya have been able to pursue issue-linkage strategies that manipulate migration interdependence by linking the management of cross-border population mobility to extracting foreign policy and economic benefits from European actors (Tsourapas 2017a; 2018).

Two questions remain unresolved in existing theorisations of refugee host-states' policymaking: firstly, what is the full gamut of foreign policies that these states may employ in seeking to exploit the presence of a refugee population group on their soil, beyond encouraging generations of outflows? Greenhill argues for three types of refugee host-states, namely 'generators', *'agent provocateurs'*, and 'opportunists' – which does not consider states that aim to profit from forced displacement without resorting to coercion. A second, related question is: why do some refugee host-states have more aggressive foreign policy preferences, while others develop strategies of policy coordination rather than coercion? In other words, when do refugee host-states adopt a more coercive stance – reminiscent of Libya under Gaddafi – and when do they employ a more cooperative one, as in the case of Pakistan or Nauru? In addressing these questions, this chapter contributes to the literature by presenting a more complete picture of refugee host-states' foreign policy decision-making, as well as the rationale behind it.

Beyond labour migration, existing international relations work on forced displacement may also be placed in conversation with the literature on rentier states and interdependence. The earlier examination of the economic benefits accrued to host-states by virtue of having refugee populations within their border points to the need to conceptualise refugee populations as a resource from which rent may be extracted. The political science literature on rent and rentier states is intimately connected with Global South and, in particular, Middle East politics, albeit focusing primarily on benefits provided by oil and other natural resources to regional states (Sayigh 1991; Ehteshami 2003). A rentier state needs to meet a number of criteria, mainly that it accrues at least a significant amount of its national revenues from foreign sources in the form of unearned income, or *economic rent* (Beblawi 1987).[8] At the same time, its government needs to be the principal recipient of this rent, while host-state actors are not engaged in the generation of such rent, but on its distribution or utilisation (Mahdavy 1970). In a rentier economy,

> reward – income or wealth – is not related to work and risk bearing, rather to chance or situation. For a rentier, reward becomes a windfall gain, an *isolated* fact, situational or accidental as against the conventional outlook where reward is integrated in a *process* as the end result of a long, systematic and organized production circuit. The contradiction between production and rentier ethics is, thus, glaring. (Beblawi 1987, 385–6)

While rentier state theorists do not discuss cross-border population mobility, I introduce this framework into the international politics of refugees. I argue that refugee host-states may adopt characteristics of a rentier state with regard to their management of forced migration, given that their governments are able to derive similar forms of unearned external income from a specific resource – namely, the presence of refugee populations within a state's borders. For the purposes of this analysis, a *refugee rentier state* is a state that hosts forcibly displaced population group or groups, and which relies financially on external rent linked to its treatment of these group(s). External rent may come from international organisations or third states in a variety of forms, including direct economic aid or grants, debt relief, preferential trade treatment, and so on. Similar to rentier state theory, refugee host-state actors are not engaged in the generation of such rent, but on its distribution or utilisation, which may or may not directly relate to the domestic management of forcibly displaced population group(s). Finally, a refugee rentier state's government remains the principal recipient of this rent.

Some empirical examples allow the clarification of the refugee rentier state concept: Libya's reliance upon European economic aid under Colonel Gaddafi in order to prevent the outflow of sub-Saharan African refugees into the Mediterranean suggests that it is a refugee rentier state: the Libyan state was not involved in the creation of these refugee flows out of sub-Saharan Africa, and the Libyan government was the primary recipient of substantial European economic aid. In contrast, the 1923 population exchange between Turkey and Greece generated over 2 million forcibly displaced persons and significant international economic support; yet, given the involvement of both states' governments in the refugee-generation process, neither Turkey nor Greece qualify as refugee rentier states. Since its creation in 1948, Israel has witnessed the inflow of millions of Jewish refugees, notably from the Arab world and the Soviet Union; yet it does not constitute a refugee rentier state, for Israeli governments do not receive any external income with regard to their treatment of these refugees. In contrast, the significant economic aid afforded to the Pakistani government in response to the influx of 6 million Afghan refugees since 1979 renders it a refugee rentier state.

As discussed in the previous section, the argument that refugee host-states may seek material gains from the presence of displaced communities within their borders is not novel. In fact, already in 1984 Weiner had asserted that international migration may constitute a kind of 'national resource' (quoted in Teitelbaum 1984, 447). In this line of thought, the rentier state framework allows for a better understanding of states' foreign policy decision-making and the rationale behind it, if examined via the prism of *refugee rent-seeking behaviour*. I introduce two key terms from the literature on interdependence: *blackmailing* and *backscratching*. For Oye, a central aspect of contemporary diplomacy within a world of asymmetrical power distribution involves the use of cross-issue linkage (cf. Haas 1980), via two forms. Firstly, blackmailing involves 'threats to do something one does not believe to be in one's interest, unless compensated; and promises to refrain from doing something one does not believe to be in one's own interest, if compensated'. A main example is the Organisation of Arab Petroleum Exporting Countries' (OAPEC) oil embargo against the United States in 1973, which was not in the interests of its member-states. On the other hand, backscratching involves 'promises to refrain from doing something one believes to be in one's interest, if compensated; and threats to do something one believes to be in one's interest, unless compensated'. One example of this is the post-1973 tacit agreement between Washington and Saudi Arabia to maintain oil production in excess of Saudi financial needs (Oye 1979, 14). Keohane and Nye summarise the difference between blackmailing and backscratching by arguing that the first involves 'making a threat one does not wish to carry out', while the second refers to 'offering a *quid pro quo* bargain' (Keohane and Nye 1987, 735).

Importing this model into refugee studies, I argue that there are two ways through which a host-state may exercise rent-seeking behaviour in its foreign policy: via *blackmailing* – threatening to flood target states with refugee populations within its borders, unless compensated; or via *backscratching* – promising to refrain from taking unilateral action against refugee populations within its borders, if compensated. Although backscratching and blackmailing may be considered as two sides of the same coin and the choice made by refugee rentier states may often be less clear-cut, there is value in understanding how the two policies may differ. I operationalise them as follows: on the one hand, a blackmailing strategy often includes threats of unilateral actions to be taken by a refugee host-state. Blackmailers often frame their actions around potential losses that a target state(s) may incur and show little interest in international laws or norms. On the other hand, a backscratching strategy is usually framed around common benefits accrued by cooperation. Backscratchers tend to value multi-lateral negotiations rather than bilateral ones, and they believe that references to international laws or norms strengthen their case.

Migration and subject-making processes

Finally, recent work within anthropology, cultural studies, and sociology has questioned the image of the migrant as the rational utility-maximising actor by undermining the economic logic of studies on return migration (Morawska 2003), as well as emphasising cross-national familial, social and religious ties, global political agendas, and social – rather than merely economic – remittances. However, an (over-) emphasis on agency shifts focus to migrants' intentions rather than the ordering of politics *per se*: if one questions the consciousness of citizens' act of migration (and return), or the degree of freedom to do so within specific social norms and expectations, then this literature's analytic utility falls somewhat short. On the other hand, the validity of purely determinist accounts, under which one's actions and roles cannot be modified, or even challenged, is similarly dubious: the history of political participation, and the practice of migration in particular, abound with instances of interpellated subjects resisting their ascribed roles or reneging on their social expectations.

How can the effects of migration be approached not simply through the interaction between the citizen and state regulations, but also through interactions with practices spread across the social body? In an attempt to bypass the pitfalls of the aforementioned epistemologies, this chapter treats migration as a political act of citizens who are neither autonomous subjects nor inherently rational actors. Rather, their contingent choices and experiences take place within a wider system of rights and obligations, reinvented traditions, personal or familial networks, and religious normativity. Political acts are, thus, produced – and contested – through discourses and practices that emanate from both the government and the social world. By drawing upon the writings of Foucault, this approach allows a shift of focus away from the limiting concept of the state, which now 'appears simply as one element – whose functionality is historically specific and contextually variable – in multiple circuits of power, connecting a diversity of authorities and forces, within a whole variety of complex assemblages'. At the same time, once we are able to 'escape the neat division between state and society', this reading enables an examination of 'practices of power as they are deployed at the micro level of everyday life'.

How would such a conceptualisation shed light onto the complex phenomenon of migration? Anthropologists like Ong and Coutin provide ethnographic examples of how citizenship can be dialectically produced by Asian and Salvadorian immigrants in the United States, yet their analyses leave out any discussion of similar processes within immigrants' country of origin (Ong 1996; Coutin 2007). The issue of whether power structures in immigrants' home countries affected them, or continue to affect them, is left unanswered. In a recent examination of migration processes in the Philippines and India, Rodriguez and Schwenken (2013) attempt to answer this question by arguing that 'labour-sending states set the regulatory frameworks and co-produce "ideal migrant subjects" from which other social actors draw or contest'. Their examination, however, eschews social processes by focusing on institutional mechanisms – such as formal recruitment processes and training centres – that emphasise the state as an object separate from society. At the same time, a broader theoretical question remains with regard to migration processes in non-democratic contexts. If authoritarian regimes are sufficiently concerned about population movements to establish migration-related institutions,[9] how do they shape the structure of the imaginative frameworks within which their subjects participate?

Notes

1 Earlier versions of parts of this chapter have been published in Tsourapas (2018, 2019b, 2020a).
2 While Erdoğan blamed the group for the insurrection, his long-time rival Fethullah Gülen denied any connection to the coup.
3 Hirschman has also introduced the concept of 'loyalty', which he downplayed in later work (see Hirschman 1993), and which is not discussed here. For more information and a broader debate on Hirschman's contribution to migration studies, please refer to Dowding et al. (2000).
4 An exception here is Greenhill's work, which, however, only ascribes Global South states as coercers in these processes, with a broader focus on understanding Western states' responses (see Greenhill 2002, 2003, 2010, 2016).
5 Similar to research on the effects of economic remittances on sending-states, a debate continues on the benefits of such outward mobility, with a number of scholars arguing that it constitutes a form of 'brain drain' for sending-states. This chapter is merely interested in identifying the perceived importance of emigration for sending-states.
6 At the same time, labour migration within the Middle also arguably constitutes an element of cooperation – rather than coercion – between resource-rich/labour-poor and resource-poor/labour-rich autocracies (for comparison, Erdmann et al. 2013;

von Soest 2015; Tasney 2016). However, this is beyond the scope of this book's research questions.

7 Indicatively, Nauru's 2001 GDP was $19 million.

8 Beblawi's 1987 canonical text on rentier states does not define what a 'significant' amount may be. I adopt this approach here, given that it allows for maximum flexibility in understanding states' behaviour.

9 On the Middle East context, see Brand (2006).

2

Migration and the state in the modern Middle East: a history

This chapter provides a broad introduction to the politics of migration in the Middle East, from the colonial era to the present day, paying particular attention to the importance of state policies. There are, roughly, four time periods in the evolution of the Middle East migration system that should be discussed: the *colonial* period, encompassing the era of the Ottoman Empire and the colonial Mandate period that ended, roughly, in the years following the end of World War Two. This is a period characterised by a rather free circulation of movement within this broad region, as well as long-distance emigration to the Americas, Europe, and sub-Saharan Africa. It is also marked by waves of immigration into the region from Europe. The *postcolonial* period, from the late 1940s until the late 1960s, coincides with the rise of Arab nationalism, as cross-border population mobility is driven mainly by political, rather than economic, factors. The *oil boom* period, from the late 1960s until the early 1980s, is dominated by economically driven cross-border migratory flows, although national and regional politics continues to play an important role. Finally, the period of *de-Arabisation*, from the 1980s to today, is characterised by an influx of Asian and sub-Saharan migrants and the rise of irregular migration, as well as increasing cooperation between Arab and European states.

Middle East migration and the colonial period

The history of the Middle East has always been associated with mobility. For historian Ibn Khaldun, the very creation of the Arab world was due to the movement of the Banu Hilal tribes from the Arabian Peninsula into Egypt and, subsequently, across North Africa during the eleventh century. Their victories over the Berber populations brought the Arabic language and the Islamic faith to the Maghreb and continued a long process of migration in the region that had existed ever since the introduction of Islam in seventh-century Mecca. Despite some restrictions put in place by the Ottoman Empire, merchants, nomads, clerks, and others would not hesitate to traverse the vast area of the Middle East (Hourani 2013). Modest population movements across the Muslim world persisted, notably in the historic region of the *bilād al-shām* (Syria, Lebanon, Palestine, and Jordan), in the Sinai Peninsula, in Cyrenaica, as well as in parts of the Arabian Peninsula (the Hejaz, Yemen, and Oman). This was particularly true with regard to the processes of the *Hajj*, the annual pilgrimage to Mecca that all adult Muslims must perform at least once in their lifetime. Caravans of tens of thousands of pilgrims would set out across the Middle East to Mecca along well-established routes, the *darb al-Hajj*. Many pilgrims never returned to their homelands but established their new homes across these routes. Beyond religion, education was another reason for temporary or permanent migration – the *al-Azhar* University in Cairo, established in 970, has welcomed students of the Qur'an and Islamic law ever since. The founding of *Dar al-Ulum* in Cairo, a Training College for Teachers of Arabic, and a separate Teachers' Training College in 1886, substantially increased the number of students into Egypt (Matthews and Akrawi 1949; Tsourapas 2016).

At the same time, Egyptian scholars and professionals traversed the region, primarily as teachers of Arabic, which earned Egypt the affectionate nickname *al-Shaqiqa al-Kubra*, or the Big Sister of the Arab world. Egyptians were recruited to work in Kuwait's first two public schools, *al-Mubārakiyya and al-Aḥmadiyya*, from the mid-1930s onwards and in Iraqi schools from 1936 onwards (FO 141/660/12–1937). In fact, in the pre-1956 period, secondary school students across the Arab world would receive the *Tawjīhiyya*, the Egyptian Secondary School Certificate, upon graduation (Misnad 1985). Administrators and legal scholars were also sent abroad: one notable example is 'Abd al-Razzāq al-Sanhūrī, who had drafted the Egyptian Civil Code. al- Sanhūrī travelled to Baghdad to found the city's School of Law in the mid-1930s, and drafted the Iraqi Civil Code in 1943 (Saleh 1979).

Meanwhile, the Levant (referred to also as the *Mashreq*, or the historical region of Syria now encompassing Lebanon, Jordan, Syria, Israel, Iraq, and Palestine) witnessed two particular types of mobility: one, was the rise of emigration out of Mount Lebanon and Syria in the mid-nineteenth century, arising out of communal strife but, also, deteriorating local economic conditions (Khater 2001). Waves of emigration out of Lebanon continued throughout the twentieth century, particularly in the context of the Lebanese Civil War, creating a thriving Lebanese diaspora across the Americas and sub-Saharan Africa (Pearlman 2013). Palestine witnessed successive waves of Jewish immigration, or *aliyot*, mainly out of the Russian empire. Jews sought shelter from the waves of anti-Semitism in Europe and the frequent pogroms, but also to establish themselves in the Land of Israel.

Middle East migration and the postcolonial period

A number of factors contributed to the rise of Arab nationalism in the Middle East in the inter-war period, including the collapse of the Ottoman Empire, the failure to create a unified Arab state at the end of World War One, as well as the strengthening of colonial rule – either directly, in North Africa, or indirectly, in terms of League of Nations Mandates in the Levant and Iraq – paved the way for the rise of Arab nationalism across the Middle East. The continuing immigration of European Jews into the *Eretz Israel*, as per Zionist expectations, also triggered Arab nationalism that culminated in the 1948 Arab–Israeli War. Migration flows in this period are characterised by two monumental events: firstly, the Arab–Israeli conflict, particularly the 1948 and 1967 wars; secondly, the rise to power of Arab nationalist forces – most notably, Egyptian President Gamal Abdel Nasser (1954–70).

The Arab–Israeli conflict has historically resulted in the largest migration movements among Arab populations, both directly and indirectly. In terms of its direct effects, Palestinian emigration to the West increased in light of their continuing struggle with the British authorities over the influx of Jews that increasingly abandoned Europe in the aftermath of World War One. But it was the 1948 War and the creation of the Israeli state that resulted in the *Nakba*, or catastrophe, for the Arabs, as over 700,000 Palestinian Arabs fled violence, or were expelled from their homes. The United Nations Relief and Works Agency for Palestine Refugees in the Near East (UNRWA) was created in 1949 to provide relief to refugees in Jordan, Lebanon, Syria, the Gaza Strip, and the West Bank. It became even more important once the 1967 Six Day War created an additional 300,000 Palestinian refugees. The dire economic and political situation in the West Bank and the Gaza Strip contributed to continuing outflows of Palestinians, primarily across the Arab World.

Indirectly, Zionist and, since 1948, Israeli policies provided the impetus for Arab states to demonstrate their solidarity with the Palestinians through organised expulsions of their Jewish populations. The Jewish exodus from Arab states was a continuing, violent process of 'un-mixing' populations that had co-existed for centuries. In North Africa, Jews faced organised persecution following 1948, which led to their exodus either to Israel or to European countries, notably France. Their population in Libya, Morocco, Tunisia, and Algeria diminished from hundreds of thousands in each state, to a few hundred by the end of the twentieth century. Similarly, Nasser's ascent to power in Egypt and, in particular, the aftermath of the 1956 Suez Crisis led to organised expulsions of Egyptian Jews. In some cases, Israel was instrumental in organising these movements, as in the 1950–1 exodus of Iraqi Jews via *Operation Ezra and Nehemiah*, or in the 1949–50 *Operation Magic Carpet* in Yemen. Through these two operations, approximately 120,000 Iraqi Jews and 49,000 Yemenite Jews were brought into Israel.

Politically minded emigration also came to include Europeans who had been living in the Middle East, particularly across North Africa and Egypt. Reminiscent of the 1922 Greek–Turkish population exchange that formed part of the creation of the Republic of Turkey, Arab nation-states encouraged – sometimes passively, sometimes more violently – the exodus of their European communities. The 1969 ousting of King Idris by Colonel Gaddafi in Libya instigated a process of expulsion for both Libya's Jewish and Italian communities, numbering some 37,000 and 20,000 citizens, respectively. Italians, in particular, were ordered to leave the country by 7 October 1970 – a day that the regime would annually commemorate as the *Day of Revenge*. Most residents of French Algeria with European ancestry, some 800,000 *pied-noirs*, were evacuated to France after the country's 1962 independence. A similar fate awaited the Greek community of Egypt, which amounted to over 25,000 by the time of Nasser's ascent to power, but of whom roughly 7,000 remained by 1966. Italian Egyptians and Syrians also fled the country in this period.

The era of Arab nationalism also encouraged the emigration of thousands of political dissidents – from *ancien régime* royalists or communists to members of the Muslim Brotherhood. In Egypt, despite regime repression, hundreds of Muslim Brothers managed to flee to Saudi Arabia in this period (Kandil 2015, 32), Kuwait, Bahrain, or elsewhere – Yusuf al-Qaradawi, for instance, relocated to Qatar; 'Abd al-Latif Mikki fled to Syria (Kandil 2015, 65). Others, such as Sa'id Ramadan, 'Abd al-Hakim 'Abidin, Sa'd al-Din al-Walili, Muhammad Najub Juwayfil, and Kamil Isma'il were accused of 'treason to the [Egyptian] nation', stripped of their nationality while they were in Syria, and forbidden from returning to Egypt (Mitchell 1969, 141). In the Gulf, Palestinian migrants as well as high-skilled, leftist Egyptians were able to organise frequent protests and demonstrations.

But the political nature of cross-border migration in the Middle East is best articulated in two broader conflicts, one involving the rivalry between conservative and revolutionary republics in the Arab world – or the Arab Cold War, and the other being the rivalry between high-skilled Egyptian and Israeli professionals dispatched across sub-Saharan Africa. In this process of intra-Arab antagonism, the Egyptian regime was able to employ regional migration as an instrument of soft power partly given the massive developmental needs that the Arab world faced at the time. In particular, Egypt's secondment programme (*nizam al-i'ara li-l-kharij*) gradually became a main component of the Nasserite propaganda machine across the Arab world, together with a variety of other elements, from radio broadcasts of the *ṣawt al-'arab* (Voice of the Arabs), to the distribution of Egyptian newspapers abroad, as the literature has already identified, within the context of the Arab Cold War (Kerr 1978; James 2006). Nasser himself, in fact, made the connection between political influence and education by calling the Voice of the Arabs 'an open university' that provided 'education in national consciousness' (quoted in Abou-El-Fadl 2015, 232). A British report on Sudan details how 'Egypt's cultural leadership in the Arab world is unrivalled and her present Government exploits it to the full in pursuit of political aims. Egyptian teachers are sent to the Sudan; Sudanese teachers are trained in Egypt' (TNA – FO 407/237, 1957).

In Africa, Egyptians were pitted against Israelis, as both countries aimed to sway the newly independent African states to their favour. According to *The New York Times*, 'the Egyptians [made] themselves heard everywhere in Africa and play[ed] the part of self-chosen leaders' (*The New York Times*, 1 March 1956). Indeed, as Muhammad Hasanayn Haykal, a close advisor of Nasser, declared: 'Egypt must send selected missions of experts in science, religion, politics, economics, commerce and social services to aid the African peoples, to support them, to collaborate with them and light the path before them' (Haykal 1956). Again, the foreign policy aspect is prominent, for two reasons: firstly, Egypt believed it stood to gain potential support at the United Nations from the newly independent African nations (Cremeans 1963); secondly, and perhaps more importantly, it aimed to battle the involvement of Israel in the continent. In 1965, Nasser wrote:

> The struggle of the Asian and African peoples is not waged in isolation from the struggle of the Arab nation. In addition to the responsibilities of the development of the African continent following its liberation call for gigantic efforts so that imperialism should not infiltrate and return to it under the pressure of underdevelopment or behind a deceptive mask, such as the Israeli mask, which imperialism tries actively to make use of in Africa. (Nasser 1966, 12)

Middle East migration and the oil boom period

In the late 1960s, a number of important events contributed to the end of the postcolonial period in the politics of migration in the Middle East, including the Arabs' defeat in the Six Day War with Israel in 1967, the death of Nasser in 1970, as well as the increasing concentration of wealth in the oil-producing states of the Gulf (as well as Libya). The gap between oil producers and non-producers in the Middle East widened even further following the 1973 Arab–Israeli War, in which an embargo on oil exports led to the quadrupling of oil prices. As wealth soared into Libya and the

Gulf, labour migration across the Middle East assumed a new form, dominated by economic rather than political forces, as hundreds of thousands of Egyptians, Yemenis, Palestinians, and Jordanians pursued employment abroad (Seccombe 1985). The small numbers of migrants working on fishing and pearling in the Gulf gave way to thousands of workers in Bahrain, Kuwait, Qatar, Oman, Saudi Arabia, and the United Arab Emirates. These had numbered around 800,000 before the 1973 War; by 1974, they had reached roughly 4 million. This is not to imply that all these workers were employed in the oil industry; in fact, most of them worked in sectors that experienced a boost because of oil revenues, such as construction, services, or education. With the centrality of the Gulf as a work destination of young Muslims remaining undiminished to this day, migration has dramatically altered the population make-up of oil-producing countries: indicatively, only 9% of the United Arab Emirates' population is currently native-born. Similarly, a number of smaller labour migration flows occurred elsewhere in the region, including cyclical labour migration of Syrian unskilled workers into Lebanon, as well as Sudanese workers into Egypt. Significant permanent emigration flows also occurred out of the Maghreb: taking advantage of the post-World War Two economic reconstruction processes in Europe, thousands of Tunisians, Moroccans, and Algerians settled permanently in European states, primarily France, creating large diaspora communities.[1]

This is not to say that state politics retreated from migration management in the region; yet such politics were pursued according to national interest, rather than anything else. North African states developed established institutions of monitoring the activities of their diasporas in Europe, the *amicales* (Brand 2006). Gaddafi's Libya repeatedly linked its immigration policy to its Arab foreign policy priorities, not hesitating to evict or mistreat Egyptian, Tunisian, or Palestinian immigrants in order to force respective political elites into specific policy shifts. Intra-Arab relations have equally been affected by the Palestinian exodus, with the events of Black September in 1970 that saw the expulsion of the Palestine Liberation Front from Jordan and the Lebanese Civil War (1975–90) being two striking examples. Mirroring the Turkish state's Turkification policies towards its Kurdish minority, the Iraqi state engaged in forced internal migration processes of Yazidis and Kurds in Northern Iraq – as part of broader Arabisation campaigns – aiming to shift regional demographics in favour of Iraqi Arabs.

Middle East migration and the de-Arabisation period

Finally, a long period of de-Arabisation has characterised regional migration politics since the early 1980s, marked by an influx of Asian and sub-Saharan migrants and the rise of irregular migration, as well as increasing cooperation between Arab and European states. This is evident in shifting immigration policies across the Gulf states, whose elites are traditionally worried about the political effects of immigration within their states. As the Qatari Minister of Labour, Abd al-Rahman al-Dirham, stated:

> The question of foreign labor is of great concern. Our social customs are threatened by foreigners. The problem is not just in Qatar but also in other Gulf countries. We prefer it if we can get suitable people from Arab countries who can live in the Gulf area without changing it. (Middle East Economic Digest (MEED), August 1982, 40)

Not surprisingly, the rise of PLO militant activism in the 1970s gradually resulted in expulsion of Palestinian labourers. 'Statistics show', Haddad argued, 'that both Saudi Arabia and Kuwait reduced the recruitment of Palestinian laborers' after 1970, opting instead to employ 'large numbers' of Egyptians who would not 'function as a fifth column and eventually endanger the host countries' (Haddad 1987, 248). Since the late 1970s and, in particular, the 1979 takeover of the Grand Mosque in Mecca and the Iranian Revolution, workers from Southeast Asia have gradually replaced Arab labour as the most populous migrant group in the oil-exporting countries of the Gulf (Kapiszewski 2006a). This was the result both of a continuous, large migratory wave out of Pakistan and Bangladesh, and the political decision to expel large numbers of Arab workers, particularly in the aftermath of the 1990–1 Gulf War: believing that the Palestinian and Yemeni political leadership supported the Iraqi invasion of Kuwait, the Gulf states expelled roughly 800,000 Yemeni workers, while the vast majority of Palestinian migrants were also forced to leave from Kuwait, where they had sought shelter in the aftermath of the 1948 and 1967 wars (Van Hear 1998; Tsourapas 2015b). The regional instability of the early 1990s also led to the return of more than 700,000 Egyptians and roughly 200,000 Jordanians.

A similar process of de-Arabisation occurred in Libya, where Gaddafi attracted an increasing number of sub-Saharan African immigrants into the country. From the early 1990s onwards, Gaddafi became less interested in Arab unity and, instead, sought to spearhead closer ties among African states under pan-Africanism. This included the signing of a 1990 integration charter with Sudan, a 1994 agreement with Chad, as well as the 1998 creation of the Community of Sahel-Saharan States (CENSAD) which contained numerous objectives regarding the free movement of people. Gradually, Gaddafi employed Libya's position as a host-state for African labour in order to further his diplomatic openings towards African states (Tsourapas 2017a). While immigration had distinct economic advantages for the Libyan

Table 2.1 Phases of Middle East migration

Timeframe	Movement from	Movement to	Numbers	Type of regulation	Role of state
To 1973	High-skilled Egyptians and Jordanians	Across the Arab world	c. 1970 – 880,000	Individual secondment	Direct regulations by both sending and receiving countries
	Algerians, Yemenis, Sudanese	France, Saudi Arabia, Egypt		State-to-state missions	Minor individual migration
1973 and period immediately following	Workers from oil-poor Arab nations	Services, construction, administration to Gulf countries and Libya	1975 – 1,800,000	Relaxation on restrictions from labour exporters because of perceived benefits of remittances	Arab migration largely individual or project-based
	Some Indians and Pakistanis				
Late 1970s	Workers from oil-poor Arab nations	Oil-rich and Gulf countries	Late 1970s – 2,100,000 to 2,500,000	Government agencies set up by Asian labour exporters to regulate their workers	Arab sending governments encouraged and even competed against other labour exporters
	Indians, Pakistanis, Bangladeshis	Many labour markets of Arab Middle East		Receiving countries not allowing integration of labour	Asian states played direct role in regulating the outflow of their workers

Table 2.1 Phases of Middle East Migration (Continued)

Timeframe	Movement from	Movement to	Numbers	Type of regulation	Role of state
1980–82	Chinese; Taiwanese; Indonesian; South Korean; Filipino; and Thai workers Selected Asians	Most labour-importing countries of the Middle East Egypt	Early 1980s – 3,500,000 to 4,650,000	The receiving communities assumed direct responsibility for managing the flow 'Package deals' and bilateral arrangements	State-to-state interactions ensued
1983–90	Highly skilled workers rather than unskilled manual workers	Most labour importers	Only select estimates for Gulf	Labor importers beginning to cut back on labour Attempts to train local nationals	Labour importers playing a more regulatory role
1991 and beyond	Asian workers and to a lesser extent Arab workers abroad Returnees Refugees due to interstate war and civil war	Their respective home countries (return flow), points of transition and alternative destinations New opportunities in the Middle East	The returnees due to market adjustments are variously estimated Refugees due to violence are estimated at 5.5 million Recycling patterns unclear	Labour contracts not being renewed Expulsions and cutbacks in staffing needs Forceful expulsion Improved record keeping	Labour importers playing increasingly regulatory role Labour exporters search for alternative destinations Emergence of potential regional approaches

Source: Choucri, 1997, pp. 106-7

economy at the time, 'the regime sought a leadership role in the international arena to counter its increasing isolation from Arab countries and the West' (Paoletti 2010, 86).

Table 2.1 summarises migration trends across the Middle East. The oil-producing states' shift in their immigration policies away from the recruitment of Arab labourers produced two important results in the regional politics of migration: firstly, this created the impetus for Arabs' and sub-Saharan Africans' irregular migration through the Mediterranean into Europe (Talani 2010; Tsourapas 2017a). This phenomenon reached considerable proportions in the aftermath of the 2011 Arab Spring events. Secondly, this has created the need for the involvement of non-Middle East states in the management of regional migration, namely the EU and EU member-states. Over the past few years, a number of Middle East states have taken advantage of their position as migrant-sending or migrant-transit states in order to sign 'Mobility Partnerships' with the EU – such as Jordan, Morocco, and Tunisia (Collyer 2012), or to negotiate *ad hoc* agreements – as the 2016 EU–Turkey Statement.

Notes

1 This process had already begun in the 1960s, similarly to Turkish emigration into Europe.

3

Constructing the migrant as a subject of power in Egypt

'Keep away from those who stuff themselves after they have starved.'

Egyptian proverb

This first empirical chapter sets the stage for an analysis of the politics of migration in the contemporary Middle East via an in-depth analysis of the linkages between emigration and foreign policy in the case of Egypt. Modern Egypt was chosen as a case study based on two factors. Firstly, the country has a historical standing as the largest regional provider of migrant labour. Secondly, the qualitative variety of migratory processes throughout the history of modern Egypt, and their quantitative increase in the post-1973 period, have endowed the Egyptian case with a vast array of writings, debates, customs, and social rituals on migration, whose discursive importance has been unexamined by the literature. This chapter argues that Egyptian practices demonstrate key linkages between emigration, subject-making processes, and foreign policy in the 1952–2011 era. The discourse on migration under Nasser reflected a broader collectivist ethos, under which the theme of population movement was employed to discipline Egyptian citizens in accordance with the regime's ideology of statism-developmentalism. In sharp contrast to this, migration and, more specifically, return migration under Sadat and Mubarak was employed to promote an individualisation of responsibility, as citizens disciplined themselves to use their freedom in making responsible choices under a broader turn towards neoliberalism.[1]

Emigration and subject-making processes under Nasser, 1954–70

'To build factories is easy; to build hospitals and schools is possible; but to build a nation of men is a hard and difficult task.'

Gamal Abdel Nasser, *National Assembly Speech*, 1957

The 1952 creation of the modern Egyptian state and Nasser's subsequent ascent to power coincided with a rise in diverse forms of emigration, despite various institutional restrictions on such population movements. The exodus of Egyptian Jews was coupled with the emigration of political dissenters (royalist supporters of the *ancien régime*; communists; Muslim Brothers) and foreigners (primarily Greeks, Italians, and Syrians). As will be seen below, more than 40,000 Egyptians were working abroad in the Yemen Arab Republic, as were a few thousand in Syria during its short-lived unification with Egypt. Rising numbers of high-skilled Egyptians would pursue temporary work across the Middle East and Africa under the aegis of the Egyptian Ministry of Education. A significant number of Egyptian students studying abroad never returned to Egypt, while a growing percentage of Copts permanently left Egypt for North America, Europe, and Australia, particularly following the introduction of the 1956 Constitution, which introduced Islam as an official religion.

What is striking about these movements is that, in their vast majority, they were not openly acknowledged by the Egyptian regime, despite the fact that Nasser was wise to the political importance of emigration – as can be deduced from his privately aired concerns about rising Jewish migration to Israel and the Israeli presence in newly independent African states. Partially in response to Israeli policy, which Nasser termed a 'mask of imperialism', the president significantly expanded upon the policy of targeted temporary emigration (particularly Egyptian teachers, nurses, scientists, or military experts) to Arab and African states; once there, they contributed to the spreading of Nasserist 'political propaganda', according to the doctrine that Egypt 'as a revolution' would not maintain the territorial boundaries of Egypt 'as a state'. As a result, in Libya, as elsewhere in the Arab world, Egyptian high-skilled professionals were subject to frequent deportations as a result of their political activism. The overarching political character of such emigration is further stressed by the fact that most of these emigrants' wages abroad were paid by the Egyptian government rather than the host-states. Nasser's concern regarding mass emigration is also evident in the numerous measures he adopted and resources he devoted to prevent such movements in his earlier years, while governmental reports further show how the regime would later consider emigration as a solution to Egypt's problem of 'astronomical' over-population.

Throughout his tenure as president, Nasser would rarely publicly discuss the issue of migration. The Egyptian state never released details concerning the emigration of Egyptian Jews; rather, one has to rely on private accounts or the reports of international organisations. State statistics on the departure of Egyptian Copts are, similarly, unavailable. This lacuna comes in sharp contrast with a long history of state record keeping in Egypt, and the otherwise detailed statistical accounts collected and methodically published by the state under Nasser. Even the word diaspora (*al-shatāt*) has been, to this day, largely shunned in official rhetoric due to its association with the creation of the Israeli state. Instead, if asked about migration, Nasser would brush it off, often stating that 'Egyptians don't migrate'. In doing so, he generalised upon the longstanding belief in the Egyptian *fallāhīn*'s (farmers') attachment to the land and their 'state of apathy' towards emigration, a belief that traces its roots to the nineteenth century. Of course, the phenomena of internal migration and urbanisation in Egypt throughout the twentieth century – let alone the population movements listed above – had long debunked the validity of this myth. Yet, as the political act of migration (or, more precisely, the dismissal of migration as an act) became associated with a distinct field of meaning, the belief in an 'attachment to the land' was made credible within the Nasserist social order.

The plausibility of this narrative relied upon a strong degree of association and cohesion with the regime's overall ideology. Behind Nasser's public assertions that 'everybody knows that Egyptians do not like to emigrate', the President constructed a broader belief system about the duties, rights, and expected conduct of a citizen. The belief system operated in line with other frames of reference, particularly Egyptian nationalism coupled with distrust of 'reactionary' neighbouring countries and the two Cold War superpowers, and a statist-developmentalist programme whose success relied on ample domestic manpower. At the same time, normative guidelines were put in place that omitted migration from subjects' repertoires of action: the rejection of migration attained a moral weight as the broad demonisation of migratory movements ultimately enabled life outside of Egypt to be presented as a type of punishment. The regime would duly publicise how it stripped communists, members of the Muslim Brotherhood, or other 'traitors to the state' of their Egyptian nationality, barring their return to the country.

The discourse on migration, in effect, allowed Nasser to 'construct' the citizen, individually and collectively, around the regime's broader ideational priorities. On an individual level, the president would repeatedly demonise any cases of greed or corruption, discouraging the self-interested pursuit of profit in favour of collective concern for the state. This was the explicit rationale behind Nasser's policy of *taklīf* (mandatory work), which forbade migration of specific professions until one had been employed within Egypt for a set number of years. More broadly, Nasser would applaud practices that discouraged consumerism, thereby delineating Egyptian citizens' fields of action within specified parameters of socio-political disposition. Overall, a citizen who wished to migrate came to contradict the oft-stated principles of autarky and frugality upon which the Nasserist regime relied:

> There are certain notions which should be discarded like extravagance and
> luxury. Today I would like to say a thing or two about extravagance. Every
> pound we save in constructing a factory contributes to the national wealth
> and, by increasing these savings, we can build another factory and thus provide,
> for example, one hundred individuals with work [...] No one should think
> only of himself. Those of us who lead a comfortable life do so at the expense
> of others. (United Arab Republic Information Department, 1958)

On a collective level, the perceived absence of migration helped pave the
way for the establishment of 'the new society'; one, the regime argued, that
was being 'built along the lines of a democratic, cooperative socialism. The
principal aims of the government are to raise the standard of living, and
to afford equal opportunities to all citizens.' The lack of emigration, the
regime argued, mirrored a sound economic policy. Put differently, there
was no need to move abroad given the ample employment opportunities
within Egypt. 'Ours is not a poor state, brothers, but a rich one', Nasser
would emphasise (United Arab Republic Information Department, 1959).
In associating the lack of migration with state development, the regime
associated the act of emigration with a lack of belief in the Nasserist state, or
a wish to undermine it. Complementary government policies entrenched the
absence of migration within broader modes of action: the Land Reform Law,
for instance, discouraged migration by providing ample work opportunities
for Egyptian farmers. Nasser's 1964 *siyāsat al-ta'yīn* (graduate appointment
policy), which stipulated that the state would provide public sector employment for every Egyptian citizen who graduated from university, further
undermined economic incentives for emigration.

   Overall, despite the fact that population movements were not only visible
by, but highly disruptive to, Egyptian society, the regime discursively downplayed such movements in delineating the framework in which political
subjects were encouraged to participate. Thus, the regime's approach to
migration shaped subjects' conceptions of meaningful political participation
and introduced a degree of disconnect between the 'model' Egyptian citizen
and those who had left the country. Remaining in Egypt, in other words,
made sense, whereas emigrating largely did not. Indications of the regime's
success in making this discourse hegemonic can be found in the commonly
held view, still promoted today, that Egyptians did not emigrate under
Nasser, and that view's routine reproduction in the relevant scholarship as
a broader truth, further obscuring the socio-political importance of population
movements that occurred during Nasser's reign.

   As a result, this period's diverse population movements have essentially
been relegated into aberrations, or unintentional mishaps, hindering their
examination as part and parcel of the regime's production of power. More
importantly, the Nasserist regime was able to morally justify its restriction of

subjects' repertoire of actions, by putting forth social norms that it professed to be more important than individual freedom: 'When will Egyptians [...] be permitted to travel freely abroad [?]' an American journalist asked Nasser in 1959. 'When we have a surplus of foreign currencies which we can spend on luxury and on summer vacations in Europe and America', he replied tersely.

Broadly, a strategy of cultural diplomacy developed after 1954, which aimed at disseminating ideas of an Egypt-led Arab unity, anti-colonialism, and anti-Zionism across the Middle East (Barnett 1998; James 2006). This had a number of components: for one, Egypt sponsored radio programmes, notably *al-Sawt al-'Arab* (Voice of the Arabs), which were broadcast across the Middle East and enjoyed enormous popularity. The distribution of Egyptian newspapers abroad was also employed in the context of the Arab Cold War as an instrument of Egyptian propaganda (Kerr 1978). Education was also a very important foreign policy tool, particularly in allowing Arabs to pursue degrees in Egypt, frequently under Egyptian state scholarships. In fact, Nasser himself made the connection between regional political influence and education by calling the Voice of the Arabs 'an open university' that provided 'education in national consciousness' (quoted in Abou-El-Fadl 2015, 232). But how was high-skilled regional emigration linked to cultural diplomacy?

In Libya, Egyptian professionals promoted Nasserite ideals, particularly Arab unity and anti-colonialism, in a number of ways. Britain's ambassador to Libya, Sir Alec Kirkbride, reported in 1954 how 'Egypt is the nearest source of supply for Arab officials, many parts of the Libyan administration are modelled on the Egyptian pattern and lastly the Egyptian Government continues to pay the salaries of Egyptian civil servants seconded to Libya and allows them to draw, in addition, the Libyan salaries attached to their posts.' But it was Egyptian teachers that the British were worried about. Kirkbride warned that 'the most damage to British interests is being done by the considerable number of Egyptian teachers who are employed in the Libyan schools. These people are in a position to poison the mind of the rising generation of Libyans against the Western Powers in general and against Great Britain in particular' (TNA – FO 371/108687, 1954). One example of this phenomenon is the Libyan secondary school curriculum, as developed and taught by Egyptian teachers:

> The presence of Egyptian teachers explains why so many classrooms show the influence of Egyptian propaganda. Pupils do crayon drawings of Egyptian troops winning victories over Israel or Britain. In Benghazi, Libya, a complete course in Egyptian history is given to secondary school students. A display in a high school art exhibit showed pictures of the leading rulers of Egypt; on one side were the 'bad' rulers, on the other the 'good' rulers. The bad rulers began with the Pharaoh Cheops, who enslaved his people to build the pyramids,

and ended with Farouk. The good rulers began with the idealistic Pharaoh Ikhnaton and ended with, of course, Gamal Abdel Nasser. (Wynn 1959, 137)

Nasserite cultural diplomacy across the country was aided by the fact that Libyan schools were using Egyptian textbooks. The seventh-grade textbooks featured a dedicated chapter entitled 'I am an Arab' that stated: 'I am an Arab. Yes, I say it with all pride and happiness. I am not alone. Every Arab is my brother in language, religion, feeling and nationhood ... Yes, I am an Arab from Libya' (Obeidi 1999, 37). But, importantly, Egyptian cultural diplomacy in Libya involved the dispatch of other professionals – the Libyan labour code was drafted by Egyptian legal scholars, while the country's first university, the Libyan University, was initially run by Egyptian academics (*Middle East Report* 1961, 150). More broadly, *The New York Times'* coverage of the country described how Libya had

> large contingents of Egyptian teachers, advisers, and government administrators [whose] penetration into almost every field of Libyan life has become a matter of Western alarm. For these Egyptians are also helping carry on Premier Nasser's anti-Western campaign. There are almost 500 Egyptian teachers in Libyan secondary schools. (*The New York Times*, 24 May 1956)

Beyond North Africa, Egyptians 'played a major role in the development of the political and cultural consciousness of [Arab] nationalism in Bahraini society' (Chalcraft 2010, 8). Similarly, Egyptian teachers in Dubai were involved in attempts to spread Nasserite ideas and foster students' political activism, as 'many young boys were encouraged by senior students and expatriate staff to demonstrate in the streets while carrying banners and photos of Jamal Abdel Nasser' (Davidson 2008, 41). The diary of Donald Hawley, a British diplomat and writer stationed in Dubai at the time, describes in detail a variety of forms of Egyptian-led political activism, including the decoration of school classrooms with pictures of Nasser and the recitation of Nasser's speeches. In Iraq, the government claimed that

> teachers were a potent factor in the spread of Nasser propaganda and that they helped incite youths to demonstrations that resulted in eleven deaths [in November 1956], mostly in Mosul. [Teachers were found to] have agitated against the regime by encouraging students to howl on streets for severance of relations with Britain and France. (*The New York Times*, 17 May 1957)

Beyond educational staff, Egyptian professionals were recruited in 'the Codification Department of the Ministry of Justice, in the Oil Affairs Department of the Ministry of Economics, and in the Government Oil Refineries Administration [...]' (TNA – FO 481/12–1958).

British archival sources paint a similar picture in Kuwait, where the Director of Education had been Egyptian himself until 1950 (TNA – FO

464/12, 1956). In the aftermath of the 1956 Suez Crisis, Egyptian teachers were reported to have organised a countrywide boycott of foreign goods, enforced by 'young women patrols (mostly Egyptian teachers) who started going round in twos and threes visiting shops and preaching to the shopkeepers the sin of selling to the foreigner'. The report highlighted how 'it would appear that all [women patrols] are Egyptians' (TNA – FO 371/120558, 1956). While it is imperative that the alarmist nature of these reports be put into the broader historical context of de-colonisation and Great Britain's concerns over the power of Nasser across the Arab world, multiple sources acknowledge how the Kuwaiti 'education system and the social clubs [appear to be] completely Egyptian influenced' (*The New York Times*, 15 March 1957). A British account of a sports gala organised in May 1957 in Minaa' Shuweekh indicates the extent of the interplay between the export of Egyptian teachers and cultural diplomacy dissemination in Kuwait; it describes how 2,100 Kuwaiti secondary school students participated in the event:

> The tune which welcomed spectators just before the gala began was that of the favourite song of 'Voice of the Arabs.' It was entitled, 'Woe to the Colonisers' … The historical tableaux which appeared in the program included: a representation of the battle of Port Said [in the context of the Suez Crisis], which took the form of a float bearing a boat with sailors and an effigy of a descending parachutist. The sailors in the boat were shooting down the parachutist. Written in large letters on the side of the float was: 'Get out of my Canal' … A physical training display which was the last event in the programme, consisted of exercises performed to the tune of a song specially composed for the occasion by an Egyptian inspector of education. Each verse of this song recalled one of the Arab states: Egypt was represented as the champion of Arab freedom and the repeller of the aggressors; Yemen as the protector of Aden who was called upon to liberate her; Syria was described as the home of true nationalism, while Iraqis were the subject of sarcastic praise for their skill in picking dates with their finger-tips … These points together with the lengthy displays in which hundreds of small boys took part with air-rifles, made this gala nearer in character to a military rally than to a sporting event. (TNA – FO 371/126899, 1957)

How effective was the export of high-skilled Egyptians across the Arab world in constituting an effective strategy of cultural diplomacy under Nasser? The difficulty of accurately measuring both soft power and its effects is well established. That said, one indication of its effectiveness – besides archival and media sources cited above – lies in local elites' responses. In Libya, King Idris reportedly attempted to identify Egyptian teachers engaging in the dissemination of pan-Arabism by using secret police agents disguised as students: 'the planting of secret police in class-rooms in secondary schools may seem grotesque, but it is to be remembered that many of the twenty-one and twenty-two year old pupils are very grown up in appearance' a British 1965 report argues, concluding that eighty Egyptian teachers were duly deported, with Libya bringing in Tunisians instead (TNA – FO 371/97338). Iraqi elites employed similar strategies to counter Nasserism, where twenty-five teachers were expelled in 1957, although this was 'carried out with restraint' and without targeting higher education professionals 'who are still needed' (*The New York Times*, 17 May 1957). Beyond elites' attempts at combatting the phenomenon, a wide variety of anecdotal data points to the soft power effects of Egyptian high-skilled migration on the 'hearts and minds' of the Arab world – Hawley's memoirs include a notable event in which a group of young boys shouted at him on a Dubai street, in 1961: 'Down with colonization and long live Gamal!' (Hawley 2007, 116).

The use of high-skilled migration as an instrument of soft power did not rest solely on the dissemination of cultural diplomacy abroad. Across a number of host-states, Egyptian migration diplomacy facilitated the dispersal of development aid, either in the form of expertise or in terms of infrastructural support. This is most evident in Egyptian emigration in sub-Saharan Africa, particularly across newly independent African states. As regime stalwart Muhammad Hasanayn Haykal declared in 1956: 'Egypt must send selected missions of experts in science, religion, politics, economics, commerce and social services to aid the African peoples, to support them, to collaborate with them and light the path before them' (Haykal 1956). Egyptian development aid across Africa had a distinct foreign policy component: firstly, Egypt believed it stood to gain potential support at the United Nations from the newly independent African nations (Cremeans 1963); secondly, and perhaps more importantly, it aimed to battle the involvement of Israel in the continent. In 1965, Nasser wrote:

> The struggle of the Asian and African peoples is not waged in isolation from the struggle of the Arab nation. In addition to the responsibilities of the development of the African continent following its liberation call for gigantic efforts so that imperialism should not infiltrate and return to it under the pressure of underdevelopment or behind a deceptive mask, such as the Israeli mask, which imperialism tries actively to make use of in Africa. (Nasser 1966, 12)

In terms of Israel, it was also engaged in a sustained effort to increase its visibility across Africa via the work of MASHAV, the Agency for International Development Cooperation in the Ministry of Foreign Affairs. Founded in 1958, MASHAV organised development projects across Africa, usually centred around three stages: (i) a survey on the potential development of a certain field (cooperative, institutional, agricultural, scientific, and so on) led, and usually funded, by Israel; (ii) African citizens coming to Israel for a short period to study at educational institutions affiliated with MASHAV;

(iii) a team of Israeli experts going to a given African state to complete or initiate a project, usually funded by the African state or through a joint venture with an Israeli company (Kreinin 1964, 18). This initiative was rhetorically associated with the ancient Jewish concept of *tikkun olam*, or 'repairing the world' – providing a mythological source for an altruistic discourse of Third World empowerment, which discounted more immediate Israeli goals: firstly, ensuring African states' support for Israel at the United Nations (where the African bloc was gaining significant voting power, given the General Assembly's one-state one-vote policy); and, secondly, strengthening ties with Western states, particularly the United States, by precluding African states from obtaining development support from the Soviet Union.

Egyptian policy in sub-Saharan Africa came into competition with Israel. This is not to say that Cairo did not attempt to include cultural diplomacy aspects. Mostly, however, Egypt was concerned with Israel's development policy. According to *The New York Times*, Nasser was particularly keen to preclude Israeli influence across these states; as a result, 'the Egyptians [made] themselves heard everywhere in Africa and play[ed] the part of self-chosen leaders' (*The New York Times*, 1 March 1956). As Haykal describes,

> The day a newly independent African country celebrates its independence, a delegation arrives from Israel bringing with it a deep and detailed study of the problems of the country. While all other delegations are offering their congratulations the Israeli delegation is speaking about the problems [that] the newly independent country faces. Most delegations return home after the celebrations but the African ruler keeps the Israeli envoy because he can discuss post-independence problems with him [...] In many cases, an Israeli mission returns bearing with it economic, technical and/or cultural agreements. Israel usually chooses one or two fields and concentrates its activities on these. For example, construction is considered the easiest and profits are positive. Any building [that] rises in any African country continues to be a symbol of Israel's activities. After comes trade and maritime companies, then agricultural centres. Also, Israel chooses her men in Africa very carefully. And its embassies in Africa are comprised of the most efficient men from the foreign ministry. (*Arab Observer*, August 1964)

Beyond Africa, Egyptian use of emigration as a form of development aid is most evident in the case of Yemen between 1962 and 1970. Despite Egyptians' political activism, the Yemeni leader, Imam Ahmad bin Yahya, found it very difficult to send them away for he relied on them for the country's development. Aiming for the institution of a revolutionary movement in Yemen that would align with Egypt, Nasser came into a protracted, direct conflict with conservative Arab leaders – particularly Saudi Arabia's King Faisal – who saw in this an attempt to destabilise the region and threaten their survival. The conflict in Yemen escalated into a proxy war between

Egypt – or, as it was then called, the United Arab Republic – and Saudi Arabia (Dawisha 1975). Beyond a heavy military engagement of over 60,000 soldiers, Egypt also organised the short-term emigration of thousands of professionals – teachers, engineers, doctors, nurses, and so on – to the country.

Already in March 1958, Egyptian teachers had organised a crowd of 500 protesters, who marched to the Palace and demonstrated against the Imam. The extent to which these Egyptians constituted a form of soft power in the proxy war against Saudi Arabia became evident in Sana'a: as British sources recount, 'all Egyptian teachers [marched] together with 2,000 demonstrators' towards the Saudi Arabia Delegation in Sana'a, where they 'broke into the courtyard and smashed all the windows'. The Imam was forced to issue a formal apology to the Saudi King saying: 'we are Arab brothers and must accept sorrow with good heart' (TNA – CO 1015/1267–1959). Yemen's heavy dependence on Egyptian professionals for its development highlights the foreign policy importance of Egyptian regional emigration at the time. Only a few months following the protest, the Imam 'welcomed' new Egyptian professionals in Hodeida, saying that Yemen was waiting for Egyptian 'experts to start building the first Yemeni spinning and textile factory' (BBC, 19 January 1959). O' Ballance explains:

> Partly because there was no alternative, Egyptians working in the country as military instructors, school teachers and doctors, all subtly and insidiously aided the spread of Nasser's views ... All this had a profound effect on young, restless, impressionable minds in the Yemen [resulting in August 1962] demonstrations in some of the secular schools against alleged approval by the Imam of the American bases in Saudi Arabia. (O'Ballance 1971, 63)

In late 1959, a number of different pamphlets, originating from Egypt, were intercepted by the British in Ta'izz. They read:

> Oh sons of Yemen, the army and the people! ... Do not clap for Gamal. O sons of Yemen whose hearts are shaken whenever Gamal is mentioned and whose tongues constantly speak of him. Gamal Abdel Nasser does not need your applause nor does he require your admiration ... Your biggest compliment to Gamal would be when you unite together and organise yourselves, eliminating the monarchy and declaring the birth of the new Yemeni People's Republic. (TNA – CO 1015/1267–1959)

Egypt intensified its soft power strategy in Yemen following the Imam's death in September 1962. Abdullah al-Sallal, the main challenger to the Saudi-backed Yemeni monarchy, declared the creation of the Yemen Arab Republic and, immediately, 'appealed to Egypt primarily for support against potential foreign intervention, from Saudi Arabia or the British in Aden, and for Egyptian technical and administrative help' (Tsourapas 2016). Following al-Sallal's appeal, 'Egypt moved into Yemen, not only with tanks, jets and soldiers, but also with almost 300 primary and secondary school teachers, administrative advisors, doctors for the new hospitals' (Rahmy 1981, 143). In terms of development aid as soft power, as the Egyptian Director of the Technical Aid Office for Yemen argued:

> [Cairo] took great care to send to Yemen the best teams and experts in spite of their being badly needed in [Egypt ...] Experts from the ... Ministry of Scientific Research and the Ministry of Agriculture were sent to Yemen ... Economists and finance experts were also seconded to Yemen and the result was the emergence of a State Budget covering the expenses and revenues for a whole year; the first of its kind in the history of Yemen. (Quoted in *Arab Observer*, 5 October 1964)

Egypt's involvement in Yemen highlights not merely the importance of labour emigration as a soft power strategy, but also the degree to which soft power interacted with economic and military power. Dana Adams Schmidt, *The New York Times*' correspondent, produced a detailed account of the military conflict in Yemen, while also paying particular attention to Egyptian soft power policy:

> I was impressed also by the extent of the Egyptians' 'hearts and minds' campaign among the Yemenis [such as] installing water pumps, school-teaching and providing all kinds of professional services and advice – agricultural, engineering and medical. These were all ways of introducing the Yemenis to modern life, ways in which the Egyptians could do things for the Yemeni people which their traditional leaders could not. The Egyptians had also brought 100 Egyptian ulema [Islamic scholars] into the country, in the hopes of persuading the Yemenis that there were really no important differences between the Sunnis and the Shia in general, and the Shaffei and Zeidi sects in particular. They may even have tried to persuade the Zeidis that they did not really need an Imam. (Schmidt 1968, 208)

Emigration and the neoliberal subject under Sadat and Mubarak, 1970–2011

> '[The President] dressed in the latest fashion while we slept ten in a room.'
> Slogan of the 1977 'Bread Riots'

By September 1969, Nasser had decided to completely abolish emigration, suspending all exit permits. His successor, however, saw matters differently: Anwar Sadat introduced migration into the Egyptian subject's repertoire of political action in 1971 – a year after he assumed the presidency following Nasser's death. The new president proceeded to abolish the long tradition of exit visas, border controls, and other restrictions, while he negotiated bilateral agreements that would allow Egyptians entry to foreign countries such as Libya or Syria with any official document of identification. Meanwhile, the press ran frequent articles about 'an increased demand for Egyptian manpower' abroad. Newspapers would duly list foreign countries' labour shortages that were to be filled by Egyptians: '2,500 Egyptian building workers leave for Bulgaria'; '15,000 workers for Czechoslovakia', and so on – statements of profound importance given the dire economic conditions within Egypt.

The regime now rejected Egyptians' attachment to the land as an 'old stereotype'. Wage differentials between Egypt and foreign countries were widely publicised – schoolteachers, for instance, earned more in four years' work in the Gulf than in their entire working life if they stayed in Egypt. By 1978, one account estimated that 15–18% of Egypt's active workforce was employed abroad. As the regime stated in its five-year plan:

> Growing numbers of Egyptians work abroad for very high wages, if compared with domestic salaries. These individuals return to Egypt possessed of high purchasing powers, which they usually direct not to saving and investment but to flagrant and luxurious consumption [...] Therefore, our manpower and resources must be planned to meet the prerequisites of progress for trained manpower, and supply trained personnel to the Arab countries.

In this rupture with past practices, the Sadat regime replaced Nasser's pseudo-historic repertoires about Egyptians' attachment to the land with a sustained language of liberalisation. This was made clear by the inclusion of the right to migration in the 1971 Constitution: Article 52 stipulated that 'citizens shall now have the right to permanent or temporary migration'. In the past, as Sadat wrote in his 1978 autobiography, Egyptians were 'turned into puppets. They became dummies in the hands of their rulers, who did with them as they pleased. People were not allowed to travel [...].' Now, however, a subject's repertoire of actions was to be guided by freedom. 'I want to make it clear,' Sadat repeatedly argued, 'that if we do not hold to the complete freedom of the individual in the shadow of competition, we cannot realize any progress. He who wants to travel, let him travel.' In line with the shift towards freedom of movement, the state retreated from administering any effective control over emigration, including keeping count of emigration-related statistics. Thus, the Sadat regime was able to grossly inflate estimates of Egyptians abroad, further fuelling social pressure towards emigration. Already in 1971, Sadat would publicly boast that 'there had never been as many young people migrating as there have been this year' (Middle East News Agency (MENA), 10 October 1971). Without official statistics, figures became exaggerated, as state officials would broadly refer to 'millions' of workers living abroad. In 1978, for instance, while the

International Labor Organization estimated 403,908 Egyptian emigrants to be working in Arab countries, *al-Ahram* put the number at 1,390,000 (Oweiss 1980, 203).

At the same time, to sustain this radical shift towards migration, particularly to the oil-rich Arab countries, Sadat also drew upon an ethical repertoire hedged around the issue of religion. The new president presented himself as the *al-ra'īs al-mu'min* (the pious president); rarely would his speeches not begin, or end, with a reference to the Qur'an, while state media began duly reporting the mosques where Sadat would perform his Friday prayers. The importance of religiously conservative Arab countries – mainly Saudi Arabia – for Egypt's future was highlighted in newspapers, with reports repeating how Egyptian manpower and Saudi wealth could complement each other for mutual benefit. Egypt's military victory against Israel in 1973, with the help of the oil embargo imposed by neighbouring Arab countries, was contrasted with the defeat of Nasser's Egypt in 1967, further normalising the centrality of oil-rich Arab countries to Egypt's new social order. Sadat promised that the 1973 War – or the 'crossing of the Canal' – would be followed by Egypt's 'second crossing, the crossing to prosperity'. Egyptian migration, in this context, would also be a gesture of help towards the Saudi state's large demand for labour, and would add to the intended interdependence between the two countries. This, for Sadat, was a matter of pride: the president was initially adamant on naming one of the Suez Canal districts after the Saudi king. In his reconciliation with the Gulf states, the president also made clear that the state was now willing to receive all 'her sons' who had been forced to reside abroad and reinstate Egyptian citizenship to them – marking the return of Muslim Brothers who had escaped to the Gulf and had been stripped of their nationality by Nasser.

This shift in discourse radically modified Egyptian citizens' repertoire of political behaviour according to the new regime's priorities. On an individual level, the return of religiously radical elements that had emigrated under Nasser marked a steady shift towards conservatism in universities, professional associations, and, gradually, in the overall socio-political landscape of Egypt. At the same time, migration to Saudi Arabia was normalised through the Egypt–Saudi rapprochement: 'Recall the writings of [philosopher] Ibn Khaldun,' one interviewee argued, 'who wrote that the defeated eventually imitates the victor: the *Naksa* [Egypt's defeat or, literally, "setback", in the 1967 War], on one side and the importance of oil from the conservative Gulf in the [1973] Ramadan War, on the other, explains the allure of Saudi Arabia for Egyptians in the 1970s, and their rejection of Nasserism.' Ostentatious piety was the Egyptian subjects' reaction to religious practices of power introduced across the entire social body: this pressure was magnified through patterns of conspicuous consumption among return migrants from the Gulf,

complementing the President's own, widely reported penchant for extrava-
gance. Interviewees would easily recall, some forty years later, the finely
made, and conservative, clothing that migrants wore upon their return to
Egypt in the late 1970s, or their imported record players, blasting Qur'anic
recitations in the evenings – both serving as simultaneous indications of
lavishness and piety.

Gradually, the Sadat regime introduced status hierarchies that, predicated
upon the question of migration, were to become bases of social discrimination
and exclusion. How these practices of power came to be deployed at the
micro-level of everyday life has been most obvious in one of the central
tenets of Egyptian life, marriage, which became intertwined with emigration
and return. While, under Nasser, renting a new apartment was easily attainable
for newlywed couples, Sadat deregulated rent controls, and shifted the state's
priorities towards home ownership. The social expectation of moving into
a new apartment – a near-necessity for any newly married Egyptian couple
– became predicated upon sufficient prior savings for the hefty down-payment.
New apartments' soaring prices (due, in part, to Egypt's urbanisation and
over-population issues), together with the rising costs of furnishing an
apartment, entrenched migration into the normative frames of young
Egyptians' quotidian lives. Whereas in the pre-1970 period, Egyptians could
afford to get married after a couple of years of public sector employment,
Egyptians after Sadat now either choose to emigrate or, if they remain in
Egypt, accept being unable to marry for the foreseeable future.

Thus, the traditional social expectation that the prospective couple must
save a certain amount of money so as to move into a new home after the
wedding is now achievable primarily through work abroad. As a result,
young return migrants tend to be highly sought after as bridegrooms. A
prospective groom's status as a returnee from the Gulf countries (or, pre-2011,
from Libya) is typically highlighted in social interactions, contributing to
his valorisation as a financially successful and, at the same time, pious
Egyptian. Through marriage, relations of power that involve the act of
migration become materially grounded in the local setting. Egyptians who
have secured a position of work abroad also enjoy a dominant role under
these social conditions; in this case, an engagement takes place, following
which the fiancé departs for abroad, where he saves money for a few years
before he returns to his new home, and family, in Egypt. Periodic journeys
abroad for additional employment are not rare.

Collectively, the regime's discourse on migration highlighted the shift
towards individualism and de-politicisation.[2] Every Egyptian citizen, Sadat
would argue repeatedly, has the right to 'get married, own a villa, drive a
car, possess a television set and a stove, and eat three meals a day'. The
socio-economic autarky professed under Nasser was duly replaced as the

Sadat regime shifted towards economic liberalisation, a trend that would be intensified under Mubarak's turn to neoliberalism. Stressing this even further, Sadat introduced Presidential Decree No. 73 in 1971, allowing Egyptians who had emigrated to regain their old civil service position in Egypt within a year, if they were unsuccessful in finding employment abroad – a period later expanded to three years. At the same time, newspapers featured articles lauding the success of Egyptians abroad. In one instance, Ali Amin, editor of *al-Akhbar* wrote:

> Egypt's youthful skills have stolen the limelight and come to be the country's staple crop. Some of them get higher salaries than [US Secretary of State, 1973–77] Dr. Henry Kissinger and [UK Prime Minister, 1974–76] Harold Wilson while still in their forties. Some lead the same lavish life as Hollywood stars. They own villas with fragrant gardens and as many as three cars each. One of them travels by private helicopter from his country home to his place of work inside New York! But our country will not lose the brains we export to the outside world. For a successful Egyptian must be back home one day to drink again from the Nile and to live with the generous people. An Egyptian travels but does not go for good, for he always returns. (*Al-Akhbar*, 30 June 1975)

Gradually, with the extension of market rationality into every aspect of life, Egyptian citizens were constructed as entrepreneurial subjects, and any preoccupation with formal politics became largely irrelevant. Instead, they became obsessed with waiting for *dawuruhum* (their turn) to move abroad. Migration came to be associated with fast profits of dubious origin, as Egyptians began debating the issues of the *quṭaṭ sumān* (fat cats) – numerous Egyptians who had grown mysteriously rich, mysteriously fast, including the members of the president's family who were later convicted of economic crimes.

Thus, migration aided in fulfilling a chief policy goal under Sadat, which he termed the ending of *al-ḥiqd* (rancour) in domestic politics. As long as the option to pursue employment abroad remained, the inefficiency of the Egyptian state could afford to be taken for granted, and existing power structures would remain unchallenged. Even one of the most controversial decisions of Egyptian foreign policy, the 1979 peace treaty with Israel which resulted in Arab states' economic embargo on Egypt, was presented in the Egyptian media together with front-page reports that Egyptian emigration routes would not be threatened, and that Arab states would continue to receive Egyptian workers. 'Egypt,' Sadat once mentioned to Kissinger, 'needed no more heroes.'

Put differently, with 'exit' being an option, Egyptians rarely 'voiced' demands of the Sadat and Mubarak regimes. The massive January 1977 'Bread Riots', partially based on the growing perception of inequality between a small section of society (who had profited from migratory processes) and the masses (which had not), was one of the last major mass protests in Egypt for more than thirty years. The regime attempted to secure legitimacy by 'claiming to provide for the well-being of the population', as Mubarak argued that the decision to protest should be weighed against its potential monetary cost. Mubarak would shun responsibility, as neoliberal policy professed that Egyptians should worry about their job or, as Mubarak would frequently argue, 'go back to work' (and, essentially, pursue employment abroad) rather than worry about politics. In response to those Egyptians who protested, Mubarak publicly argued, *mish bitū' shughl* (they are not the working type). Even the few notable resistance movements that did emerge, such as the *Kifāya* (Enough), or the Egyptian Movement for Change, were mostly elite-led projects rather than bottom-up campaigns.

Overall, through social norms and expectations, the Egyptian regime under Sadat and Mubarak refocused subjects' fields of action around the issue of migration. Having succeeded in normalising migration as a political act since the early 1970s, the regime proceeded to tie it to specific meanings – freedom, piety, individualism, and neoliberal de-politicisation – and shape citizens' engagement with power around them.

Conclusion

'The days when a citizen living abroad was regarded with suspicion, as if he had not fulfilled his national duties, are over ... We must all guarantee, in deeds and not in words, that an Egyptian working abroad is a good citizen, who has not renounced his identity.'
Hosni Mubarak, Speech to Egyptian Expatriates' Meeting, 1983

This chapter has explored how approaching migration as a political act within a community sheds light onto the effects of cross-border population mobility upon migrants' countries of origin. Specifically, it examined how processes related to migration are embedded in both governmental practices and social norms of interaction, and how these processes affect the subject. In this reading, migration is deeply entrenched within different structures of power; the act of migration arguably signifies less an act that affirms agency, or the subject's sovereignty, than a deeper entrenchment of the subject within social norms and practices, as well as within the governmental techniques of power that govern and delineate conduct. In this sense, migration carries moral weight, designating the field within which political participation takes on meaning.

In examining population movements in the empirical case of the post-1952 modern Egyptian state, the chapter traced how migration discursively supported the Egyptian regime, both under Nasser and under Sadat and Mubarak.

The divergent ideological priorities of each period were duly reflected upon migration: the citizen as a migrant was, in the first case, demonised and, in the second, praised. Thus, social expectations, in tandem with formal governmental policies, contributed to different definitions of citizenship – the Egyptian citizen was constructed as a self-sustained, frugal subject under Nasser, and as a 'free,' profit-seeking subject under Sadat and Mubarak. In either of these cases, migration as an act became firmly embedded within a broader, socially constituted frame of reference that distinguished between the migrant and the non-migrant subject, and defined citizens' engagement with political power.

Notes

1 An earlier version of this chapter has been published in Tsourapas (2017b).
2 For a broader discussion on this see Tsourapas (2015b).

4

State–diaspora relations and regime security in North Africa

The 2 October 2018 assassination of Jamal Khashoggi, a Saudi journalist, inside Saudi Arabia's Istanbul consulate, served as a brutal demonstration of the long arm of the state in the Middle East. Khashoggi, living in self-imposed exile in the United States since 2017, was confronted with the complex mechanisms that states have developed to engage with political dissent beyond their territorial borders. This chapter identifies the trade-off that authoritarian states face between migration and security: on the one hand, they wish to reap the economic benefits associated with large emigrant populations – primarily an influx of remittances, but also diaspora's investment in the home country, skills acquisition and training, a reduction in unemployment, and so on; on the other hand, authoritarian states also face the political need to maintain control of emigration flows, to monitor the movements of political dissenters, and to contain diasporas' activism abroad. Authoritarian states' diaspora policymaking can best be understood via the management of the trade-off between the political imperative to prevent emigration and the economic urge to embrace it. The chapter aims to unpack this dimension of Middle East states' migration diplomacy further by shedding additional light on the state–diaspora relations as they have developed across North Africa. The examples of Algeria, Libya, Morocco, Tunisia, and Egypt demonstrate how states are torn between 'controlling' and 'courting' their diasporas residing in Europe and North America. Regime security considerations have led the first four states to develop intricate control mechanisms that aim to prevent political activism abroad and to minimise diasporic acts of dissent against the ruling regime of the sending-state. In contrast, Egypt's diaspora policy has evolved more inclusively: while acts of repression are not unheard of, the main tenets of Egyptian policy have revolved around the desire to engage their citizen diaspora groups into the country's development ambitions since the 1970s. The chapter discusses these policies in detail and employs the tenets of the *illiberal paradox*, as described in Chapter 1, in order to shed light on the rationale behind this divergence.[1]

Maghreb: controlling the diaspora

Algeria marked the first attempt by an authoritarian emigration state in the Middle East to address the tensions of the illiberal paradox. After the brutal Algerian War, the country gained independence from France in 1962 (McDougall 2017), while Algerians continued to enjoy a degree of freedom of movement between the two countries (Gillette and Sayad 1984). By 1965, over half a million Algerian nationals resided in France. Despite rising restrictions on immigration by the French state, this number would grow exponentially via family reunification processes. The large population of Algerians constituted a significant development opportunity, primarily with regard to remittances (Trebous 1970): numerous bilateral agreements with France as well as Belgium and Germany demonstrated the economic importance of emigration for the Algerian state – at the time, freedom to leave the country was guaranteed as a constitutional right. But how did the authoritarian emigration state address potential security issues that could arise from its citizens' freedom of movement?

Algeria was the first state in the Middle East to develop an institutionalised mechanism aimed at reconciling the economic need for large-scale emigration with the security imperative for control over expatriates' political behaviour. The strategy involved the transformation of the Federation de France organisation belonging to the National Liberation Front (Front de Libération Nationale, or FLN, a major party in the Algerian war of independence) into the Friendship Society of Algerians in France (the Amicale des Algeriens en France, or AAF) in 1957. The AAF ostensibly constituted an organisation that represented the interests of Algerian emigrants abroad, tasked with the provision of Arabic-language classes and culture to the growing expatriate community across France. It also mediated between the Algerian community and the French institutions. Early on, Algeria identified the need to reach out to those migrants who were integrating into European societies. As one AAF official in France stated:

> In Algeria the children are Arabs in an Arab milieu ... The children born in France are in a completely different milieu ... The immigrant child is a bit deprived. He feels a stranger in school, and then on holidays over there he doesn't speak Arabic. His cousins treat him as French. (Grillo 2006, 193)

The AAF staff were always recruited from Algeria, rather than from the expatriate community. Over the years, the organisation established offices in every part of France that had an Algerian consulate. The AAF would also organise numerous events, film shows, and annual celebrations – at some point, it even published a French-language journal entitled *L'Algérien en France* (Grillo 2006, 270). Overall, the AAF 'enjoyed a complete monopoly of the organisation of the Algerian emigrant community in France' (Collyer 2006, 840).

In addressing the tensions of the illiberal paradox, the Algerian state identified the developmental benefits of emigration (cf. Collyer 2012); thus, it proceeded to securitise its diaspora policy. It did so via the AAF's transformation into an extension of the Algerian state in France. The AAF provided effective surveillance of Algerians abroad, and reported directly to the Algerian Ministry of the Interior: 'the structure of the Amicale's links outside the offices resembles the cell organizations favoured by the FLN during the Algerian War. Some of those now prominent in Algerian affairs in Lyon were also active locally during that war.' In fact, 'this network enables the Amicale, and thereby the consulate, to be informed about what is happening to Algerian citizens in the quartiers and the factors' (Grillo 2006, 270).

> Under [President Houari] Boumediene, the Algerian state has a clear vision of the role it wants to play in Paris. Europe is divided into nine regions, themselves divided into sections. The Amicale employs up to five hundred people led without qualms by its first president, Mahmoud Guennez, an excellent instructor and a good organizer during the War of Independence. In 1959, this colonel was sent to France to help the FLN activists. Six years later, this 'terrorist' chairs the first meeting of the Amicale des Algeriens en Europe. (Beau 1995, 87)

Given the responsibility to 'maintain the allegiance' of emigrant communities, the AAF aimed to prevent its compatriots from succumbing to the 'cancers' of liberalism, socialism, and communism, which were expected to plague 'naïve' migrants residing in 'decadent' host societies (Laurence 2012, 56). Its second president, Abdelkrim Gheraieb, would boast about how the AAF was tasked with monitoring dissent and reporting back to Algiers: 'once a month, Boumediene would summon me, very worried about the actions of political opponents in France' (Beau 1995, 88). At some point, the AAF 'reportedly sent daily detached reports to Algiers regarding developments in the community in France' (Brand 2011, 5). Driss El Yazami, a Moroccan educated in Paris and, since 2004, the president of the Euro-Mediterranean Foundation of Support to Human Rights, recounts how the AAF would direct its members to harass North African expatriates affiliated with the Arab Workers Movement (Mouvement des travailleurs arabes, or MTA):

> They were really savages ... the Amicale people, they would punch us ... many times, they came to take our leaflets and throw them out, all that ... And we would physically fight them many times ... Let's just say that the movement we were most opposed to ... was the AAF. (Fillieule and Sommier 2018)

A distinct policy shift in 1973 further attests to the expectations of the illiberal paradox: when increasing immigration restrictions in France and across Europe diminished the developmental value of labour emigration, Algeria shifted towards the securitisation of labour emigration. It was able to use its oil resources to relax its dependency on migration; in fact, on 19 September 1973, Boumediene banned Algerians from emigrating to France altogether (Fargues 2004, 1360). As the illiberal paradox thesis would expect, the post-1973 Algerian state put all its efforts into controlling emigration instead (cf. Collyer 2012). Partly because of the shift in the Algerian state's interests and partly because of domestic politics in Europe, the AAF gradually lost its power and centrality in managing the affairs of the Algerian diaspora. At the same time, the Algerian state prioritised the development of a 'discourse that discouraged emigration and policies that offered socio-economic securities as part of a nascent welfare state' (Natter 2014, 12). Overall, the Algerian experience demonstrates how the illiberal paradox sheds light onto the workings of the authoritarian emigration state: when approaching cross-border mobility as a developmental opportunity (1962–73), Algeria attempted to securitise its diaspora policy via the AAF; from 1973 onwards, once the developmental importance of cross-border mobility diminished, Algeria shifted towards a securitisation of emigration policy instead.

In contrast to Algeria, oil-rich Libya is traditionally approached as a country of immigration or, more recently, transit migration (Bredeloup and Pliez 2011; for an overview of Libyan history, see Vandewalle 2012). Political scientists have examined how Libyan elites employed the status of the country both as a transit- and as a host-country of migrants for economic and foreign policy gains in its migration diplomacy (Tsourapas 2019b, 188–96); yet, little has been written on the country's complex emigrant policy. While emigration flows never reached the high figures of other Middle Eastern and African states, Libya experienced sustained labour emigration, particularly temporary mobility of students and high-skilled professionals, dispersed across multiple host-states. Initially, under King Idris, the first ruler of post-independence Libya (1951–69), the state did not see any clear developmental benefit to cross-border mobility and chose to prioritise the control of borders and the provision of tight exit restrictions for Libyan citizens. The need to use migration in order to train the country's workforce was not an issue: Libya relied on foreigners (primarily Egyptian and Palestinian professionals) to staff its bureaucratic apparatus, as was standard practice with other newly independent Arab states of the time (Tsourapas 2019b, 74–7).

The shift towards perceiving cross-border mobility as a developmental opportunity for Libya came in the last few years of Idris' rule and under Muammar Gaddafi, who seized power in 1969. Eager to rid Libya of its dependence on foreigners and consolidate a process of 'Libyanisation' of the country's economy (Maghur 2010, 3), Gaddafi encouraged the emigration of Libyans for skill-acquisition purposes and expanded a programme for scholarships to study abroad. Gradually, the regime would grant exit visas to allow Libyan youth to pursue training and educational opportunities abroad (the requirement of exit visas was formally dropped in 1991). Already in 1968, Prime Minister Abdul Hamid al-Bakkoush would state that an educational priority for Libya was 'to establish specialised schools to promote competence in foreign languages, in order to enable the student to continue his higher studies abroad' (*Libyan Review*, 1968): 3,939 students were sent abroad in the 1976–7 academic year alone; by 1981, 2,900 Libyans were studying in the United States and some 2,000 in the United Kingdom. In 2010, it was estimated that approximately 12,000 students were dispatched to over fifty-two countries worldwide (Aldoukalee 2013).

As the Gaddafi regime loosened the grip on emigration, the illiberal paradox thesis suggests that there would arise the need to address the security vacuum with regard to emigrants' behaviour abroad. Indeed, the Libyan state gradually securitised its diaspora policy that aimed to extend control over Libyan emigrants' activities abroad (Tsourapas 2020a, 358–61). Unlike Algeria, however, the Libyan regime relied less on surveillance and more on overt violence. In the United Kingdom, this included efforts toward mobilising Libyan students against potential anti-regime activists, organised by Omar Sodani in the 1980s. This is not to suggest that the Libyan diaspora was composed solely of political opponents to the Gaddafi regime – many Libyans decided not to return home for family or economic reasons, for instance; yet, the Gaddafi regime tended to view these Libyans as traitors to the state. Gaddafi would refer to them as *kullab dala* ('stray dogs') and promise vengeance on behalf of the state. 'Teams of rough and ready revolutionaries moved in and took over the Libyan embassies (now named "people's bureaus") around the world and began rooting out the "stray dogs" who were engaged in anti-regime activities' (Pargeter 2012, 103–4).

The long arm of the Libyan state went beyond national borders as state agents attempted political assassinations of citizens who had relocated abroad. Many of these campaigns were reportedly spearheaded by Moussa Koussa, nicknamed *mab'uth al-mawt* ('envoy of death'). In 1980, Koussa was formally removed from his position as public envoy in London when he publicly admitted these practices to the London *Times*: 'We killed two in London and there were another two to be killed … I approve of this' (*The Times*, 11 June 1980). Earlier in May, the assassin of Salem Fezzani, a Libyan living in Italy shot dead in his restaurant in Rome, declared 'I was sent by the people to kill him. He is a traitor and an enemy of the people' (quoted in Pargeter 2012, 105). As Salem al-Hassi, once Libya's Intelligence Chief recounts:

For years, the Gaddafi intelligence services went after opposition leaders in the capitals of many countries, in Europe, the United States and Arab countries. A great number of opposition leaders were handed over Gaddafi by Arab and European countries. A great number were kidnapped in Arab and European countries. (Quoted in Asharq al-Awsat 2012)

The illiberal paradox arguably allows for a better understanding of how the Gaddafi regime's wish to employ emigration as a developmental opportunity contrasted with its wish to maintain firm control over all Libyans' activity. Thus, the regime addressed this paradox via the intense securitisation of Libya's diaspora policy. In a 1994 report, the United States' Department of State notes:

Libyan nationals' right of return is theoretically fully protected, even for opponents of General Qadhafi. However, this 'right' may be more nearly an obligation; the regime often calls on students, many of whom receive a government subsidy, and others working abroad to return on little or no notice and without regard to the impact on their studies or work. Libyans who study abroad are interrogated on their return home. (US Department of State 1994)

One of the most chilling was the case of Al-Sadek Hamed al-Shuwehdy, who had emigrated to pursue an engineering degree in the United States. He was publicly executed in 1984, in the middle of a stadium full of thousands of school children and students, who had been brought in for the occasion. After he tearfully confessed that he has joined the 'stray dogs', a gallows was brought into the arena and al-Shuwedhy was hanged on live state television (Black 2011).

Overall, Algeria's shift from the securitisation of diaspora between 1962 and 1973 to the securitisation of emigration, from 1973 onwards, was reversed in the Libyan case. Libya's initial securitisation of emigration between 1951 and 1969 was replaced by the securitisation of diaspora, from 1969 onwards. As per the illiberal paradox, these shifts are dictated by domestic elites' understanding of the developmental value of emigration: Algeria's oil resources allowed it to relax its dependency on economic remittances, particularly when faced with Western European restrictions on North African labour. In Libya, Gaddafi recognised the developmental value of emigration for skills acquisition and training, rather than economic remittances; thus, Gaddafi's post-1969 aim of developing its national workforce became linked with the securitisation of the Libyan diaspora.

Moving beyond Algeria and Libya, it can be argued that labour emigration has been part and parcel of the Moroccan state since gaining independence in 1956 (see Iskander 2010). Similar to Algeria, patterns of mobility were affected by the long experience of colonialism that had led Moroccans to France, primarily through Algeria. Recruitment agreements with France and

Germany in 1963, as well as Belgium and the Netherlands (in 1964 and 1969, respectively), formalised a pattern of migration into Europe that was regulated by the Ministry of Labour. The Moroccan state, or Makhzen, prioritised the economic benefits of emigration early on: from 1968 onwards, state economic development plans were based on maximising labour emigration – primarily as a way to attract economic remittances, as in Algeria. The tightening of Western European immigration rules led many Moroccans to pursue employment in Libya and the Arab oil-producing countries from the 1970s onwards. More recently, Moroccans have also sought irregular entry channels into Europe.

The tensions that the illiberal paradox highlights are evident in Morocco's emigration and diaspora policies. The decision to adopt a liberal emigration policy for developmental reasons suggests a need to securitise the Moroccan diaspora. Indeed, both Mohammed V and his eldest son Hassan II – the two monarchs that ruled Morocco in the twentieth century – extended significant resources towards the country's diaspora communities in Europe. Morocco appeared to have based its approach to Algeria, as it developed friendship societies under the Federation des Amicales des Marocains, or *amicales*, from 1973 onwards. Reminiscent of the Algerian case, Moroccan *amicales* 'openly intimidated and harassed oppositional groups, and engaged in public violent encounters with opponents', while in the Netherlands they were consistently referred to as 'the long arm of King Hassan' (Bouras 2013, 1226; cf. Van Heelsum 2002). The organisations' leaders were often recruited from the Moroccan intelligence services and would supply names of activists and trade unionists back to Rabat; these migrants would be duly detained upon their return home (Sahraoui 2015, 525). Under Hassan II, particular attention was paid to mosques, ensuring that they were loyal to the monarch's religious leader, who is Amir al-Mu'minin, or the Commander of the Faithful, according to the Moroccan constitution (Obdeijn, De Mas, and Hermans 2012, 229). Overall, the Moroccan *amicales* were tasked with preventing migrants from organising themselves politically and, by extension, becoming a force of political opposition abroad (De Haas 2007).

The timing of the Moroccan state's decision to institute its *amicales* in 1973, as Algeria shifted away from the securitisation of its diaspora policy, can be explained by the illiberal paradox framework. Morocco lacked Algeria's oil resources and considered labour emigration more important for its development – thus, the shift in the economic salience of emigration led to a stronger securitisation of the Moroccan diaspora. This is demonstrated by the fact that, unlike Algeria, the Makhzen also sought to avoid Moroccans abroad being perceived as political agitators by the host-states; involvement in European politics would jeopardise migrants' status and, by extension, the inflow of valuable remittances into Morocco. It is not accidental that the participation of Moroccans in post-1968 French industrial strikes via the

Association des Marocains de France (AMF), organised by exiled leader of the Left Mehdi Ben Barka, was perceived as a treasonous act by Rabat. Migrants who had participated in these strikes would have their passports seized upon return to Morocco (Iskander 2010).

Not surprisingly, many Moroccans who did not belong to the *amicale*, or who had participated in the AMF or other organisations, were afraid to return home (*Official Journal of the European Communities* 1976). Brand describes how, 'concerned with the image of the country abroad, the regime sought to discourage social agitation by or among its nationals'. In fact, 'Moroccans who were active in labor union struggles in Europe often encountered difficulties upon returning to the kingdom, having been denounced either by consular authorities or by members of the Amicales' (Brand 2002, 9).

The Makhzen did not treat emigration as a politically suspect act, as in Libya; nor did Morocco attempt to strengthen linkages with a diaspora that had integrated – albeit only partially – in European host-states, as in the case of Algeria. Instead, King Hassan II tackled the illiberal paradox by treating populations abroad as 'subjects', addressing them as such and denying that they may ever lose their marocanite. 'They will never be integrated' he declared on French television in 1993. 'I discourage you, in relation to my people, the Moroccans, from attempting a misappropriation of their nationality because they will never be 100% French' (Sahraoui 2015, 525).

Overall, Morocco suggests a different approach to the illiberal paradox than Algeria or Libya, which did not hesitate to shift their securitisation policies in 1973 and 1969, respectively. The fact that post-independence Morocco has highlighted the importance of labour emigration in its developmental strategy led to the consistent securitisation of its diaspora policymaking. The tightening of immigration in Western Europe after 1973 led the Makhzen to intensify this process of securitisation via the feared *amicales*. The fourth case study discussed below, Tunisia, pursued a similar approach to the migration–development nexus.

Finally, Tunisia is considered an archetypical emigration state, which perceived of cross-border mobility as a main mechanism for addressing structural unemployment and other political economy issues that plagued the post-independence North African state (see Brand 2006; Natter 2015). Traditional destinations initially included France and Germany, with whom Tunisian elites signed recruitment agreements in 1963 and 1965, respectively. Additional agreements with Belgium (1969), the Netherlands (1971), and Libya (1971) followed, while Italy has emerged as a major country of destination in the last three decades. Achieving high rates of emigration has traditionally been considered a developmental goal for the Tunisian state; remittances covered approximately 42% of its trade deficit in the late 1980 (Brand

2002). More than 11% of its population (or, approximately 1.2 million Tunisians) were residing abroad in 2012 (Natter 2015, 9).

The recognition that labour emigration constitutes an important instrument for economic development within the authoritarian setting of post-independence Tunisia suggests – as per the illiberal paradox thesis – the securitisation of the state's diaspora policymaking. Indeed, the Tunisian regime developed an extensive network of *Amicales des Travailleurs Tunisiens en France* in Paris, Lyon, Marseille, and Nice in the late 1950s (and later in other locations within France and across Western Europe). Similar to the other two North African countries, Tunisia presented these as socio-cultural institutions (Simon 1979). They were presented as relatively innocuous institutions that sponsored 'folk groups from Tunisia, sports teams, the celebration of certain religious occasions, and Arabic language instruction. Thus, they were meeting places where the Tunisian community could gather for events that helped preserve ties with the homeland' (Brand 2006, 111).

Interestingly, the post-1973 Western European restrictions on immigration led to an intensification of the Tunisian state's efforts to control its citizens abroad, as in the case of Morocco. Reminiscent of the Moroccan state's appeals against migrants' politicisation in their host-states, the Tunisian Minister of the Interior advised Tunisians in France that 'your role is to preserve this outstanding image of Tunisiens résidents à l'étranger and to fight with us against these intruders who are generally as useless at home as they are abroad' (Brand 2006, 112). At the same time, Tunisia's weak post-1987 economic performance and its increased reliance on economic remittances coincided with the intensification of its repressive tactics against Tunisian expatriate communities abroad and the denial of passport renewals for political activists abroad (cf. Natter 2015). This confirms the expectation of the illiberal paradox framework.

While little is known on the activities of the Tunisian *amicales*, a broad consensus exists that they were considered to be 'extensions of the consulates, if not the ... police' of the Tunisian state (Grillo 2006, 193). Their ties with the ruling Socialist Destourian Party in Tunisia (Parti Socialiste Destourien, or PSD) were clear from early on (Bel-Air 2016). Geisser conducted interviews with Tunisians in France who argued that 'the majority of [the institutions'] presidents were ignorant and barely knew how to read or write. They applied party orders without thinking' (Geisser 2012). Attempts at intimidation, particularly vis-à-vis Tunisian members of the Islamist Ennahda Movement, were common: 'Yes, the Tunisian amicale watched us [and their leaders] would even come to see our parents in order to dissuade us from participating in this or that activity, threatening to transmit this information to the consulate' (Geisser 2012, 163).

What distinguishes the Tunisian state's approach vis-à-vis the illiberal paradox from its North African counterparts lies in its attempts to address the tensions between security and economics by involving the diaspora communities in the state apparatus. In this, Tunisia did not employ explicit violence or repression abroad in the way that the Libyan or Algerian sending-states did. Instead, the Tunisian *amicales* followed Morocco's example of putting forth the image of the 'good citizen abroad' but took it to its logical conclusion: Tunisia aimed to implicate the migrants themselves in the enforcement of certain sets of rules and practices that, ultimately, aimed to lead to control and obedience. *Billadi*, for instance, the Arabic-language journal that was disseminated to the diaspora from 1974 onwards, featured articles written by Tunisians abroad. The *amicales* did not behave in an overly top-down manner, as an extension of the state abroad; instead, by inviting Tunisian diaspora member to partake in their administration, the *amicales* aimed to become part of the diaspora itself. This is reflected in the oft-quoted saying that *al-Tunisiyuun f-il-kharij fi qalb al-watan* ('Tunisians abroad are in the heart of the homeland').

Rather than persecuting political opponents by arresting them upon their return home – as in the cases of Algeria, Libya, or Morocco – the Tunisian state employed return migration as a reward for loyalty: select members of the Tunisian diaspora were invited back to Tunis every year in annual expatriate conferences, where they met with party and government officials. The sending-state's response to the participation of Tunisians abroad in protests or demonstrations was not to exercise violence, but to task the diaspora itself with ostracising these agitators. In 1973, in his address to a group of emigrants, Tunisia's minister of the interior would state that 'your role is to preserve this outstanding image [of Tunisians abroad] and to fight with us against these intruders who are generally as useless at home as they are abroad' (cited in Simon 1979, 144). This instrumental appeal to patriotism, which tasked diaspora members with surveying and enforcing a state-led image of Tunisia abroad, was indicative of how power also worked in a more diffuse manner within the home-state itself (Tsourapas 2013).

Overall, the first part of this chapter has analysed four North African states' diaspora policymaking via the 'illiberal paradox', which allows a focus on the tension that authoritarian states face between the economic benefits and political risks associated with cross-border mobility. In Morocco and Tunisia, state elites' view of labour emigration as vital for economic development led to consistent attempts at securitising diaspora policymaking. In fact, the securitisation of diaspora policymaking became more pronounced when remittances became more important for the Moroccan and Tunisian economies (post-1973 and post-1987, respectively). In Libya and Algeria, however, elites chose to securitise the state's emigration policy when cross-border mobility was not expected to reap developmental benefits (before 1969 and after 1973, respectively).

Egypt: courting the diaspora

'No one can believe that America has turned, in two-hundred years, to be the most powerful, richest country in the world. I am asking my people to start like you started, the drive to the West. Everyone can achieve his ambitions. But leave this old valley [of the Nile], go out and find it in the western desert! Go West, young man! And fight like fighters! Like America!'
                    President Anwar Sadat (quoted in Carroll 1982, 95)

In Egypt, the emergence of a pro-active diaspora policy coincides with the Egyptian state's shift away from the Soviet sphere of influence, and its firm entrenchment within the Western camp and, in particular, the United States. This section, firstly, contextualises this foreign policy shift within Egyptian political history. It proceeds to examine how Egyptian diaspora-engagement efforts had distinct political and developmental dimensions that were linked with the country's Western orientation: in terms of its political aspect, the Egyptian state's migration diplomacy aimed to project an image of a liberal, pro-Western, democratising state abroad, and thus strengthen the links between Cairo and Washington. In developmental terms, Egypt aimed to convince high-skilled Egyptians abroad to contribute to the socio-economic advancement of the homeland. This was expected to take place either via short-term visits back to the homeland or, more ambitiously, via return migration. Ultimately, neither developmental strategy bore fruit; frequent protests by Egyptians abroad (under Sadat and Mubarak, as well as during the events of the Arab Spring) marred the ruling regime's discourse of democratisation; similarly, while the linking of migration and development attracted a range of American aid on the issues of population control and population mobility, it did not encourage Egyptians abroad to contribute towards the homeland's development.

In order to best understand the foreign policy rationale of Egypt's diaspora policy development, a brief background note on the US–Egypt relationship is needed. The bilateral relations between Cairo and Washington vacillated significantly in the first twenty years of the 1952 Revolution (Hahn 1991; Mufti 2012), as Nasser would repeatedly try to juggle between the United States and the Soviet Union in the hope of maximising Egypt's economic and military aid. Initially, Washington supported the Free Officers' overthrow of British-backed monarchy, for it shared the view of King Farouq as a corrupt and ineffective leader. The early cordial relationship between the United States administration and the Free Officers is well-identified (Gerges

2012, 42); in fact, one of Nasser's early nicknames had been 'Colonel Jimmy' because of his presumed pro-American stance (Jankowski 2002, 24). Gradually, however, these amicable relations were replaced with alarm as the Free Officers' regime developed its ambitious regional foreign policy and formed closer ties with the Soviet Union. At the same time, Egyptian opposition to American policies in the broader Middle East increased with the 1955 creation of the Central Treaty Organization, or the Baghdad Pact, a Cold War US-backed alliance between Iran, Iraq, Pakistan, Turkey, and the United Kingdom (Gerges 1994, 24–8). Operating within the Cold War context, Washington was also concerned with Nasser's participation in the 1955 Bandung Conference of the Non-Aligned states, and his subsequent rhetoric of 'positive neutrality' (Sayyid-Marsot 2007, 132; cf. Abou-El-Fadl 2015). As a result, Americans decided to freeze any possibility of funding Nasser's ambitious, and costly, Aswan Dam project that aimed to control the waters of the Nile river. In response, Egypt moved closer to Moscow and purchased Soviet weaponry from Czechoslovakia, a move that paved the way for the 1956 Suez Crisis, a coordinated military operation by France, Israel, and Great Britain to capture the Suez Canal and to force the abdication of Nasser.

US–Egypt relations improved after the low point of early 1956, once the Eisenhower administration forced Great Britain, Israel, and France to abandon military operations against Egypt despite their early victories – an event that Nasser duly appropriated as a national victory against colonialism for both Egypt and for the Arabs (see Chapter 2). By 1958, bilateral relations deteriorated further following the creation of the United Arab Republic and Washington's decision to dispatch marines in Lebanon under the Eisenhower Doctrine. The fact that Washington continued supplying arms to Israel, while Arab countries were still under an arms embargo, added to bilateral tensions (Dekmejian 1971, 58–9). A period of *rapprochement* during the administration of President Kennedy, with whom Nasser corresponded and initially developed a working relationship, translated into economic aid and technical assistance, the 'chosen instruments of US policy' (Haykal 1973, 169–97; Hopwood 1991, 70–1; Gerges 1994, 155).

This bilateral cooperation, however, did not last into the Johnson administration (Haykal 1973, 201–19). The two states' relationship was exacerbated by the growing ties between the Americans and the Saudis, the conservative monarchical regime that was antagonising Nasser's pan-Arab rhetoric and revolutionary agenda, as well as Nasser's involvement in the Yemeni Civil War. Rising economic problems led Nasser towards a closer relationship with the Soviet Union, which he authorised to dispatch thousands of Soviet experts across the country as part of its financial aid to Egypt. American demands in exchange for aid to Egypt always angered Nasser, who in 1964 famously invited US ambassador Battle to 'drink from the sea', or to 'go to hell' in Egyptian slang. 'And if the water of the Mediterranean is not enough for him,' Nasser continued 'we offer him the Red [Sea] as well!' As a result, food aid to Egypt, delivered by the US 'Food for Peace' programme, was terminated in 1965 (see Ferris 2013). Once the 1967 War broke out, Egypt severed diplomatic relations with the Americans altogether, and US interests in Egypt were represented by the Spanish embassy (Waterbury 1983, 124). While Nasser's death coincided with a particularly dire relationship between the two countries, Sadat proved able to transform Egypt from a belligerent force into the most important US partner in the broader Middle East region following Israel (Brownlee 2012).

The history of post-Nasserite *rapprochement* between Washington and Cairo is well known (Gerges 2012, 50–4). Sadat's decision to expel 15,000 to 20,000 Soviet advisers working across Egypt in July 1972 signalled the beginnings of a pro-American policy (Haykal 1978; Beattie 2000; Brand 2014a, 70). The reasons behind this monumental shift towards Washington are still debated, but a mainstream explanation argues that 'Sadat seemed to feel that the more he attacked the Soviet Union the more he would gain from American support', as Egyptian Foreign Minister Mohamed Ibrahim Kamil wrote in his memoirs. 'He therefore stepped up his attacks to a point that carried him beyond the limits which govern normal international relations – especially when one is dealing with a superpower that can help or hinder the shaping of affairs' (Kamel 1986, 12). The result was a steady improvement of ties between Cairo and Washington, particularly post-1973 (Figure 4.1). This was evident in Sadat's frequent declaration that the US 'holds 99% of the cards' (Brand 2014, 79). Sadat's approach to Washington was 'premised on the hope of building a "special relationship" with the US, equal to, if not better than that between the US and Israel' (Ayubi 1991, 336). Sadat was hoping to extract distinct economic and geo-strategic benefits:

> With her vast capabilities, the United States is bound in duty, even naturally expected, to assist all those striving for a better future alike for themselves and for the whole world. (Sadat 1978, 126)

As Kamel remembered:

> Relations between Egypt and the United States were practically non-existent since President Nasser severed diplomatic relations in protest at the role played by the Americans in the 1967 War. But following the October War in 1973, these relations soon revived [...] Relations between Egypt and the United States continued to improve through Nixon's presidency. Nixon paid a State visit to Egypt, and when Gerald Ford came to power after Watergate, Sadat fostered Egyptian-American relations by developing personal and working ties with the new President. This was accompanied by a corresponding distancing from the Soviet Union. (Kamel 1986, 11–12)

العم ،سام – شكلك أنمر كبرعن سنة ٦٧ . . . .
أين البلد – وانت كمان شكلنـأتفير . . !!
تغييرات آكتوبر ::

Figure 4.1 Uncle Sam saluting the Egyptian peasant. ('The October Changes: Uncle Sam: You have changed a lot since 1967... Egyptian Citizen: You have changed a lot as well ... !' *al-Akhbar*, 2 March 1974)

This deep shift in Egyptian foreign policy has attracted a wealth of scholarship (Kerr and Yasin 1982; Korany and Dessouki 2008), and Sadat's contribution to this US–Egypt rapprochement has been analysed extensively, from his early decision to expel the Soviet experts, to his emphasis on developing personal ties with Henry Kissinger (Kissinger 1982); and from his realisation that the Cold War has entered the *détente* phase (Lippman 1989, 24), to his efforts to place the Egyptian economy within the Western sphere of influence. An issue that has been left unexamined, however, is how Egyptian efforts at the diaspora's mobilisation featured in this, with regard to both the political and developmental benefits that the Egyptian state aimed to receive.

Egyptian emigration towards North America, Europe, and Australia only became prominent in the aftermath of the 1967 War and, in particular, under Sadat and Mubarak (see Table 4.1). Two main factors contributed to this shift in the popularity of permanent emigration to the West and, in particular, to the United States. Firstly, as discussed earlier, Egypt's defeat increased a popular sense that the Nasserite system of beliefs – with regard to the political, economic, and moral system it had put forth since the Free Officers Revolution – had failed to produce results for Egyptian citizens. This affected the entire social body of Egypt, but it was particularly felt across the educated middle class – those Egyptians who had taken advantage of Nasser' 1962 decision to make higher education free for all Egyptians, and who were now stuck at low-paying, public sector jobs. Kerr describes the late 1960s situation aptly:

Table 4.1 Immigrants admitted to the US from Middle Eastern countries, 1953–73

Year	Total immigrants	Egypt	Iran	Iraq	Jordan	Lebanon	Syria
1953	170,434	168	160	125	304	261	124
1958	253,265	498	433	215	528	366	209
1963	306,260	760	705	426	752	448	226
1965	296,697	1,429	804	279	702	430	255
1968	454,448	2,124	1,280	540	2,010	892	644
1970	373,326	4,937	1,825	1,202	2,842	1,903	1,026
1971	370,478	3,643	2,411	1,231	2,588	1,867	951
1972	384,685	2,512	3,059	1,491	2,756	1,984	1,012
1973	400,063	2,274	2,998	1,039	2,450	1,977	1,128
Total	6,521,145	29,417	21,213	11,641	26,341	16,392	9,206

Source: United States Department of Labor 1973

thousands of non-so-bright young men in their soiled collars and cheap suits eke out a shabby and insecure but desperately respectable existence on ten pounds a month as minor clerks, bookkeepers, schoolteachers, and journalists. They are assured from time to time in the press and in the President's speeches that as educated men they are the 'vanguard' of the nation's progress, but they are impotent to fashion even their own progress and they can only listen anxiously to the officially propagated theme of equal and widening opportunities under the new socialist economic development plan which ambitiously pledges to double the national income in ten years. (Quoted in Wickham 2005, 32)

The 1967 defeat of Nasserism encouraged these Egyptians to seek their future elsewhere, further emboldened by a second factor – the 1965 Immigration and Nationality Act, which was enacted in 1968. Abolishing the nationality quota system that had dominated US immigration law since the 1920s, this shift allowed a diverse mix of immigrants to settle permanently in the United States, including Egyptians. By June 1969, thousands of requests were being submitted weekly for emigration to the United States (whereas only 151 visas for immigration to the United States were issued in Egypt in 1963, for instance). Hundreds of Egyptians would 'line up each morning in growing numbers' outside the United States Consulate, which operated as a part of the Spanish Embassy due to the 1967 severance of diplomatic ties (*The New York Times*, 23 June 1969). *The New York Times* reports from an immigration officer of the Australian embassy, stating that 'until about the middle of the nineteen-sixties, nearly all the emigrants we processed from here were foreign residents – Greeks, Italians, Armenians and so forth [...] The Egyptians just were not interested.' Yet, by July 1969, approximately 28,000 requests for emigration were submitted to the Egyptian authorities, in contrast to a sum total of 15,500 for the six preceding years (*al-Ahram*, 4 July 1969). Al-Najjar (1972) reviewed data from CAPMAS (now unavailable) to show this increase quantitatively.

Following Sadat's rise to power and the espousal of permanent migration in the 1971 Constitution, the Egyptian state gradually developed pro-active diaspora-building mechanisms that targeted the needs – both actual and anticipated – of Egyptian citizens that had left their homeland for the West. It would appear that a number of state agencies, in addition to the executive itself, developed a variety of strategies towards these emigrant communities. Interestingly, very little exists in terms of a publicly available data on Egyptian diaspora policy, suggesting that this developed in a rather *ad hoc* matter over a period of years. Yet, we are able to identify these policies as they were publicised across Egyptian media. For one, a large number of Egyptians would frequently be invited back to Cairo and Alexandria, where they would be entertained by the president and the first lady, at great cost. This highly publicised practice was common under both President Sadat (*al-Gomhuria*, 4 August 1976) and Mubarak (*al-Ahram*, 2 August 2010). In the aftermath of the 1973 Arab–Israeli War, about 1,500 emigrants from North America would receive annual complementary tours of the Suez war front hosted by various cabinet ministers (*al-Ahram*, 17 June 1974; *al-Gomhuria*, 27 August 1976). This pattern becomes more striking if one takes into account Egypt's mid-1970s economic situation.

The regime also paid generous attention to those who had recently emigrated, particularly to students. Those Egyptian studying in Europe and North America, for instance, would receive financial support from the Egyptian president on an *ad hoc* basis. A well-publicised grant of $50,000, or $212,000 today, was given to the Union of Egyptian students in North America, for instance (*al-Ahram*, 9 August 1976). On the occasion of North American Egyptian students visiting Cairo, Sadat instructed the Ministry of Information to 'offer L.E. 6,000 to consolidate the budget of the Egyptian Student Union in the United States and Canada' (*al-Gomhuria*, 12 August 1977). This was not an isolated occurrence, for any problems were to be dealt with immediately, regardless of cost. As mentioned earlier, Sadat did not hesitate to dispatch the presidential airplane to transport home Egyptian students that were unable to find employment in France (*al-Gomhuria*, 12 July 1975). For Egyptians studying in Britain, Sadat offered 'eleven pilgrimage tickets, an Islamic library of 2,000 volumes and a large number of recorded recitations of the Qur'an' (*al-Gomhuria*, 12 May 1974). As *al-Gomhuria* described:

> In response to requests from Egyptians in the United States, [Deputy Premier] Dr. Hatem promised the establishment of an American centre for the marketing of Egyptian films, the creation of model Arab libraries, [...], the dispatch of periodical bulletins, pictures, and films on Egypt. He promised to provide

emigrants with a monthly newssheet giving the most important events, political talks, and songs. He also acceded to the delegates' further request to send the Egyptian National Troupe to the United States to present its folklore programs. (*al-Gomhuria*, 9 January 1972)

What was driving such policies? A main goal behind Sadat's diaspora-engagement strategy was to demonstrate to his Western counterparts that the Egyptian state was undergoing a process of political liberalisation. 'It seems to have been an extension of his "foreign complex," as his critics called it – that determination to show the West how Westernised and "with it" he was' (Hirst and Beeson 1981, 214). The Egyptian regime viewed the liberalisation of Egypt's migration policy and, in particular, the ability of Egyptians to settle permanently in Europe and North America as a strong indication of its liberal nature, and the distance it had travelled from the restrictive Nasserite regime. In the past, he wrote, Egyptians had been 'turned into puppets. They became *duma* [dummies] in the hands of their rulers, who did with them as they pleased. People were not allowed to travel [...]' (Sadat 1978, 289). Now, however, an Egyptian's repertoire of actions was shaped around the ideal of personal freedom. Sadat often repeated similar assertions:

> First, I want to make it clear that if we do not hold to the complete freedom of the individual in the shadow of competition, we cannot realize any progress. He who wants to travel, let him travel (Quoted in Cooper 1982, 97).

'All young people want to go abroad', 'Ali Hamdi al-Jammal summed up in his 'People's Talk' column for *al-Ahram*. 'This is their right, which no one can deny' (*al-Ahram*, 6 July 1974). Under Nasser 'censorship was in force. Travel was restricted. Economic activity was calcified by restraints', Lipmann argued, espousing the Sadat-era rhetoric. In turn, 'Sadat peeled this structure away layer by layer. In 11 years as president, from 1970 to 1981, Sadat lifted from Egypt the fear of war and death that had hung over every family for a generation' (Lippman 1989, 6). As Sadat wrote in his memoirs:

> Freedom is the most beautiful, holy and precious fruit of our culture; an individual should never be made to feel that he is at the mercy of any force or coercion or that his will is subjected to that of others. (Sadat 1978, 78)

A variety of symbolic efforts were utilised to put forth an image of Egypt that corresponded to the foreign policy priorities of the time – a politically liberal state that cared for its citizens in the West. In December 1981, Mubarak appointed a minister of state for migration from the Christian Coptic community of Egypt, which 'underlined the conception that permanent migrants were the key constituency, since many Egyptian Copts had settled abroad during the 1950s and 1960s' (Lesch 1986). Ayubi highlighted how 'restrictions on emigration will negate the "democratic" image that the regime has tried to cultivate, and would invoke an atmosphere reminiscent of the frequently criticised policies of the Nasirist period' (Ayubi 1983, 446). More ambitiously, the Egyptian regime tried to employ the liberalisation of Egypt's emigration policy to portray an image of Egypt as a democratising, liberal country. This formed part of a broader strategy that some scholars called 'cosmetic democratization' (Waterbury 1983, 383), or one 'for the Yankees to see' (Ayubi 1995, 411). Sadat 'loved playing democracy. It was so quintessentially American. [But] since the Egyptians were not yet ready for freedom or democracy, since they were not even capable of playing the game by his rules, he was periodically forced to silence those players who had the temerity to pretend the game was real' (Kays 1984, 162–3). Already in 1972, Sadat was talking about the need to introduce 'correct democratic practice' to Egypt (Brand 2014, 75). Writing in 1975, Waterbury argued that Sadat's 'espousal of liberal political principles is sincere. But Egypt's liberalism in the post-Nasser era is not yet rooted institutionally; it is so far the creature of President Sadat' (Waterbury 1975, 15).

To what extent, one could ask, was Egypt's diaspora-building strategy a genuine reflection of Sadat's espousal of liberalism? One cannot be sure, particularly given the president's secretive nature: Sadat was a 'one-person show' recalled Dr Badran, the former minister of health, also adding that 'Sadat realised that America was the only way forward'. For Choucri, the Egyptian government had 'viewed [migration] as an indication of good will and a reflection of domestic political liberalization' (1977, 7–8) . But evidence does point to the instrumentalisation of Egypt's diaspora-building strategy as a means of projecting the image of a liberal state to the West. When asked how the US–Egypt relationship impacted upon Egypt's migration policy, former Prime Minister Hegazy declared that there was 'definitely a link between migration to the West and the president's emphasis on liberalisation'. Former Minister Dessouki agreed: Egypt under Sadat 'was now a free country, and Egyptian migration was acceptable to the West. So yes' (*Personal Interview*, 13 April 2014).

A second aim behind Egypt's strategy towards its permanent migrants was to ensure their return – not merely for developmental reasons (as will be explained below), but for distinctly political ones. It would be a major political victory for Sadat – both domestically and internationally – to convince these migrant groups to return to the homeland, choosing Egypt over Europe, Canada, or the United States. It would serve, arguably, as further testament to the regime's socio-economic and political success, for migrant groups in Europe and North America represented an idealised version of Egyptian elites, the 'cream of the crop' of Egyptians. As *al-Akhbar* writes:

> Egypt's youthful skills have stolen the limelight and come to be [America's] staple crop. Some of them get higher salaries than Dr. Henry Kissinger while still in their forties. Some lead the same lavish life as Hollywood stars. They own villas with fragrant gardens and as many as three cars each. One of them travels by private helicopter from his country home to his place of work inside New York! But our country will not lose the brains we export to the outside world. For a successful Egyptian must be back home one day to drink again from the Nile and to live with the generous people [of Egypt]. An Egyptian travels, but does not go for good, for he always returns. (*al-Akhbar*, 30 June 1975)

Not incidentally, the regime frequently employed the support of permanent emigrants, for instance by publicising telegrams that expatriates in Europe and North America had sent to Sadat or Mubarak, expressing their enthusiasm for the regime's political programme, and publishing them in the press.[2] On 21 April 1974, for instance, *al-Akhbar* details how, in their cable, 'expatriates thanked the President for meeting them and speaking to them as well as for his obvious care for them. They also greeted the President and pledged allegiance to their great people' (*al-Akhbar*, 21 April 1974). Through such acts, he hoped to gain both domestic as well as international points, mainly from Washington. One example was the August 1977 Conference of Egyptian students in North America, for which seventy Egyptian students were flown to Cairo on President Sadat's private plane for a two-week event. Reported on all three major newspapers was a cable the students sent to Sadat:

> Addressing President Sadat as a father, the cable said that, on approaching the air strip of their dear fatherland, they would like to express sincere thanks and gratitude for honouring them by providing them with the opportunity to visit their dear Egypt and mother country aboard the President's private plane. The cable said that the President has always been acting like that. (Middle East News Agency (MENA), 9 August 1977)

Interestingly, population mobility as a means to a closer relationship with the United States was also employed by the Sadat regime with regard to Egyptian Jews. The Egyptian Jewish community, once thriving, had been reduced to a few hundred people by the early 1970s, as the majority of them emigrated to Israel in the post-1948 era. Within the process of Egypt–Israeli reconciliation (in which Washington played a leading role), Sadat declared his willingness to have the Jewish community return to Egypt. Initially, the regime sought the return of Egyptian Jews to Egypt from Israel, following the example of Sudan, Iraq, and Morocco (in the latter, 4,000 Jews were reported to have returned home). The media reported that Arab leaders realised that these Jews 'are nationals who have the right to return, and that the Arabs are not against the Jews' (*al-Gomhuria*, 13 April 1977). Isma'il Fahmi, deputy premier and foreign minister, declared this issue was part of President Sadat's 'comprehensive Egyptian strategic plan to reach a stage of firm peace based on justice in the area' and promised the creation of high-level committees to prepare for the return (*al-Ahram*, 20 July 1977). Sadat picked up this topic in an interview with CBS:

> Well, at some point Rabin said, how could we achieve peace with those people who do not even want to exchange any salute with us, in the United Nations? Very well. I said, well, I am ready to have the Jews that have gone to Israel, the Egyptian Jews, and I am sure they prefer Egypt to any other place. I am sure of it. (MENA, 31 July 1977)

How politically successful have the Egyptian regime's diaspora-building strategies been? For one, the Egyptian Jewish community has continued to wither, with no evidence of return migration, another testament to the fact that the regime's wish to see them return was aimed squarely at Washington. At the same time, these policies carried with them an exorbitant economic cost. The 1978 five-year plan estimated the cost of supporting educational training abroad to the state at over $8 million per year, or double the total annual budget for all scientific research within Egypt itself until then (Ministry of Planning, 1978). 'Then,' Ayubi bluntly observes, '40 percent of these people do not return' (Ayubi 1983, 444). Askari and Cummings' 1977 research identified that 'individuals with high degrees of personal skills dominate the ranks of both emigrants and status changers' to the United States (Askari and Cummings 1977, 76). A survey of migrant scientists and engineers from the Middle East at time of entry in the United States, and in 1970, proved illuminating (see Table 4.2).

Table 4.2 Intentions of highly-skilled migrants at time of US Entry and 1970 (%)

Category	Egypt	Iran	Other Middle East	All migrants
Remain in the USA	75.6%	27.8%	37.6%	43.7%
Return home	14.4%	40.7%	33.5%	18.1%
Undecided	9.0%	31.5%	27.7%	36.7%
		In 1970		
Remain in the USA	96.4%	66.7%	63.0%	56.9%
Return home	-	-	6.4%	7.2%
Within 1 year	-	-	2.3%	1.4%
More than 1 year	-	-	1.2%	2.5%
Undecided when	-	-	2.9%	3.3%
Undecided	3.6%	33.3%	28.9%	34.3%

Source: National Science Foundation 1973

At the same time, and perhaps more importantly, a large percentage of Egyptians living in the United States and Canada – a population that includes many Copts – were rumoured to have abandoned Egypt for political, rather than purely economic, reasons (Tadros 2013). As a result, they did not wish to affiliate themselves with the Sadat or Mubarak regime. This explains the failure of the second goal in Egypt's diaspora policy – the projection abroad of a liberalising, democratic polity. In fact, anti-Sadat and anti-Mubarak protests quickly overshadowed such pro-regime actions. Once Egyptians in Europe and North America began voicing their dissatisfaction with presidents Sadat and Mubarak, the ruling regime was no longer able to argue that it enjoyed expatriates' support, in domestic or international politics. Such protests tarnished the image of Egypt abroad even more than the 'brain drain' issue, given the emphasis that both Sadat and Mubarak placed on their perception in the West: one of the most prominent protests was staged during Sadat's final visit to Washington in 1981, which was 'embarrassing' for the regime (McDermott 1988, 192). March 1980 was a highpoint of tension between Copts and Muslims in Egypt, with bombing of Coptic properties around the country, and Pope Shinuda cancelling all Easter celebrations in protest. Two months later, migrant Copts in the United States and Canada demonstrated openly during Sadat's visit to the United States in May of that year. In June 1981, armed clashes erupted between Muslims and Copts (Brand 2014a, 91). Sadat reacted by accusing Shinuda publicly of conspiring to erect a separate Christian state in Upper Egypt' (Haykal 1983, 230), and threatened a variety of sanctions, including the withdrawal of citizenship (Ayubi 1983, 447).

Infuriated and 'betrayed', the President duly jailed 1,536 perceived political opponents within two days following his return to Cairo, including prominent political, religious, and intellectual figures – Heikal, Fuad Serageldin, Fuad Morsi, and Omar Tilmassani, the head of the Muslim Brotherhood (Lippman 1989, 219; Brand 2014a, 91). As Waterbury described, 'leftists, Nasserists, rightists, Wafdists, extremists, and gadflies. Anyone, it seemed, who had ever seriously crossed swords with Sadat was picked up' (Waterbury 1983, 384). Such acts detracted from Egypt's image as a stable, democratising country – an image that Sadat and Mubarak were eager to present to the Western world. As the *Guardian* put it, Sadat 'reviled Egyptian critics abroad' (the *Guardian*, 18 October 1981).

> The newspaper *al-Dawa* is the organ of the Muslim Brotherhood. I allowed this newspaper to be published although the Muslim Brotherhood was dissolved by order of the Revolutionary Command Council in 1954, a decision that has never been repealed … You all know that I have released every Muslim Brother from the detention camps and prisons and reinstated them in their jobs. I let the newspaper continue publication. Today it came out to confuse our young people about the United States … In whose interests are our children being

told these days that the United States had warned the Mamdouh Salem government against the religious movements and to eliminate the religious movements?
(Lippman 1989, 246)

Political diaspora mobilisation was not common throughout the majority
of Mubarak's rule, save from the activities of the Coptic diasporic community.
The American Copts were quite vocal in their demands for the protection
of the Coptic community within Egypt, particularly with regard to human
rights abuses and religious freedom. They also pushed for adequate representation of the Coptic community across governmental and state institutions.
Research has identified how the diaspora community engaged in lobbying
efforts against the Mubarak regime, aiming to have Washington exert pressure
on Egypt to reform its domestic policies (Brinkerhoff 2009). Collaborating
with Cairo's Ibn Khaldun Center for Development Studies, the US Coptic
Association, in particular, developed a number of demands which they
disseminated via their website, including the end of all discrimination against
Copts, the revision of school curricula to include the history of the Coptic
community, as well as equal time on government-controlled television and
radio stations. These activities have been well-researched in the literature
(Brinkerhoff 2005; Hanna 2013), although the extent to which they have
had any success in convincing Washington to jeopardise its relationship
with Egypt over the Coptic community is debatable.

The Egyptian explained politically in a more sustained manner over
the past decade, in the run-up to the 2011 Arab Spring events. With the
support of key political figures in the diaspora, including Nobel laure-
ate Mohamed el-Baradei, Egyptian communities across Europe and the
United States mobilised against the Mubarak regime, and in support of
the country's democratic transition. A number of initiatives developed
within the United States – such as the Alliance for Egyptian-Americans,
the American-Egyptian Strategic Alliance, and Democracy for Egypt. At
the same time, Egyptians abroad extended their support to organisations
within the homeland – for instance, el-Baradei's Association for Change,
which was instituted in February 2011 in Cairo, relied on social media tools
to relay information abroad and gain support from the diaspora. A variety
of social media instruments, including the 'We are all Khaled Said' page
that highlighted the police-instigated torture and death of a young Egyptian
in Alexandria, were incorporated in the diasporas' political mobilisation.
This mobilisation continued throughout the rule of Mohamed Morsi,
whose presidential campaign included videos and messages to Egyptians
living abroad, and who instituted out-of-country voting provisions for the
Egyptian diaspora – a long-requested provision. The return of military rule
in mid-2013, however, put an early stop to this wave of diasporic political
activism.

A second function that the Egyptian state's diaspora-engagement strategy aimed to achieve was economic development. Egypt was expecting certain material benefits from these migrants – for one, as discussed above, these migrants are traditionally perceived across Egyptian policy circles as the core of the state's 'brain drain' issue (*al-Akhbar*, 27 October 1978). Statistical data on Egyptian migrants' levels of education in each host-state is unavailable, but the dominant perception of state elites in Egypt remains that 'as far as permanent migration to more developed countries is concerned, this has always mainly interested more educated workers' (Talani 2010, 184). While high-skilled Egyptians did emigrate across the region, particularly after 1990, the literature agrees that 'brain drain' occurred mainly to the West and, particularly, towards the United States and Canada. This, again, is linked to the 'temporary/permanent' divide (Zohry and Harrell-Bond 2003, 47–8). Ayubi explained this perception:

> [I]t is possible to argue that temporary emigration does not represent a kind of brain drain in the proper sense: first, because it is by definition temporary; second, because its output is still made use of within the same region; and third, because such people disburse a significant proportion of their incomes back to their home country [...] In addition, although temporary migrants feature a reasonably high percentage of personnel who were employed in Egypt in scientific, professional and technical occupations [of about 38 per cent], this percentage is not as high as it is with permanent migrants, and its internal composition is also quite different. (Ayubi 1983, 438)

Not unlike in other developing countries, the Egyptian social body tends to ascribe an elevated status to Egyptians living in Europe and North America, for they have escaped the socio-economic and political conditions plaguing Egypt. Aswany described:

> In the 1980s I applied for a grant to study in the United States and one of the conditions was to pass an examination in English as a foreign language [in a room] full of young doctors and engineers who, like me, were applying to go abroad to study. That day I asked everyone I met if they would like to stay in the United States if they had a chance, and the answer was a firm yes [...] Why did these young people want to escape Egypt? Poverty was not the reason because with a little patience and hard work they could work in Egypt for reasonable salaries, whereas in the West they would often have to do menial work well beneath their qualifications. The fundamental reason they were emigrating was frustration and a sense that the situation in Egypt is unfair and topsy-turvy. [If] you are talented in Egypt, you face a major problem and would be better off if you were average or even a dim-witted failure, first because the system is designed for average people and suffocates those with talent, and second because your future depends first and foremost on your relationships rather than your just deserts. To have talent in Egypt is a burden

because it gives rise to malice and envy, and many people will come forward to crush it. If you are talented in Egypt, you face three options: you can emigrate to a democratic country that respects talents and appreciates competence, where you can work hard day after day until you become like Ahmed Zewail, Mohamed ElBaradei, Magdi Yacoub, and their like; you can offer your talents to a despotic system, agreeing to be its servant and a tool for oppressing, abusing, and cheating Egyptians; or you can decide to preserve your honor, in which case you will meet the same fate as Ibrahim Eissa [the *al-Dustur* editor dismissed by the Mubarak regime]. (Aswani 2011, 198–9)

As Sadat frequently repeated, 'I do not oppose emigration to highly developed countries for the purposes of becoming acquainted with the latest technological advances' (quoted in Tsourapas 2015b, 2204). Interestingly, Egyptians residing in the West have been perceived as more susceptible to Israeli influence – the media frequently published stories of Israel attempting to recruit Egyptian youth abroad: in one case of an Egyptian abroad, 'the Israeli intelligence who is always watching for [Egyptians] to recruit for work, was ready for him and flooded him with money, women, and red nights' (*al-Gomhuria*, 29 November 1975). While such reports are frequently exaggerated, they nonetheless reveal the state's feared loss of control over 'permanent' emigrants. Egypt's policy towards these migrant groups extended to public pleas for these emigrants to 'contribute materially' to the homeland's development (*al-Ahram*, 28 February 1977). As Sadat stated, 'a considerable number of Egyptian scientists work abroad. Some have attained extremely high levels of education, and there is no objection to having them come back to contribute to the country's scientific development. With their experience acquired abroad, those scientists could offer much' (*al-Akhbar*, 11 October 1971). State policy extended beyond mere financial incentives (for instance, beneficial access to housing – another policy area in which the state favoured 'permanent' over 'temporary' migrants), or the *ad hoc* creation of 'Visiting Professor' posts in universities to be occupied by Egyptian scientists residing abroad (*al-Ahram*, 21 April 1974). This was the rationale behind the agreement signed between the Egyptian state and the United Nations Development Programme, which would invite Egyptian scientists working abroad to return to Egypt for an average period of one month, financed by the Academic of Scientific Research and Technology, in order to transfer expertise and build contacts with local Egyptian staff (*al-Ahram*, 3 January 1981). This continued under Mubarak, who argued in his 1987 address at the Expatriate Workers Conference organised that year:

It has always been a source of pride for me during my travels outside the country to hear things about Egyptians who work and study abroad [...] Many Egyptians have displayed an intellectual brilliance and have become noted pioneers sought by people from various parts of the world for their knowledge [...] All these distinguished and outstanding Egyptians have not forgotten their Egyptian nationality. Their international fame has not prevented them from maintaining a profound and firm link with their homeland [...] Undoubtedly, you have noticed new developments and new accomplishments every year when compared to the year before [despite] the shortage of resources, the terribly increase in population, and the debt problem which is facing all Third World countries without exception [...] You have not come to attend this conference, travelling all this way, for a mere discussion by committees that end up in northing, or for debates in which you merely exhibit your knowledge. Rather, you have come to Egypt to participate in the process of construction [...] The people expect a great contribution from you to the advance of the march.

The faith that the regime placed in these emigrants is apparent by the fact that, just before the massive 1977 'Bread Riots', Sadat 'asked Egyptian scientists abroad to participate in solving Egypt's food and housing crisis' (*al-Ahram*, 5 January 1977), much as he had sought their expertise when presenting his plans to fully liberalise the Egyptian economy (*al-Ahram*, 21 April 1974). Mubarak did not steer away from this: 'Please allow me to tell you frankly that the people expect you to adopt practical recommendations', he mentioned in his address to Egyptian expatriates in 1987. He continued to say that

> The people are your kinfolk. These recommendations, the number of which is not important, should be subject to immediate implementation. We need positive recommendations that should deal with reality and that should be implemented in a way that will achieve your interests and those of all citizens.

Mubarak outlined exactly what the Egyptian regime was expecting of its expatriates, based upon what other countries had achieved:

> Friendly peoples in Third World states have set examples in this regard. Their expatriate citizens have, through sincere efforts, contributed to consolidating their countries' economic and social development process, especially where the transfer of technology appropriate to their conditions and requirements is concerned. They have also helped establish self-financing small- and medium-scale industrial projects; promoted their countries' exports and opened up markets for them; and set up regular channels for liaison between research and education institutions in their country and similar institutions abroad, so that they may keep abreast of the latest scientific developments and modern discoveries. (Quoted in Middle East Contemporary Survey 11, 1987)

At the same time, the belief that 'permanent' emigrants will aid in the country's development is further documented in the themes of the bi-annual, state-sponsored conferences organised through the 'Friends of Egypt' organisation since 1974 (see Table 4.3). The target of these events were Egyptians

Table 4.3 Titles of *Friends of Egypt* conferences

Year	Conference Title
1974	Organising Modes of Communication with Egyptian Scholars Abroad
1974	Development of the Desert
1978	Development of the Countryside as a Source of Complete Development
1980	Development under the Umbrella of Peace
1982	The Role of Science and Technology in Egyptian Development
1984	Environmental Problems of Development
1986	Economic Development in Egypt
1988	Education in Egypt
1990	Egypt's Human Resources
1992	Water Resources and Development in Egypt
1994	Energy and Continuous Development in Egypt
1996	Unemployment in Egypt
1998	Development of the Desert in the Third Millennium
2001	Modernizing Egypt
2003	Human Development in the Third Millennium
2005	Information Technology and its Role in Development
2009	Care, Communication and Development

Source: Tsourapas 2015b, p. 2210

residing in Western countries, according to organiser and former Minister of Health Dr Badran, and the professed aim was to 'bring successful Egyptians back to the homeland' (*Personal Interview*, 21 January 2014).

Egyptian outreach for economic development aid from its diaspora in the United States produced negligible results. Few migrants returned, according to most estimates and secondary accounts.[3] 'Many ["permanent" emigrants] realised that a return would mean a lowering of standards and much overtime to keep income levels up. There was apprehension that contact might be lost with developments in their academic fields abroad' (McDermott 1988, 241). Overall, government bureaucracy and suspicion from many Egyptians abroad have been obstacles to a significant flow of permanent migrants' investments into the country (Zohry and Debnath 2015). A survey study by Saleh on the country's 'brain drain' problem in the 1970s identified similar sentiments by Egyptians abroad. One Egyptian interviewed for the project stated:

I came back with hopes that with the degree and experience I got, I could help Egypt, but I was shocked. My efforts in England didn't help Egypt … There is a shortage of [professorial positions] that I could fill, but I am not taken … Even my salary, that they cut for two years in England, was not given back to me. I am treated as a "colored" where I work (army), for I have a doctor's degree ... I feel that colleagues have envy and hatred for me and my degree. (Saleh 1979, 55)

Another returnee recalled:

I was shocked by many things in Egypt as soon as I arrived. I stayed in a state of unbalance for a long time ... During that time I met the worse difficulties that a returning scientist meets ... at the customs, bribery of government employees and all that ... just to get my car out ... Difficulties came one after the other ... At present I am trying to acclimatise to life in the framework of the actual reality around me. (Saleh 1979, 64)

Overall, the second part of this chapter has examined how Egypt's diaspora policy was markedly different from that adopted by the other four North African states by examining, firstly, the Egyptian state's development of a pro-active diaspora policy towards Egyptians living in Western Europe and the United States and, secondly, the impact of emigration policy upon the *rapprochement* between the Washington and Cairo. The first did not yield the expected results, as the Egyptian diaspora neither appeared to engage fruitfully either in the economic development of the Egyptian state, nor did it respond to the regime's calls that it should return to Egypt. This was not entirely unexpected, given that Sadat's outreach efforts and its promotion of a 'democratising' image of Egypt were unconvincing, and marred by the Egyptian regime's resort to authoritarianism. On the other hand, the issue of migration did bring Washington and Cairo together – much in the way cooperation on issues of migration allowed the Egyptian regime to upgrade its relations with neighbouring Arab states, so did technical cooperation and aid in issues of migration and population control pave the way for more elaborate projects that tied the two countries together.

Conclusion

The securitisation of diasporas by authoritarian sending-states has become commonplace, from Central Asian republics' targeting of political exiles to African states' monitoring of diaspora activities. A few cases make international headlines: beyond the Khashoggi murder, the March 2018 poisoning attempt on former Russian military officer Sergei Skripal and his daughter in England was also widely reported. Most such cases, however, remain out of the public eye. For example, few Western media outlets reported Kuwait's extradition of eight migrants who belong to the Muslim Brotherhood – an Islamist religious and political group – to Egypt in July 2019, where they await long prison sentences. Similarly, eyebrows were not raised in the West when Azerbaijani emigrant and former parliament member Huseyn Abdullayev (who led the 'Let's Not Keep Silent' opposition campaign while abroad) was arrested by Turkish authorities in April 2018 and later extradited to Azerbaijan – despite the fact that Germany had granted him political asylum a few years earlier.

This chapter has taken a look at the range of policies available in terms of North African states' engagement with diasporic groups. A cursory examination of other authoritarian states identifies similar responses to the trade-off between security and development, both within the Arab world and beyond. Those that approach cross-border mobility as a developmental opportunity – such as Jordan, Turkey, and China – have all attempted to securitise their diaspora policies to varying degrees. In light of worries about religious extremism or anti-regime political activism, they respond to the trade-off between development and security via extraterritorial authoritarian practices of repression, monitoring, and control. However, those states that do not see cross-border mobility as producing strong economic benefits – such as Iran, the Gulf Cooperation Council states or, in the past, Cuba or Egypt under Nasser – have been more likely to securitise their emigration policies. They attempt to tackle the trade-off between migration and security via tighter restrictions on citizens' cross-border mobility.

Notes

1   An earlier version of this chapter has been published in Tsourapas (2020a).
2   Naturally, this does not imply that all Egyptians abroad were politically active, nor that pro-regime activism was unheard of.
3   A complete evaluation of whether Egyptian diaspora policies positively contributed to the return of Egyptians (and shifted their attitudes towards their home country) would not be possible within this book's methodological framework and given the unavailability of statistical data. That said, I encountered very few elites or experts willing to argue that Egyptian policy was a success in this aspect. The wider literature corroborates this.

5

Inter-state cooperation and labour migration to the Gulf

'The Arab world is now in what may be termed the Saudi epoch in modern Arab history.'

Muhammad Hasanayn Haykal (*al-Anwar*, 20–23 May 1977)

Earlier in this book, we analysed in detail the extent to which the short-term migration of Egyptian professional staff featured into the workings of the Arab Cold War and Egypt–Israel rivalry, thereby constituting an instrument of Egyptian soft power in the 1954–70 period. Yet, the regional realities of the post-1970 Arab world had changed dramatically, as Egypt was faced with an unprecedented economic downturn at the same time as Arab conservative monarchies enjoyed massive oil rents. No longer was Egypt willing or, indeed, able to export high-skilled emigrants across the region for soft power purposes. At the same time, Saudi Arabia and other oil-producing states in the region were in dire need of unskilled and low-skilled labour, particularly in the fields of construction, and shared a deep distrust of Nasserite-era politicised migration. In this period, Egyptian migration diplomacy targeted its unskilled and low-skilled labour and focused on ensuring bilateral coordination with Arab host-states that, in turn, led to *inter-state cooperation*. Egypt coordinated its emigration policy as per host-states' needs and political sensitivities: it realised Arab oil-producing states' labour demands, and institutionalised unrestricted short-term, or temporary, emigration across the region; the ruling regime also understood these states' reticence to politicised migrants, and it discursively linked this form of migration to its repudiation of Nasser and his regional foreign policy, within the context of 'de-Nasserisation'. Similarly, Arab host-states coordinated their policies to Egypt's needs and political sensitivities: seeing an opportunity for massive numbers of unskilled and low-skilled migrant workers from Egypt, they prioritised their recruitment over other nationalities;

second, they acknowledged the Egyptian regime's desire to 'save face' in terms of Egypt's deteriorating economic condition, and framed their recruitment of Egyptians as compensation for the Egyptian state's shouldering of the burden of the Arab–Israeli conflict. By the end of the 1970s, short-term migration of Egyptians had resulted in inter-state cooperation in other policy fields.

A brief description of the regional balance of power in 1970 is necessary in order to contextualise Egyptian migration statecraft in the region. The Egyptian economy in particular had evolved dramatically over these two decades: marked by an early nationalisation wave of foreign banks and companies that had been initiated in 1956 with the French-owned Suez Canal company, it had experienced relatively high rates of growth and significant industrial development early on. Throughout the 1950s, the elimination of foreign interests had given way to new opportunities for Egyptian capital, and the public sector expanded massively under the various expropriations organised by 'Aziz Sidqi, the minister of industry and a long-time Nasser associate. The private sector was steadily being put under increased state authority through a variety of regulations, such as Law 28|1958 that granted the ministry of industry the responsibility to provide licenses to any new industrial establishments (Dekmejian 1971, 126–7; Waterbury 1983, 69–70).

Yet, by the mid-1960s, Egypt faced a number of issues that would contribute to a long process of *al-inkimāsh* (economic shrinkage): for one, the policy of state-led economic growth, import-substitution industrialisation, and sectoral monopolies stopped bearing fruit by mid-1960s, with GNP growth falling from 6.4% (1963–4) to 4.4% (1965–6) to 0.3% (1966–7). Egypt's involvement in the North Yemen Civil War was extremely costly, amounting to roughly $60 million annually. The situation became even more difficult following the failure of the 1961 cotton crop, the rising costs of maintaining the fight against Israel, as well as the post-1965 suspension of American food for peace shipments to Egypt (Amin 1995). Through his decision to sever diplomatic relations with West Germany, Nasser had also jeopardised some $290 million in bilateral aid. At the time, Egypt's domestic debt exceeded $1.5 million, while its foreign one was estimated at over $2.5 billion (Gerges 1994, 205). Furthermore, the 1967 War accentuated Egypt's economic decline: GNP growth reached -3.1% in the 1967–8 fiscal year, as the closure of the Suez Canal, which had been in Egyptian hands since 1956, deprived the state of another valuable source of revenue. On top of this, 80% of military equipment had to be replaced, and Nasser continued prioritising the war effort during the 1967–70 'War of Attrition' with Israel. By the time of Nasser's death in 1970, the country was in dire straits. 'Egypt thus ended the sixties devoting almost as low a share of GDP to investments as it had in 1947', argue Hansen and Nashashibi (quoted in Waterbury 1983, 83). 'But public consumption had more than tripled (to almost 25%) while that of private consumption had shrunk by one fourth (to about 65%). A largely unchanged payments deficit persisted' (quoted in Waterbury 1983, 83).

Egypt's new president, Anwar Sadat, realised that the time was ripe for a reappraisal of Egypt's regional policy. This was a particularly pressing matter after the '1970s oil boom [when] the differential between the rich and the poor Arab states reached a peak [...]' (Ayubi 1995, 159). At a time when Egypt was suffering from a massive balance-of-payments deficit, the oil-producing Arab states were entering a new phase of unrivalled economic prosperity. The repercussions of the 1973 'oil boom' were, according to Kerr and Yasin, 'nowhere more dramatic than in the Arab states', effectively dividing the Arab world into rich and poor states (Kerr and Yasin 1982, 1). The 'unprecedented' increase in oil revenues for Saudi Arabia (its GDP more than doubled, from 40.5 billion Saudi riyals in 1972 to 99.3 billion riyals in 1973) signified that it, together with other oil-exporting Arab countries, had 'entered the age of affluence' (Al-Rasheed 2010, 133). Already in 1972, the GCC countries held 26% of all Arab GNP, but only 7% of the total Arab population – a decade later, they contained 8% of the population, but 52% of all Arab GNP (Ayubi 1995, 159). At the same time, by 1970, Egypt's population had grown from 21 million in 1952 to over 33 million. Egyptians were faced with 'increasingly bleak' job prospects in their country (Beattie 2000, 13). Given the shifting balance of power in the region, presidents Sadat and Mubarak moved steadily towards a stronger relationship with Egypt's oil-exporting neighbours, particularly the Gulf states and, chief among them, Saudi Arabia (Hinnebusch 1985, 65; Waterbury 1983, 361).

In this context, inter-state cooperation evolved out of mutual coordination of migration policies along two policy levels. Firstly, regional migration carried distinct material benefits for both parties: Egypt was in need of economic aid from the oil-rich Arab monarchies, which, in turn, were in need of Egyptian unskilled and low-skilled migrants; secondly, both sides demonstrated a desire to accommodate each other's political particularities: Egyptian policymakers had to recognise that oil-rich Arab monarchies were apprehensive of Nasserite-era migration as soft power; Arab host-states' policies had to also frame these migration flows not as direct economic aid to the Egyptian regime, allowing Sadat to 'save face' within the Arab world. The following two sections outline this degree of policy coordination along the material and political dimension, respectively, before outlining how this coordination resulted in inter-state cooperation in the chapter's final section.

The invention of 'temporary' Egyptian migration to the Arab oil-producing countries

Her son responded with another miracle: 'The Egyptians are the only Arabs who enjoy the affection of the Saudis ... it's because they have a good sense of humor.' The cousin denied this immediately. 'Not at all. It's because they don't get involved in politics, and all they're interested in is making a bit of money.'

Sonallah Ibrahim, *Zaat* (2001, 149)

This section discusses the process of bilateral coordination of unskilled and low-skilled migration policies between Egypt and Arab oil-producing host-states, focusing on Egyptian policies. One of President Sadat's decisions upon assuming power in late 1970 was to begin the drafting of a new, 'Permanent' Constitution.[1] From a migration statecraft perspective, the end result of this process – the 1971 Constitution – is important because it introduces migration as a right of Egyptian citizens for the first time in the nation's history. It is also important because it institutionalises two different forms of emigration – temporary and permanent – a distinction that was novel to Egypt and had no previous usage. Law 111|1983, still valid today, explains the difference between 'temporary' and 'permanent' Egyptian migrants, first highlighted in the 1971 Constitution: a 'permanent' emigrant is one who 'stays abroad permanently by obtaining the nationality of a foreign country and/or a permanent residence permit; stays abroad for a period of at least ten years; or obtains an immigration permit from one of the countries of destination'. A temporary emigrant, on the other hand, is 'someone (not a student or seconded worker) who works abroad for twelve consecutive months'. However, in practice, this differentiation has been based upon migrants' country of destination: Egyptians living in Arab countries are invariably considered temporary emigrants, or temporary workers abroad, even when they have lived there for decades. All those emigrating to Australia, Europe, North America, or elsewhere, on the other hand, are considered permanent emigrants, even if they just arrived in their host-countries (Zohry and Harrell-Bond 2003, 34).

The literature has typically accounted for this by citing foreign workers' inability to settle permanently in the countries of the Arab Gulf, and the relative ease of doing so in the West. Minister of Migration and Manpower Nahid al-'Ashri argued that 'Egyptians in the Arab world are not migrants. They are temporary workers, who will return home.' Former Minister of Health and President of Cairo University Ibrahim Gamil Badran told me that the Egyptian state's diaspora policy did not target 'Egyptians in the Gulf [who are there temporarily]. Egyptians do not emigrate to Arab countries.' Yet, this *post hoc* explanation is not entirely convincing, given that it does not problematise why this distinction first emanated from Egypt itself. Also, it is somewhat inaccurate, given that not all regional emigration is *de facto* temporary: Syria, Jordan, and Libya, which constitute traditional destinations of Egyptian migrants in the Arab world, have, at times, granted citizenship to emigrants, particularly to Arabs (Dib 1979). In the Persian Gulf, the United Arab Emirates and Kuwait would, until the 1980s, grant citizenship to Arabs after ten and fifteen years of residence, respectively. Iraq would also proceed to naturalise Egyptian migrants throughout the 1980s, as seen above. But even when naturalisation is not an option, it is not unusual for Egyptian migrants to remain there for over two or three decades or, even, to stay abroad until their death. If the 'transformation of temporary immigrants into settlers cannot be ruled out' in the Gulf, then Egypt's decision to bifurcate its policy merits deeper analysis (Kapiszewski 2001, 193).

As I have shown elsewhere (Tsourapas 2015b, 2208), by emphasising the temporary aspect of regional migration, Egypt arguably wished to coordinate its migration policy along the wishes of the Arab oil-exporting countries. The institutionalised non-permanence of Egyptian migrants aimed towards mollifying Arab countries' misapprehensions about opening their borders to potentially millions of Egyptian immigrants.[2] Oil-producing Arab countries had clearly stated their need for migrant labour well before the 1973 oil embargo dramatically increased their monetary resources and labour needs. Already in 1970, the Saudi five-year plan reported that:

> The employment of non-Saudi personnel is considered a partial answer to the Kingdom's needs of manpower necessary for development processes because of the number of Saudis working in both the private and public sectors who possess academic qualifications and adequate training required for fast development will continue to be relatively low. (Quoted in Barsalou 1985, 136)

At the same time, however, they were extremely cautious of the potential social and political disruptions that may ensue from such mass immigration – partly because of these states' demographic make-up, in which nationals traditionally comprise a very small percentage of the total population (see Table 5.1). The type of migration that would most appeal to these states would be temporary, in which foreign workers would be able to return to their homelands once they were no longer needed in the Gulf (Kapiszewski 2001). 'The intent of Saudi Arabia's policies are as straightforward as those of Kuwait', writes Sell. 'The Saudis wish to keep migrants temporary and have them return home when their labour is no longer wanted' (Sell 1988, 95). As the Qatari Minister of Labour Abd al-Rahman al-Dirham, stated:

> The question of foreign labor is of great concern. Our social customs are threatened by foreigners. The problem is not just in Qatar but also in other

Table 5.1 Saudi Arabian work permits and remittances to Jordan
(millions of dinars)

Year	Permits	Remittances	Year	Permits	Remittances
1980	668,000	16.1	1986	564,000	3.7
1981	632,000	15.2	1987	591,000	7.3
1982	663,000	13.6	1988	641,000	18.8
1983	819,000	13.9	1989	615,000	13.5
1984	950,000	9.9	1990	605,000	11.2
1985	802,000	10.4	1991	580,000	4.5

Source: Wilson 1994, p. 284

Gulf countries. We prefer it if we can get suitable people from Arab countries who can live in the Gulf area without changing it. (Quoted in Middle East Economic Digest, August 1982, 40)

If one takes the Arab host-states' preferences into account, then the Egyptian shift into bifurcating its migration policy makes perfect sense. Sadat would claim that Egyptians 'have a small cultivable area of land, a big population that is increasing maybe by the biggest rate in the world' (interview with President Sadat: *Time*, 18 March 1974). Indeed, one of the goals of the Higher Council of Manpower and Training, newly formed through Presidential Decree No. 795, was the 'fulfilment of the needs of Arab and other friendly countries' (Messiha 1980, 12). At the same time, Egypt introduced training regulations that ensured the state 'provides the specialized manpower required and regulates the supply of workers whose services are sought by the sister Arab states' (*al-Ahram*, 30 April 1974). In 1974, the regime announced that 'within the framework of planning to meet the requirements of [workers] in building, electricity, factories and services, practical technical training centres will be set up in order to meet increased demand for Egyptian workers' (MENA, 3 July 1974).

A year later, Prime Minister Mamduh Salim officially declared that 'Egypt's policy is to encourage export of its manpower to the Arab world [...] so that Egyptians can participate in the development plans of sister Arab states' (*al-Akhbar*, 15 August 1975). In October 1975, Egypt officially announced that its formal policy was 'to export its surplus workers to other Arab countries and elsewhere' (*The Middle East*, October 1975). This carried on under President Mubarak. In 1984, the undersecretary of the ministry of immigration highlighted the continuity in terms of Egyptian migration statecraft: 'we must supply the Arab countries with the manpower to develop [...] This is our duty. They need our manpower and we have good relations.

They are our brothers' (*Cairo Today*, May 1984). Similar to the incorporation of education policy in Nasser's migration statecraft as soft power, education policy under Sadat and Mubarak was also incorporated into Egyptian migration statecraft. This time, it aimed to accentuate the temporary nature of labour emigration to the Arab oil-producing states. Egyptian school curricula now taught that 'people emigrate, just like the birds' (*Al-Ahram al-Iqtisadi*, No. 745, 1983). The 1977 preparatory school certificate exam asked students to write an essay on 'the joys of a person who could obtain work in an "Arab" country, thus managing to accumulate money and return home to start a new life' (*al-Ahram*, 18 May 1977).

Of course, it is important to note that medium- and high-skilled Egyptians also emigrated to the oil-producing Arab states in the post-1970s period. Despite public warnings from the Minister of Education Dr Mustafa Kamal Hilmi that the country suffered from a shortage of 25,000 educators in 1974, some 20,000 teachers pursued employment across 'Arab and friendly countries' in that year alone (*al-Ahram*, 17 June 1974). By 1979, the Ministry of Education would report that it had a shortage of 14,928 teachers in languages alone (*al-Gomhuria*, 30 August 1979). A report by the National Bank of Egypt argued, in 1979, that 'the main functional categories and professionals which are badly needed in Egypt ... are [those] inclined towards migration'. It estimated that shortages in technicians and skilled workers reached 40–50% (National Bank of Egypt 1979). To such criticism, Sadat would respond that as far as 'Egyptian emigration to Arab [states is concerned] Egypt will continue to meet the manpower requirements of these countries' (MENA, 5 January 1977). As he often declared, sustained emigration is part of the responsibility of Egypt towards 'our Arab brothers ... who are in need of Egyptian expertise' (*al-Gomhoriya*, 29 August 1974).

However, Gulf states' concerns over Egyptian migration were not centred solely on the issue of migrants' duration; after all, regional emigration under Nasser was also temporary, but was able to produce political disruption across the Arab world. Arab host-states were also concerned that Egyptian unskilled and low-skilled temporary migration would engage in the same type of pro-Egyptian politics that were common throughout the 1950s and 1960s – for them, Nasser's death in 1970 did not necessarily imply that ideas of Arab unity or pan-Arabism were no longer a potential source of agitation, particularly as the Palestine Liberation Organisation (PLO) had been escalating its armed struggle since the mid-1960s. A few days before Nasser's death, in September 1970, Palestinians in Jordan had attempted to overthrow the Hashemite monarchy. Having spent years acting as a state within a state in Jordan, the PLO and Yasser Arafat attempted a military takeover, before being forcibly expelled from the country into Lebanon, during what has become known as *Aylūl Al-Aswad*, or Black September.

The potentially destabilising effects of Arab nationalism did not go unnoticed across the Arab monarchies of the Gulf.

The Egyptian regime under Sadat perceived of the need to provide additional assurances to the Arab host-states, and initiated a sustained process that linked Egyptian emigration to the regime's repudiation of Nasser's domestic and regional foreign policies, including the use of migration as a soft power strategy, in a process known as de-Nasserisation (cf. McDermott 1988; Lippman 1989, 27–51). Through President Sadat's statements but, more frequently, through the media, the Egyptian regime signalled that the era of politicised migration and Nasser-era antagonism with other Arab regimes was gone. Prominent journalist 'Ali Amin underlined that 'Egypt will [now] never think of interfering with the internal affairs of any Arab state. Neither will it impose an opinion, a certain person, policy, or form of government on them, be it Beirut, Amman, Damascus, Tripoli, Kuwait, or the Arabian Gulf' (*al-Ahram*, 7 April 1974). While, in the past, 'Arab states' suspicion of Nasser's political motives was reflected in a reluctance to encourage the emigration of Egyptians, Arabs were now urged to abandon such scepticism (Choucri 1977, 6). Anis Mansur, the later editor-in-chief of the regime mouthpiece *October*, explained:

> [An] Egyptian was looked upon as the man with the 'ugly face' throughout the Arab world. For twenty years, every Egyptian had seemed to turn into a spy or saboteur. Every Egyptian teacher was thought to have come to overthrow the standing rule and to distribute subversive literature. Every Egyptian doctor was considered a spy acting for Egyptian Intelligence Service to set one class against another [...] Now he is not interested in other peoples' affairs. 'Give and take' is his motto. [Under Nasser] every Egyptian was treated as a *persona non grata* and he had to isolate himself to affirm that he had nothing to do with what happened in Egypt. [Under Sadat] this abominable picture changed and will continue to change to the better, for Egypt came to be governed by a ruler not by a leader [...] Egyptians abroad form a 'working army' for the sake of Egypt and all Arabism. (*al-Akhbar*, 13 March 1974)

These statements, which were commonplace in 1970s Egypt, cannot be explained convincingly unless one takes into account the lengths that Sadat went to in order to differentiate himself from Nasser. The former Minister of Migration and Manpower Nahed Ashry corroborated this: 'Presidents Sadat and Mubarak did not wish Egyptian workers' involvement in politics abroad' (*Personal Interview*). As Sadat himself wrote in his memoirs, Egyptians in the past had been 'turned into puppets. They became *duma* [dummies] in the hands of their rulers, who did with them as they pleased' (Sadat 1978, 289). But, in the post-1970 era, this changed dramatically. As *al-Akhbar*'s Mostafa Amin wrote, in a column entitled '"Ugly Egyptian" Image Removed', the Egyptian migrant was formerly considered:

a hooligan holding a knife in his mouth and a heavy club in his hand. Unfortunately, the Egyptians helped maintain that ugly picture by their behaviour, and this explains to a great extent the pleasure that the world showed upon our 5 June 1967 defeat. Today the situation is totally different. (*al-Akhbar*, 23 May 1976)

Overall, the Egyptian regime's strategy for closer ties with the oil-producing conservative Arab monarchies relied on the coordination of its emigration policy along two lines: the introduction of 'temporary' emigration as an institutionalised form of regional cross-border mobility, and the desire to move away from Nasserite-era antagonism by stop supporting the politicisation of regional emigration. By the early 1980s, Hosni Mubarak would emphatically declare that:

The days when a citizen [of Egypt] residing abroad was viewed with suspicion … are over … we must all guarantee, in actions and not in words, that an Egyptian working abroad is a good citizen. (Quoted in *al-Akhbar*, 15 August 1983)

How did Arab host-states coordinate their immigration policies with regard to Egyptian needs? This section highlights two key aspects of this post-1970 immigration policy coordination: firstly, the rhetoric that Gulf states developed in their recruitment of Egyptian labour centred on their need to 'repay' Egypt for its important sacrifices during successive Arab–Israeli Wars. This discourse made little sense – why would Arab leaders downplay their states' own contribution to the defeat of Israel and choose to praise Egypt instead? – unless it is examined under the prism of migration statecraft. This discourse allowed the Egyptian state to 'save face' and to receive material aid from its Arab counterparts in the form of economic remittances, without being seen as being indebted to their financial help. Secondly, Arab host-states' immigration policy coordination is evident in the preferential treatment that Egyptian migrants received across the Gulf states – with regard to both their recruitment and the duration of their stay in these host-states – particularly when compared to Palestinian and Yemeni workers.

The discourse on Arab host-states' 'repaying' Egypt for its human, material, and military losses to Israel over numerous wars emerged in the aftermath of the 1973 Yom Kippur War. Sadat would refer to an imminent military confrontation with Israel from assuming power in 1970, but it was not until October 1973 that hostilities between Arabs and Israel broke out. Through a surprise offensive, the Egyptians re-occupied the eastern coast of the Suez Canal, while the members of the Organisation of Arab Petroleum Exporting Countries (OAPEC) proclaimed an oil embargo against select Western countries. Saudi Arabia, in particular, imposed a complete embargo on exports to the Netherlands and the United States. 'The campaigns showed once more the military superiority of the Israelis,' wrote Hourani, 'but neither in the eyes of the Arabs nor in those of the world did the war seem to be a defeat' (Hourani 2013, 418). In fact, Sadat welcomed the result of the 1973, or October, War as a much-needed corrective to the devastating 1967 defeat and valuable proof of intra-Arab solidarity, and was able to highlight the human sacrifices of Egypt in the Arab–Israeli Wars, and link them with the need for Arab economic aid.

In an ingenious use of political rhetoric, Sadat now signalled that Egypt, the region's most populous state, should provide mass labour for oil-rich Arab states' developmental needs in peacetime, much as it had used its ample human resources to provide security for them during wartime. 'We believe that Egypt should call for an immediate Arab meeting,' Sadat declared in 1977, 'and that the Arab countries should be frankly told that Egypt has shouldered the burden of the Arab cause for 30 years and, as a result, has suffered hunger, become impoverished and made sacrifices' (*Akhbar el-Yom*, 22 January 1977). Even as the centre of Arab power was moving towards the oil-rich monarchies, Sadat's strategy aimed at ensuring that Egypt would continue to enjoy an important, albeit no longer central, role in intra-Arab politics. As Sadat's foreign minister wrote in his memoirs:

> The shock of the 1967 War and the defeat – psychological and moral as well as military – suffered by the Arabs, sparked a spirit of Arab resurrection, especially since this was coincident with the emergence of the area's vast potentialities in oil and manpower, making it a strategic and economic power to be reckoned with. The end of the 1973 War saw the Arab world transformed. It had become a mighty giant that had awakened from its torpor and realized its own strength as soon as it had regained its self-confidence and self-esteem. (Kamel 1986, 29)

After all, as a result of the 1973 War and oil embargo, Egypt's rationale went, 'Saudi Arabia and all the Gulf emirates were awash in surplus earnings from oil exports. Sadat was not at all reticent in claiming his share' (Waterbury 1983, 416). Securing increased financial aid from Saudi Arabia was a chief goal of Sadat (*al-Akhbar*, 21 March 1974), and promoting Egyptian migration became an intrinsic part of this strategy. This was justified in two ways: firstly, Egyptian efforts during the Arab–Israel Wars carried a moral implication that Arab states contribute to its economic well-being; secondly, the heightened need for migrant labour in the oil-producing Arab countries, combined with Egypt's labour surplus, suggested a mutually beneficial, honourable solution that allowed Sadat to save face. The conflation of these two elements occurred through a strategy that linked Egypt's 'extraordinary' sacrifices during the various conflicts with Israel to continued Arab aid, albeit in an indirect form, through the absorption of its excess labour force.

Egyptian labour, in its perceived importance for the Arab–Israeli Wars and its potential utility to labour-poor Arab countries, gradually dominated the Egyptian elite's discourse in the post-1973 period. 'Egypt is the Arabs' fortress', prominent journalist Musa Sabry wrote in *al-Akhbar*, referring to the Arab–Israeli Wars of 1948, 1956, 1967, and 1973. 'She has sacrificed 100,000 martyrs over 4 wars' (*al-Akhbar*, 21 March 1974). Implied here was an economic *quid pro quo*: according to Sadat's rationale, Egypt's sacrifice in labour necessitated not only closer relations with the Arab states, but concrete aid. Sadat, according to journalist and confidant Anis Mansur, 'considered his preoccupation with Egyptian affairs too onerous for him to add any Arab problems to them, and [felt] that to manage the affairs of the 37 million Egyptians is too heavy to be made heavier by the misery of 70 million more Arabs'. 'Egyptians abroad,' Mansur claimed, 'form a "working army" for the sake of Egypt and of all Arabs' (*al-Akhbar*, 12 March 1974). According to Sadat himself:

> In order to repel aggression, the Egyptian people lost more than L.E. 10,000 million, this besides the lives of the fallen soldiers, which cannot be evaluated in terms of money. The Egyptians did not pay this price just for their own defence, but in defence of the whole Arab nation ... the burden of military expenses adversely affected the level of development in Egypt, which dropped from 6.7 per cent during the period from 1956 to 1965 to less than 5 per cent annually. (Sadat 1974, 6)

The strategy of highlighting Egypt's importance in the fight against Israel was not new, tracing its roots to the late Nasserite era and, particularly, the 1967 Khartoum Conference negotiations, when the conservative monarchies agreed to support the Egyptian state financially 'until the elimination of Israeli aggression' without any written conditions (Gilbar 1997, 105). The Saudis had then declared that 'Egypt is not standing on its own, the Saudi government, which never hesitated to assist its big sister in the various stages of its conflict with the enemy ... feels today, as always, that it is supporting Egypt' (Feiler 2003, 7). After 1973, Egypt discursively equated the importance of the oil embargo, imposed by the OAPEC countries in shaping the war outcome, with the Egyptians who had lost their lives fighting against Israel. 'Who won the [1973] War?' *Akhbar el-Yom* asked. 'Faisal, or Sadat?' (*Akhbar el-Yom*, 22 March 1974). Sadat would similarly argue that 'other Arabs, despite their opposition, for the moment could do very little about Israel without Egypt's leadership and support; nor could they deny Egypt a role in the Arab world, by virtue of its sheer size, the dynamism of its experience and the momentum of its human resources' (Feiler 2003, 125). The president vehemently supported that 'everything [the Arabs] possess was given them by the blood of our sons in Sinai' (*Al-Siyasi*, 3 May 1981). As Sadat declared:

'The October battle would not have been possible had I not worked for two years to make the Arab nation one family again. The decision for the crossing was Egyptian-Arab; the solidarity was Egyptian-Arab; the surge forward was Egyptian-Arab. Thus from being disunited, we became united; instead of acting against each other, we developed an understanding.' Arab unity was real, for Sadat, and it was no longer dependent on 'empty slogans'. (Quoted in Brand 2014, 81)

Egypt's contribution to the 1973 War became enmeshed with the responsibility, or duty, of oil-exporting Arab states to accept Egyptian migrants in such a way that the Egyptian regime would not 'lose face': 'We do not want gratuities,' Hegazy declared; 'we do not state our needs and ask for aid. Egypt has huge trained manpower potential [...] Egyptian manpower is the most precious capital we possess' (*al-Ahram*, 27 October 1974). It is in this light that Egypt's decision to have the 'export of labor become an officially recognized policy objective' should be understood (Dessouki 1982, 59). According to Sadat:

Egypt is the heart and mind of the Arab world [...] And the biggest asset in Egypt is the human being, the Egyptian man, who is a doctor, engineer, labourer, teacher, with 13 universities here and with the pride and heritage of seven thousand years. (Quoted in Lippman 1989, 262)

In other words, if Egyptians contribute to the Arabs' well-being during wartime, it is only logical they should continue to do so in times of peace. Arab host-states willingly cooperated with this discourse and were happy to portray their recruitment of Egyptian labour as part of their responsibilities towards Egypt. As Saddam Hussein graciously acknowledged, Egyptian wartime sacrifices needed to be repaid through migration:

There is not a single Arab citizen or a single Arab country that is not indebted to the Egyptian people, and the Egyptian soldiers, for their sacrifices at all times [...] It is nationally incumbent on every true Arab to hasten to repay part of that debt so that giant and generous Egypt should continue to stand on its feet in full grandeur. We in Iraq are prepared to contribute to that duty, and that honour. Our doors are flung open to Egyptian farmers, workers, and intellectuals. They will be assured here of the same treatment as their Iraqi brothers, without the least discrimination. (quoted in *al-Ahram*, 21 February 1975)

This is not mere rhetoric: in fact, Iraq had put forth an official request for 'large numbers of Egyptian farmers to migrate to Iraq with their families, where they will be given title to agricultural land with the aim of increasing the country's wheat and maize crops' only a month earlier, in January 1975 (*al-Ahram*, 20 January 1975). By March 1975, negotiations between Manpower Minister Saleh Ghareeb and his Iraqi counterpart decided on Egyptians being remunerated ID 130/monthly and enjoying all the privileges

granted to Iraqi citizens (*al-Ahram*, 1 March 1975). It was decided that the
first 500 Egyptian *fallāḥīn* families would move to the *al-Khalsa* settlement,
some 36 miles south of Baghdad (*October*, 4 July 1982). There, they would
be assigned 20 feddans of land (later reduced to 8 feddans, or approximately
8.5 acres of land), a three-room house, a shed, and cattle free of charge
(*al-Ahram*, 8 March 1975). Importantly, the land deeds would be indefinitely
leased to the Egyptian farmers' families (el-Solh 1984). Applications for the
scheme reached 4,000 people by mid-June 1975 (*al-Ahram*, 13 June 1975).
The process was later lauded by Iraqi Minister of Information, Tariq ʿAziz,
as 'a confirmation of the necessity of Arab cooperation in the fields of
development and production' (quoted in MENA, 11 August 1976). A second
village was built in the *al-Wahdah* area of *Karrada*, a Shia-majority district
of Baghdad, while in 1983 authorities agreed to build three new villages
(*al-Ahram*, 17 December 1983).

There are numerous potential reasons as to the rationale behind Arab
states' compliance regarding this discourse. It has been often argued that
they were keen to avoid instability in Egypt, or the potential of having a
Nasserite replace Sadat at the helm of the country. Everyone knew that
Sadat was facing a precarious position in Egypt, particularly given the
country's deteriorating economic conditions. As the CIA succinctly put it
at the time, his 'domestic position depends to a considerable extent on his
international and intra-Arab stature' (Interagency Intelligence Memorandum
1976, 15). Another potential reason would have to do with securing the
Arab host-states' interests: if Egypt was willing to facilitate the emigration
of hundreds of thousands of unskilled and low-skilled labour, while also
discouraging these migrants from engaging in politics – unlike their Yemeni
or Palestinian counterparts – then they would happily coordinate their
policies to match Egyptian preferences.

Beyond discursive statements of support, it is difficult to establish with
certainty that Arab host-states coordinated their policies in order to prioritise
the recruitment of Egyptian emigrants. Haddad has argued that Saudi Arabi
and Kuwait preferred Egyptian labourers because, unlike Yemenis or Palestinians, they would not 'function as a fifth column and eventually endanger
the host countries' (Haddad 1987, 248). Indeed, Egyptian regional migrants
confirmed the regime's promises by generally developing a reputation of
political pacifism, to the delight of their host-states (Van Hear 1998). Under
Sadat the Egyptian state effectively ceased to promote migrants' political
activism abroad:

> It must be stressed that, for the most part [...], Egyptians go abroad for purely
> economic reasons. They may not like the conditions or the social values of the
> countries hosting them, but they are totally disciplined [not] to jeopardise the
> opportunity to earn money by indulging in political activities. (Roy 1991, 574)

Using multiple sources of data, Feiler (2003) estimated the astronomical growth of Egyptian labour emigration across the Arab world – escalating from an impressive 520,000 migrants in 1975 to 2.9 million by 1983. In terms of Saudi Arabia, in particular, Kerr described this systematic dispatch of Egyptian migrants as an 'unspoken bilateral relationship' (Kerr and Yasin 1982, 6). More broadly, by the end of the 1970s, as concerns over domestic labour shortages were invariably bypassed for Arab states' developmental needs and any political economy cost was set aside in favour of Egypt's bilateral relations, Egypt's role as a regional supplier of labour had 'become a tradition, an accepted part of Middle Eastern economy and society' (Birks and Sinclair 1980, 43).

Labour migration and Jordan–GCC cooperation

As in the case of Egypt, the need to export labour was evident early on for Jordanian policymakers – in this case, this was primarily due to the state's own limited resources and successive waves of Palestinian refugees. In its early decades following independence, the country was a target of external revenue from the British government, which would fund over 50% of Transjordan's budget. The country's strategic position in the Eastern Mediterranean, as well as its importance in guarding the passage to India and Iraq, underpinned the British desire to make up for Transjordan's weak domestic economic base, lacking any major natural resources or agricultural land (Baster 1955, 27). The 1949 United Nations Economic Survey Mission described how

> agriculturally this stretch of country is probably amongst the poorest land in former Palestine. From north to south it consists of a succession of hills. Some of them have become so eroded through the ages that they are now only bare rocks; others carry soil only in patches and it is so shallow that it is a matter for wonder that it is capable of producing cereal crops even of the low standard which it carries at present. (United Nations, 1949, 58)

The need for external support became more apparent in the aftermath of the 1948 Arab–Israeli War as 70,000 Palestinians sought refuge on the East Bank. As Brand describes:

> Nearly half of 'Abdallah's new subjects were refugees, many of them destitute. An additional 160,000 had been separated from their productive land by the armistice lines but did not qualify for UNRWA (United Nations Relief and Works Agency for Palestine Refugees in the Near East) assistance because they were not refugees. Just as devastating, the establishment of the state of Israel disrupted transport and commercial lines between Jordan and its outside

> markets. The fact that the conflict ended in the absence of a peace treaty also
> meant that Jordan found itself with a 650-kilometer border with Israel that
> required a diversion of resources for defence. With limited domestic economic
> resources, the kingdom, still heavily reliant on aid from Britain, was hardly
> in an economic position to absorb the refugees swiftly. (Brand 2008, 176)

An additional challenge for King 'Abdullah's leadership was that this occurred
only two years following the end of the British Mandate: on 25 May 1945,
the Mandate had officially ended, as Transjordan became the Hashemite
Kingdom of Transjordan. Arab states quickly replaced British external funding,
but this was short-lived: the king's 1957 decision to dismiss Prime Minister
Suleiman Nabulsi, who pursued Arab nationalist policies aiming to move
the country closer to Egypt, led to the termination of Arab state budget
support. External income would, now, come from the United States. Eager
to maintain the regional order, American aid flowed into the Kingdom for
roughly a decade: in the aftermath of the 1967 Arab–Israeli War, the king
would seek Arab aid yet again, accusing Washington of a pro-Israeli stance.

It is in the post-1967 context that Jordan's stability and the security of
the ruling regime became a main concern for the conservative Arab monarchies
of the Gulf, chief amongst them Saudi Arabia – indeed, Saudi Arabia has
been the country's second larger donor state since 1974, behind the United
States. At one level, this was due to Jordan's importance in the Arab fight
against Israel – an idea that also underpinned the Gulf monarchies' approach
to Egypt and traces its formal origins to the resolutions of the 1967 Khartoum
Summit. At the same time, however, the Saudis also valued the country's
buffer position against revolutionary, Arab nationalist regimes: in this sense,
the ideological leanings of the pro-Western Hashemite regime were valued
by the conservative monarchies that sought to resist the spreading of pan-
Arabism. Not incidentally, the Saudi regime would offer material, political,
and moral support to Jordan throughout the 1950s and the early 1960s
(Brand 2006, 176).

Bilateral migration diplomacy was instrumental in setting the stage for
the heightened use of cross-border mobility as a 'win-win' scenario between
Jordan and the Gulf. On the one hand, Amman was able to use the migration
of tens of thousands of its citizens as a (short-term) solution to pressures
of unemployment back home, while adding another source of foreign currency
to the Jordanian economy – namely, economic remittances. On the other
hand, Riyadh identified a way of overcoming its lack of a trained, and
ample, domestic labour force by benefitting from this influx of migration
to sustain the development of the Saudi state and its economy.

On its part, the Jordanian state facilitated citizens' exit by adopting a
liberal migration policy. Until 1962, the Jordanian state implemented an
exit visa policy that aimed at preventing the emigration of political activists:

any hint of suspicion about problems with regard to a potential emigrant's political affiliation would quickly lead to the rejection of an exit visa application (Abu-Odeh 1999, 83). However, from 1962 onwards, the Jordanian state relied on remittances and the steady outflow of emigrants and adapted its policy accordingly: it ceased keeping detailed records of emigration flows but partially liberalised its emigration policy. The 1973–5 plan recognises the importance of migrant remittances as a key source of hard currency, while Jordanians abroad are recognised as being not 'a small part' (*juz' ghayr qalil*) of the country's labour force. The plan also proposes that the government engages in bilateral labour accords with Arab host-states and ensure that it actively works towards the protections of the interests of Jordanian workers abroad (Al-Mamlakah al-Urdunniyyah al-Hashimiyyah n.d., 271). From 1973 onwards and, with few exceptions, the Kingdom pushed forth with a fully liberalised labour migration policy that placed few obstacles to prospective emigrants, reminiscent of Anwar Sadat's reforms in Egypt.

A number of bilateral agreements were signed with host-states, starting with a Jordanian–Kuwait accord in 1958, followed by agreements with Pakistan and Libya in 1978. Together with Egypt and (pre-Assad) Syria, Jordan had also signed a 1967 agreement calling for the free circulation of labour workers in the Arab world. A new Ministry of Labour was established in 1976, which proceeded to recruit and post labour attaches to key embassies abroad, first in Kuwait and the United Arab Emirates. The Ministry also negotiated and signed bilateral labour agreements with Pakistan and Libya in 1978 (Hashemite Kingdom of Jordan, National Planning Council n.d., 295). During the 1976–80 period, approximately 8,000–10,000 Jordanians emigrated on an annual basis (Hashemite Kingdom of Jordan, National Planning Council n.d., 293).

As early as 1975, approximately 175,000 Jordanian labourers (or 66% of the Kingdom's emigrant workforce) were located in Saudi Arabia alone. Worker remittances amounted for up to 50% of all the foreign receipts of Jordan in the 1970s and 1980s, while Thiollet estimates that approximately 60% of the Jordanian labour force was working in the Gulf during the 1970s, including both Jordanians and Palestinians with Jordanian passports (Thiollet 2011, 111).

As one Jordanian policymaker describes, 'there are two things that are essential: aid and labor migration. All the trade agreements put together are small fries ... the most significant factors in Jordan's relations with the world are aid and labor flows. It defines the economy. It defines politics. It defines our relations with the Arabs. It defines everything' (Ryan 2009, 55). For Brand, '[p]erhaps the most important Jordanian export to Saudi Arabia (in terms of its effect on the Jordanian economy) has been human capital in the form of expatriate labor' (Brand 2013, 104–5). Ryan describes this symbiotic relationship between Jordan and host-states across the Gulf:

> Access to petrodollars and to foreign labor markets have thus become essential considerations in the calculations and policies of poorer Arab states. Once gained, these sources of financial assistance and labor remittances remain central to the stability of Arab regimes. Such political-economic dynamics have led to a cycle of dependence, in which economic reliance on allies provides more than economic relief for Arab regimes. Indeed, these issues now comprise the economic underpinnings of political stability. (Ryan 2009, 55)

The importance of migrant remittances in Jordan's economic performance since the mid-1970s has been evident (Keely and Saket 1984, 688) (Table 5.2). They have been able to finance the negative balance of trade that has traditionally plagued the Jordanian economy, as well as contribute to the growth of money supply by allowing banks the liquidity necessary to provide credit.

Not surprisingly, Jordanian ministers would tour the Gulf in an effort to secure additional contracts for Jordanian professionals – in May 1977, the Jordanian Minister of Education 'Abd al-Salam al-Majali sought additional positions for Jordanian teachers across Gulf state schools, particularly in Saudi Arabia and Kuwait. At the time, some 8,000 Jordanian teachers were employed in Saudi Arabia.

This has affected societal views on migration as well – again, not unlike Egypt: Jordanians and Palestinians 'viewed work in the [G]ulf as the best means of avoiding unemployment, as well as a chance to break away from family dependence and obtain money to marry and establish independent households of their own' (Wilson 1994, 282). As in the case of Egypt, Jordan attempted to normalise the phenomenon of labour emigration through textbooks: the 2010 Jordanian tenth-grade civics textbook, for instance, highlights how countries such as Egypt and Jordan benefited from migration to the Gulf, and states that 'with the tremendous flow of oil in the Gulf region and in Libya, new waves of population and labour force movement began, employment opportunities expanded … and the processes of migration and movement of labour to the oil regions became one of the more important forces shaping contemporary Arab life' (Brand 2010, 105).

Table 5.2 Worker remittances as a share of Jordanian GNP (%)

1970–4	1975–9	1980–4	1985–9	1990	1991
3.0%	18.2%	18.4%	14.3%	12.1%	10.5%

Table 5.3 Estimates of Jordanian migrant stock (2013–15)

Host state	Number	% of total migrants
Arab Countries	Approximately 660,000	84%
Saudi Arabia	250,000	
UAE	200,000	
Kuwait	55,081	
Qatar	40,000	
Oman	7,403	
Bahrain	7,000	
Palestine	55,709	
Libya	20,408	
Iraq	10,336	
North America	75,018	10%
United States	65,618	
Canada	9,400	
Europe	31,541	4%
Germany	8,836	
United Kingdom	7,000	
Sweden	3,898	
Others	20,000	2%
Australia	5,960	
Total	Approximately 785,000	100%

The last major study of Jordanian workers in the Gulf, conducted in 1980 by the Economics Department of the Royal Scientific Society of Jordan, identified that they were predominantly male (over 95%) and clustered in the 20–39 age group (80%). Most Jordanian migrants were located in Saudi Arabia, with Kuwait and the United Arab Emirates following (Table 5.3). Most were married, with only about one third of them being single. They were educated, with one third of them having attended university. Over 40% of them held professional or technical positions, and stayed abroad for an average period of five years (Keely and Saket 1984, 689).

Conclusion

'The supply of Egyptian manpower was essential for the Gulf countries, and the President realized the country's potential in bringing them closer to Egypt.'
Former Prime Minister Abdel Aziz Hegazy (*Personal Interview*, 27 April 2014)

Moving beyond an analysis of migration diplomacy in the realms of subject-making and state–diaspora relations, this chapter has examined how short-term unskilled or low-skilled emigration depended on migration policy coordination between sending- and host-states, which facilitated inter-state cooperation in the case of Egyptian and Jordanian migration to the oil-rich Arab monarchies. With regard to the Egyptian side, the ruling regime made sure to drive the point across that it had coordinated its emigration policy to Arab host-states' needs. Sadat did not hesitate to signal the transience and de-politicisation of Egyptian regional migration as another distinctive feature that differentiated Egypt under his rule from the Nasserite era. Post-1970 migration was de-politicised, driven by economic rather than ideological reasons, and, above all, 'temporary'. Similarly, the Kingdom of Jordan's migration diplomacy allowed for a closer relationship with a number of Gulf monarchies based on policy coordination on matters of labour migration. Arab host-states reciprocated this policy shift and coordinated their immigration policies accordingly: they willingly demonstrated preferential treatment to Egyptian and Jordanian migrants – both with regard to their recruitment, as well as the duration of their stay.

Notes

1 The 1971 Constitution was deliberately termed 'Permanent' in order to differentiate it from various short-lived constitutions put forth by Gamal Abdel Nasser.
2 This was also later mirrored in the Gulf states' decision to shift towards Asian migrant labour that, as Thiollet puts it, was also considered less likely to settle in the Gulf, a trait that perfectly fit the agenda of many Gulf policymakers who had started to regard migration as a threat to regime stability, state formation, and national security (Thiollet 2011).

6

Managing mobility as a host-state issue-linkage strategy

In previous chapters, the management of migration featured in a range of state strategies in the Middle East – this includes the creation of the subject in post-1952 Egypt, the securitisation of diasporas in the case of North Africa, as well as the strengthening of relations with the oil-producing monarchies of the Gulf. This final chapter examines how cross-border mobility may also feature in issue-linkage strategies, as migrants and refugees are employed as instruments of leverage by host-states. The chapter focuses on two types of mobility as leverage – labour and forced migration. In terms of the former, the chapter first examines how Egypt was faced with numerous attempts by Arab host-states to target Egyptian migrant communities within their borders, predominantly unskilled or low-skilled, as instruments of *coercion*. Egyptian migrant communities were faced with various forms of abuse, including incarceration and torture, or, more frequently, expulsion from host-states seeking to take benefit from Egypt's socio-economic depend-ence on labour migration. Two types of issue-linkage strategies were employed by Arab states against Egypt: in the first, coercion emerged as personalistic cross-regime relations between the sending- and host-state broke down, namely between Egyptian President Anwar Sadat and Libyan Prime Minister Muammar Gaddafi; the second type of strategy aimed to secure specific policy concessions from Egypt, as has been the case with Iraq or, in the post-2011 era, with Libya and Jordan.[1]

But, beyond labour migration, forced displacement may also engender opportunities for issue-linkage and leverage, particularly given the growing unwillingness of Western states to accept rising numbers of refugees. The chapter's second half focuses on forced migration and issue-linkage strate-gies, examining how host-states of first asylum responded to the influx of Syrian refugees with regard to their foreign policymaking in the post-2011 era. The chapter's findings point to the emergence of a new type of state, a *refugee rentier state*, in which elites adopt policies aimed at extracting revenue from other state or non-state actors in exchange for maintaining refugee groups within a country's borders. Seeking to benefit from increasing Western fears of mass refugee inflows, Global South states are increasingly able to leverage their position in order to secure unearned external income, or *refugee rent*. The chapter focuses on the differences in terms of refugee rent-seeking behaviour in the cases of Jordan, Lebanon, and Turkey and proceeds to theorise how forced migration may constitute an instrument of leverage for this type of state. More broadly, the chapter demonstrates how the safety and well-being of varied labour and refugee communities across the Middle East often become subject to host-states' varied political exigencies.

Egyptian labour migrants as political leverage

One of the key destinations of Egyptian migrant labour in the Middle East has been Iraq, where the fate of the Egyptian migrant community fell prey to the breakdown of bilateral relations in the context of the Iraq–Kuwait War. Historically, Iraq has enjoyed a long tradition of attracting Egyptian professionals since its independence, becoming a major destination of unskilled Egyptians in the post-1970 era. This was aided by the fact that Iraq allowed Arabs to enter without a visa or work permit as per the Ba'ath Party's pan-Arabist leanings (A. M. Lesch 1986, 7), as well as the country's substantial need for migrants to overcome labour shortages that occurred during the 1980–8 Iran–Iraq War. Yet, the 1988 ceasefire with Iran created a number of problems for Egyptian migrants, as the early promises of Taha Yasin Ramadan al-Jizrawi that Egyptians would be given priority in the recruitment for reconstruction projects were not kept (Feiler 1991, 140). The socio-economic pressures from the demobilisation of Iraqi soldiers who returned to find Egyptian workers either occupying most employment positions or competing with them for any opening led to harsh measures against Egyptians in Iraq.

As a result, violent attacks by the returning Iraqi soldiers were not uncommon: 1,052 bodies were flown in from Baghdad in the first ten months of 1989, many with bullet holes and other marks of violence, while reports of police brutality and mass attacks against Egyptians multiplied. In late 1989, ten extra flights per day were ordered for the following few months between Iraq and Egypt in order to 'cope with the exodus' (*The New York Times*, 15 November 1989). At the same time, in an effort to tackle the country's severe economic problems, the state began delaying payments to foreign workers, and, in October, imposed a ceiling on the amount of remittances they were allowed to send home, from 40 Iraqi dinars to anywhere between 10 to 30 Iraqi dinars (*al-Gomhuria*, 9 November 1989). This was, according to Taha Yasin Ramadan, 'related to certain economic conditions' that Egypt should accept. By mid-November, the number of Egyptians in the country was estimated at 1 million, while delayed remittances were estimated at $350m (MENA, 16 November 1989). Egypt was forced to accept a compromise payment of $50m by the end of the year.

The Iraq–Kuwait War marked another turning point in the politicised nature of intra-Arab migration. The invasion of Iraq into Kuwait on 2 August 1990, and Saddam Hussein's proclamation of Kuwait as Iraq's 19th Province, was condemned at the United Nations Security Council (UNSC), which demanded the withdrawal of Iraqi forces. Importantly, Yemen, serving as a UNSC non-permanent member, abstained from voting; the Yemenis believed that an Arab solution, rather than an international one, was needed. The Saudis did not appreciate this, and also disagreed with the Palestine Liberalisation Organisation's Yasser Arafat's ostensible support for Iraq. Hosni Mubarak, on the other hand, was not only vocal in denouncing the Iraqi aggression, but spearheaded a military operation to amend the invasion (Feiler 1991, 134–5). As a result, by 1990, Egypt was faced with an extreme wave of return migration from Iraq and Kuwait given the regional instability, as 'more than half a million migrants returned to Egypt within two months of the invasion' (Feiler 1991, 134–5). The exodus was also generated because migrants were targeted as payback for Mubarak's lack of support for Saddam Hussein. Out of a community of 150,000–250,000 Egyptians in Kuwait, by 22 August 1990 roughly 5,000 to 8,000 were arriving from Aqaba to Nuweiba daily: 'The Iraqis, they were our brothers, but now after two weeks everything has changed', one returning migrant told *The New York Times*, reporting stories of rape and theft. Fleeing Kuwait, Egyptians said they 'had to sleep at night in desert camps, and Iraqi soldiers, they came in the night and searched our pockets' (*The New York Times*, 22 August 1990).

Once in Jordan, Egyptians fleeing from Kuwait and Iraq also had to face Palestinians, who were also disgruntled at Mubarak's foreign policy choices:

[Palestinians in Jordan] cursed them, kicked and screamed at them and charged the refugees extortionate prices for food and water, because Egypt had sided against Saddam Hussein. 'The Palestinian people, not the Jordanians, they attacked and hit us [...] When we walked in public, they shouted very bad things about Egypt and about President Hosni Mubarak. We Egyptians, we cannot stand for this, so we answered back, and the Palestinians hit us. They were kicking, beating and attacking us in the streets, they were so furious with Mubarak' Mansour Hassan Ahma said, as he lifted his full-length shirt to show the scars on his legs. 'They said, "You are a dirty nation." As bad as the Iraqi people are, they are better than the Palestinians'. (*The New York Times*, 22 August 1990)

The massive exodus created serious problems for the Egyptian state, and lends credence to the argument that, in matters of cross-regime competition, migration can be a key instrument of regime de-stabilisation. Already in the mid-1980s, the Egyptian government was struggling to find employment even for the modest number of returnees from the Gulf: the Ministry of Emigration let migrants participate in soil-improvement projects, where they would be later allocated one fourth of the reclaimed land (*Rose al-Yūsuf*, 23 June 1986), while the Egyptian government tried – unsuccessfully – to find new labour markets for Egyptian migrants in South America and Africa for these return migrants (*al-Ahrar*, 16 August 1985). But Egypt was unprepared for the massive return wave from Iraq and Kuwait. For Vatikiotis, this highlighted

> the absence of any official Egyptian state policy on the emigration of Egyptian workers to the Arab states, or anywhere else for that matter. The government had made no provision for any legislative or policy measures to ensure the protection of citizens abroad, especially in Iraq. In the Gulf in particular, the country's consular services were woefully under-represented. As large numbers of Egyptians began to return from Iraq, ruined, abused and destitute, in late 1989, negotiations between Cairo and Baghdad to agree a mutual policy regarding Egyptian migrant labour in Iraq were held in Cairo in a series of hurriedly arranged meetings between a stream of visiting Iraqi ministers and President Mubarak. The opposition attacked the President and the Atef Sidqy government for having failed to provide acceptable rules to regulate the migration of Egyptian workers seeking employment in the Arab states and other countries overseas, as well as their protection in circumstances such as those which arose in Iraq. (Vatikiotis 1991, 432)

Indeed, one of the responses of the Mubarak regime to the economic needs of returning migrants due to the Iraq–Kuwait War was to employ Nasserite-era policies, and to pledge to employ 100,000 of them in the Egyptian bureaucratic apparatus (*The New York Times*, 26 August 1990). A strong indication of regime unpreparedness was that, in scrambling to provide housing and employment opportunities for these returnees, 'senior figures in the Mubarak regime' were hoping to encourage the 'more permanent settlement of Egyptian communities in Africa, a possibility reminiscent of the establishment of the Lebanese community in West Africa 50–75 years ago' (Vatikiotis 1991, 433). This mirrors earlier attempts by Prime Minister Kamal Hassan Ali to introduce measures 'designed to direct returning workers and their families to new settlement areas, mainly in thinly-populated desert regions'. Unfortunately for the regime, 'there are already signs that few returnees will want to take on the task of pioneering new desert communities. As a result, pressure on the overtaxed housing market of the major cities is likely to increase' (*The Middle East*, January 1986).

Research points to the fact that, in 1990, President Saddam Hussein ordered the displacement of Egyptians from Iraq (at the time hosting over 44% of all Egyptian regional migrants), partly to compel Egypt to withdraw from Operation Desert Storm (Farouk-Sluglett and Sluglett 2001, 288). Despite the forced return of over 700,000 migrants (Feiler 2003, 245), Egypt did not shift its policy on Iraq. While Egypt was not able to absorb these costs domestically (only a year later, in 1991, Mubarak had to resort to the IMF and initiate an arduous process of economic restructuring), it was able to locate alternative host-states willing to shoulder the cost. Saudi Arabia and Libya, with whom Egypt had friendly relations (Vandewalle 2012, 179), absorbed the displaced migrants out of Iraq and minimised the socio-economic cost to Egypt. In terms of Saudi Arabia, Feiler writes:

> Fortunately for Egypt, Saudi Arabia offered various economic compensations for its cooperation with the anti-Iraqi coalition, and by the end of April 1991, the number of Egyptian workers in Saudi Arabia had reached 1.25 million – double their pre-war number. (Feiler 2003, 244)

But Libya also came to the help of Egypt: 'it is interesting to note that the moment relations between Egypt and neighbouring Libya improved ... over 50,000 Egyptians moved into Libya seeking employment', Vatikiotis wrote. 'So long as Egyptian migrant labour found ready employment in these Arab countries ... things went well' (Vatikiotis 1991, 432–3). While Saudi Arabia and Libya do not release detailed migration statistics for security reasons, Farrag has estimated the geographical distribution of Egyptian regional migrants before and after Operation Desert Storm. Her findings exemplify Egypt's strategy of shifting the cost of host-state coercion to alternative host-states. Overall, the fact that the Egyptian economy was not in a position to absorb the cost of Iraq's strategy of displacement did not render Egypt vulnerable to it: given that oil-producing Arab states were willing to shoulder this cost, Egypt did not satisfy one of the two conditions establishing migration interdependence vulnerability, and was able to resist Iraqi coercion.

Beyond Iraq, the breakdown of cross-regime relations resulted in similar effects for Egyptian labourers elsewhere. In 2009, Qatar's Hamad bin Khalifa Al Thani reacted to perceived personal attacks by *al-Gomhoriya* reporters against his wife, Sheikha Mozah bint Nasser Al Missned, by targeting the Egyptian community within Qatar: 'instructions were issued to Qatari employers and the directors of companies and institutions, not to renew the contracts of the Egyptian workers in all the sectors in response to the insults of *al-Gomhuria'* al-Mesryoon reported. 'These instructions also asked that no future contracts be signed with the Egyptian labor, except in rare areas of speciality that are much needed by Qatar' (*al-Mesryoon*, 11 May 2009).

Beyond Iraq and Qatar, Jordan also attempted to use the status of its Egyptian migrant community as leverage against Mohamed Morsi's government, who assumed office in the aftermath of the 2011 Arab Uprisings. According to a 2004 agreement between Cairo and Amman, Egypt is contractually obliged to supply natural gas to Jordan via the Arab Gas Pipeline to the amount of 240 million cubic feet of gas per day until 2019 (*al-Ahram*, 3 June 2013). Egypt found it impossible to continue the supply of natural gas at these levels in the aftermath of the 2011 Arab Spring, due to domestic energy shortages and frequent attacks against the pipeline itself, which was also supplying gas to Israel at reduced prices. Once in power in June 2012, Morsi unilaterally decided to curb the export of natural gas to Jordan, which saw its reliance on Egyptian natural gas fall from 89% in 2009 to 17% by the end of 2012. 'As a consequence, the state-owned electricity company, the National Electric Power Company (NEPCO), made huge losses, in 2011 amounting to 5 percent of gross domestic product (GDP)', and was faced with a $3.5 billion deficit (Henderson 2015). It was estimated that 'every time the supply is halted as a result of the frequent interruptions caused by the bombing[s], it costs the Jordanian treasury $1 million per day' (*al-Monitor*, April 2014). Indicatively, the supply of gas to Jordan was interrupted over fifteen times between February 2011 and November 2012 period alone (*al-Ahram*, 21 November 2012).

In the bilateral conflict over this issue, Jordan employed its status as host-state of Egyptian migrants for coercive purposes. Egyptian migrant labour in Jordan has a long history spanning back decades, when thousands of Egyptian workers travelled through Jordanian territory in order to reach Saudi Arabia and other oil-producing countries in the Gulf that had been recruiting Arab labour in the aftermath of the 1973 Arab–Israeli War (Amin and Awni 1986). Over the past few decades, Jordan has also become a host-state for unskilled Egyptian migrant labour. This has been due both to its fairly developed economy as well as its position: many Egyptians that were either unable to enter the Gulf states, or did not wish to return to Egypt when their employment there was terminated, chose to pursue employment in Jordan. A key characteristic of these migrant labourers is that they are unskilled or low-skilled, and that thousands of them lack legal documentation to validate their employment status in Jordan. In 2012, it was reported that only 167,000 possessed a legal working permit (*Egypt Daily News*, 19 December 2012).

In early December, Jordanian media and government sources began hinting at the need to restructure the domestic labour market. Jordanian Minister of Labour Nidal Qatamin declared 'the necessity of launching a campaign in Jordan to regulate the labour market' (*al-Ahram*, 9 December 2012). The announcement focused particularly on Egyptian workers that were employed in the Kingdom without a permit. Did Jordan's decision to regulate the domestic labour market by targeting illegal Egyptian migrants constitute a strategy of coercion against Egypt? Or, could it merely have been driven by other factors, such as the deterioration of the post-Arab Spring Jordanian economy (cf. Yom 2015)? Qatamin publicly stated that the regulation campaign was driven by a 'security' not 'political' rationale (MENA, 9 December 2012). Yet, two pieces of evidence strongly suggest that this was a clear attempt at using migration as inter-state coercion: firstly, the targeted Egyptians had been pursuing employment within Jordan for years, if not decades, making the timing of Jordan's policy shift suspect. Secondly, numerous sources confirmed that Jordan's policy shift formed part of its broader strategy on securing Egyptian natural gas. *Al-Jazeera* reported an early December 2012 meeting that Abdullah held at the house of former minister Rajaii al-Maashar. The piece, entitled 'Jordan Swaps Egyptian Labour for Gas', states:

> According to the sources that spoke to Al-Jazeera.net, the king revealed that his country is in possession of some cards that it is using to send messages to Cairo. Such cards include the presence of … Egyptian workers in Jordan and the fact that Jordan is the only passageway for the exported Egyptian vegetables towards Iraq … One of the meeting participants quoted the king as saying that the weak flow of the Egyptian gas and it being cut off Jordan 'destroyed the Jordanian economy.' He also indicated that the rise in debts over the past two years was mainly due to the losses incurred by the power plant that had to use heavy fuel instead of gas. (*Al-Jazeera*, 11 December 2012)

Al-Quds al-Arabi confirmed the meeting, adding that Abdullah mentioned how 'tens of thousands of Egyptians working in the Gulf states go through [Jordanian town] Aqaba in their movements', which the Kingdom could further use as a bargaining chip against Cairo (*al-Quds al-Arabi*, 12 December 2012). Given Egyptian inaction, Jordan adopted a strategy of displacement, as the government announced that any Egyptian workers found working illegally within the Kingdom would be subject to deportation. At the same time, the Ministry of Labour began targeting Egyptians who possessed valid permits but had been working in professions not included in their permits (MENA, 13 December 2012). *Al-Hayat* quotes a number of sources that affirm how:

> The officials in Amman are very upset with their counterparts in Cairo, and this is why they have sent a signal to the Egyptians in order to express the dissatisfaction of the Jordanian leadership. Amman is upset about a number of issues, one of which being the fact that the gas pipeline from Egypt to Jordan is no longer functioning normally. Other official sources told *al-Hayat* that 'thousands of Egyptian workers were arrested in Jordan during the last

two weeks due to irregularities in their papers and sent back to their country
…'. (*Al-Hayat*, 12 December 2012)

Deportations of Egyptian workers formally started on 8 December, when
approximately two hundred migrants lacking necessary documentation were
expelled (*al-Ahram*, 9 and 11 December 2012). By 14 December, it was
revealed that Jordan had arrested hundreds of Egyptian workers, who were
found in violation of their residency permits and faced deportation. Following
Abdullah, other Jordanian institutions underlined how the potential expulsion
of Egyptian migrants was linked to Egypt's policy on natural gas. The
Amman Center for Human Rights Studies issued a telling declaration: 'sadly
the recent procedures of deporting Egyptian workers came as a result of
poor political relationship between the two countries. While we stress the
relationship with our neighbour Egypt,' the report continued, 'it is unac-
ceptable for the new Egyptian leadership to stop the implementation of
bilateral economic agreements and sacrifice [a] profound relationship' (2012,
1). Elites also confirmed this state strategy: 'official authorities in Amman
were leaking information about the presence of [a number of] Egyptians
working in Jordan without a license and in an illegal way', *al-Quds al-Arabi*
reported. 'The collective deportation of the latter would address a harsh
message to the Egyptian government, and the Jordanian government chose
the shorter path and arrested hundreds of Egyptian workers who were in
violation of their residency conditions and indeed deported them.' The
newspaper's report concluded with a message from an unnamed, 'prominent'
Jordanian politician who wished to send a message to Cairo: 'We beg of
you. Our situation cannot tolerate having you tamper with the gas issue
any further' (*al-Quds al-Arabi*, 13 December 2012).

Egypt complied with the host-state's demands. Morsi called Abdullah
from London, where he was on an official visit on 9 December, the first time
the two leaders engaged in conversation since Morsi's electoral victory. The
Egyptian president reportedly guaranteed an increase in the supply of Jordan
with Egyptian gas and agreed to create a joint bilateral committee on the
issue, in order to appease Abdullah. Simultaneously, Morsi also dispatched
Egyptian Prime Minister Hisham Qandeel to Amman, in an effort to solve
this 'silent crisis' (*al-Quds al-Arabi*, 13 December 2012). Jordanian Prime
Minister Abdullah al-Ensour later reported to the media that Qandeel had
reiterated Morsi's natural gas assurances to Abdullah and confirmed that
'Egypt will always keep its pledges and has no intention to renege on any
agreements' (*al-Gomhuriya*, 19 January 2013). According to *al-Hayat*:

> The diplomatic contacts launched at the highest level between Jordan and
> Egypt succeeded in containing the crisis that had erupted between the two
> sides. In this respect, Egypt pledged to continue supplying Jordan with gas

and Amman promised to stop deporting the thousands of Egyptian workers present in the kingdom ... Cairo promised to keep supplying Jordan with gas after the misunderstanding that had erupted lately. The two states had signed agreements in this regard and President Morsi pledged to respect them. Jordan for its part said that it would no longer expulse the Egyptian workers whose papers are not in order. Following these contacts and the agreement that was reached, thousands of Egyptian workers were released and one thousand nine hundred people were even allowed to go back to Jordan after being deported to Egypt. (*Al-Hayat*, 21 December 2012)

The Jordanian Ministry of Labour announced the formal halting of Egyptian workers' deportation, and the Egyptian minister of migration was dispatched to Jordan to resolve Egyptian migrants' remaining administrative problems. A few days later, Morsi publicly thanked Abdullah for 'his decision to stop these measures' (*al-Ahram*, 13 December 2012). 'Egypt and Jordan overcame a labour problem that could have strained bilateral relations,' the MENA wrote, 'thanks to direct high-level contacts that were crowned by a personal phone call Egyptian President Mohamed Morsy had with King Abdullah II on Monday evening' (MENA, 13 December 2012). A minor glitch in negotiations appeared in late January 2013, when Qandeel was visiting Jordan to sign a bilateral agreement on the legalisation of Egyptian migrant workers. As was reported across Egyptian media, host-state elites identified 'a delay of pumping Egyptian natural gas to Jordan' which presented a 'new obstacle' in any bilateral migration agreement. Khaled Azhari, the Egyptian minister of manpower and immigration, went on record to state that his Ministry would coordinate with the Egyptian Ministry of Petroleum 'to remove any obstacles facing Egyptian labourers in Jordan' (quoted in *al-Ahram*, 29 January 2013).

Moving beyond Iraq and Jordan, Libya was the chief destination for Egyptian workers seeking opportunity abroad, until it was replaced by Saudi Arabia in the mid-1970s. The Egyptian state historically exercised an extensive migration diplomacy strategy of soft power in Libya, having found that it could cater to the educational and bureaucratic staffing needs of its newly independent neighbour to the west. Various ministries, particularly the Ministry of Education, dispatched thousands of teachers and white-collar employees to Libya, where illiteracy, according to the 1954 census, ran to 81% of the population. The Egyptian arrivals made up for the lack of trained manpower in the fledgling Kingdom of Libya, established only in 1951, and helped to realise King Idris' dream of rapid modernisation. Secondments increased with the discovery of the country's petroleum resources in 1958 and the commercial export of oil, which began in 1962. By 1973, Libya hosted the largest number of Egyptian migrants in the Arab world.

At the same time, unskilled and low-skilled Egyptian workers also took advantage of the porous border, crossing the Western Desert in search of more lucrative employment. Like high-skilled Egyptian migrants, they also found work due to the relative absence of qualified Libyan labourers: by 1964, only 5.2% of the population had completed primary education or beyond. Initially negligible in comparison to the numbers being seconded, this form of migration increased after 1967. Skilled migration outside the Egyptian state's secondment programme would also grow in the post-1967 period. While the statistics are notoriously unreliable, by conservative estimates roughly 229,500 Egyptians were working in Libya in 1975. That number would rise to 250,000 by 1980.

The antagonism between King Idris and Nasser, described earlier, ceased in September 1969, when Idris was overthrown while undergoing medical treatment abroad. The newcomer Colonel Muammar Gaddafi regarded Nasser as a role model and a great pan-Arab leader, and pursued an initial policy of reconciliation with Egypt (Vandewalle 2012). The resulting close collaboration between the two states allowed the Egyptian migrant community to thrive: Libya abolished entry visa requirements in 1971, allowing Egyptians into Libya with only an identity card, and the two countries prepared a union with Syria in order to create the Federal Arab Republic. Egyptian workers, skilled and unskilled, flocked in their thousands to Libya, taking advantage of the fact that most Libyans continued to work in agriculture, rather than construction or services. Gaddafi was also delighted at the political aspect of the migration, believing that the free movement of labour constituted a necessary step toward 'the unification of all Arabic-speaking people' (Cooley 1982, 101). Libyan migration diplomacy in this period employed the temporary recruitment of unskilled and low-skilled Egyptian workers as a means towards closer inter-state cooperation.

The death of Nasser and subsequent rise of Anwar al-Sadat, however, contributed to the gradual deterioration of bilateral relations and renewed turmoil for Egyptian migrants in Libya. Sadat, on the one hand, was convinced that Gaddafi was mentally ill – he did not hesitate to call the Colonel a 'lunatic'. Partly to check Gaddafi, he drew closer to Sudan's Jaafar al-Numayri, which the Libyan leader perceived as a hostile act. Gaddafi, on the other hand, found it increasingly hard to hide his contempt for what he saw as Sadat's lacklustre management of the 1973 War with Israel. The two majors on the Libyan Revolutionary Command Council whom Gaddafi had sent to Cairo to observe the war, 'Abd al-Mun'im al-Huni and 'Umar 'Abdallah al-Muhayshi, defected to Egypt, adding to the disgruntlement of the Libyan leader. Gaddafi's willingness to welcome a number of Egyptian political dissidents to Libya made matters worse: Hikmat Abu Zayd, who under Nasser had become Egypt's first female minister, holding the social affairs portfolio from 1962–65, moved to Libya in 1974 and became a vocal opponent of Sadat's policies from her post at the University of Tripoli. Following the April 1974 attempt on Sadat's life, which the Egyptian president blamed on Libyans, Egypt abandoned plans for the Federal Arab Republic and summoned home the Egyptian pilots and training staff who had been working on Libya's air defence system.

In turn, that same month, Libya deported hundreds of Egyptian unskilled migrants, many of whom were tortured and unceremoniously dumped at the border. Sadat responded by announcing that Egyptian civil servants were forbidden to travel to Libya for any purpose. It was a clear effort to starve the Libyan state and educational system of its staff. Sadat's announcement also marked the beginning of Libya's use of Egyptian migrants as a coercive issue-linkage strategy – a pattern that would be repeated often in the future. Yet Sadat did not interfere with the status of Egyptians employed in the construction sector, nor those in social services – such as doctors, nurses, and welfare workers, who had become the largest group of Egyptians within Libya, and who would come to bear the brunt of the violence meted out by the Libyan regime.

While Egyptians continued to flood into Libya, daily life for them grew harder – sometimes including unpleasant encounters with Libyan military personnel. As *al-Ahram* noted, the wife of an Egyptian in Libya travelling back to Egypt was stopped in Salloum, where 'a Libyan customs officer inspected her suitcases and tossed her underwear provocatively before his companions. When she upbraided him, he beat her, broke her glasses and insulted her with words of abuse that outraged some Egyptian soldiers who happened to be there at the Customs House. The two sides might have clashed' (*al-Ahram*, 28 August 1974). A few months later, in April 1975, Gaddafi expelled a few hundred more Egyptians. Mufrih Nasr Isma'il, a migrant from Fayyoum, died in an incident of police brutality in Derna. In Cairo, at the Arab Socialist Union and Peoples' Assembly, deputies demanded the withdrawal of all 200,000–300,000 Egyptians then in Libya. At the same time, Sadat affirmed his conviction that Gaddafi was '100 percent mad' (quoted in Cooley 1982, 115–16). On 24 April, there occurred several instances of 'barbarous' Libyan torture of Egyptians, including sleep deprivation and beatings with 'sticks, whips and pipes' (MENA, 24 April 1975).

The Sadat regime never framed the maltreatment of Egyptians in Libya as a human rights violation. In fact, official media downplayed the extent of the abuses in order to avoid shutting down the valuable route of labour export. Musa Sabri, an *al-Ahram* journalist and confidant of President Sadat, wrote on 24 April: 'Really, I do pity [Gaddafi], and I am worried for the Libyan people … The members of the Libyan Revolutionary Council should have searched for a way to treat their sick brother.' Instead, the regime treated the expulsions as a distinctly political issue, approaching other Arab countries that might host the workers who had left Libya. Following a visit by Sadat to Saudi Arabia, *al-Ahram* reported that the Kingdom 'was ready to absorb all the Egyptian migrants working in Libya who now wish to leave', though without spelling out the details. The key was to project confidence – Egyptian newspapers made sure to mention that foreign governments' requests for labourers 'exceed the number of Egyptian workers in Libya' (*al-Ahram*, 24 April 1975).

Similar statements came out in March 1976, when Libyan authorities began denying admission to Egyptians carrying only identity cards and expelled more than 3,000 such migrants. Again, the Egyptians were driven to the border and simply left there. The Matrouh governorate in Egypt declared a state of emergency, while Sayyid Fahmi, the Egyptian minister of interior, directed additional trains and buses to the border for the migrants' pickup. *Akhbar el-Yom* reported on 20 March that at least one worker died, while a second, Yunis 'Abd al-'Al, was completely paralysed and left unable to speak as a result of head injuries. At the same time, there were several reports of male Egyptian migrants being forced to enter the Libyan armed forces – later evidence showed similar attempts to press-gang Egyptians in Iraq – or to renounce Egyptian citizenship in favour of becoming Libyan. On 5 October 1976, *al-Ahram* reported that some 2,500 Egyptians were arrested in Derna and sent to recruiting stations. The men were subsequently tortured before being released to the Egyptian border authorities at Marsa Matrouh. Sadat continued to gloss over the abuses themselves, repeating instead that Egyptians working in Libya could be employed in other Arab countries. In an interview on 26 March with *Der Spiegel*, Sadat argued that he didn't 'take the situation so seriously. We are ready to absorb our workers; they can find work here, or in other Arab countries.'

In January 1977, Egypt, Syria, and Sudan announced a Unified Political Command, a move heavily criticised by Gaddafi, who also did not take kindly to the Egyptian troop build-up along the border. The inspection of these forces by the Egyptian war minister on 27 and 28 March was followed by a Libyan declaration, in early April, that 'Sadat, in his behaviour, intends to oblige us' to act against Egyptian workers. Libya stopped issuing new visas and proceeded to expel Egyptians *en masse*. Orders were given to deport all Egyptian farm workers immediately, and the governor of Marsa Matrouh prepared to receive about 10,000 returnees per day. While these workers returned safely, some were reported to have sustained injuries from riding in open-backed trucks filled to capacity. In May, Libyan Prime Minister 'Abd al-Salam Jalloud toured Eastern Europe, searching, in vain, for replacement labour.

Egyptian–Libyan relations reached their lowest point when a four-day border war broke out between the two countries from 21–24 July 1977. Border skirmishes escalated to limited Egyptian air attacks on Soviet-built installations within Libya. While tensions persisted for months afterward, by November Libya had begun issuing entry visas to Egyptians once more, ushering in a few quiet years for Egyptians there. Even then, however, the Egyptian Minister of Education Mustafa Kamal Hilmi pointed out in the People's Assembly that the majority of Egyptian teachers in Libya had requested an early end to their secondment, and had applied to return to Cairo. Despite previous periods of turmoil, 6,909 teachers had been sent to Libya for the 1976–7 academic year. Yet, their numbers dramatically decreased given the deterioration of the two states' relations leading to the border war, coupled with the continuing violence against Egyptians; by 1983, the Egyptian Ministry of Education's secondment programme in Libya was effectively terminated (Messiha 1980, 3).

Sporadic incidents occurred in the ensuing years, but no more mass deportations occurred – it is likely that the economic embargo imposed upon Egypt by the rest of the Arab world in the aftermath of the Camp David accords deterred Gaddafi from further unilateral action. It was only in 1985 that the Libyan regime, facing severe economic problems given the slump in the price of oil, decided again to dispense with the 'huge army' of 'non-productive' foreigners (see Table 6.1). At least 20,000 Egyptians were deported over August and September of that year, with some estimates putting the number of deportees as high as 100,000 out of a community of 250,000 (*The New York Times*, 18 August 1985). The Egyptians were allowed to take only half their earnings and were 'stripped of their electrical appliances and often even household goods at the border'. This mass expulsion followed a raft of measures against foreign labourers, including pay cuts and cancellation of contracts. Egyptian and other Arab workers were allowed to remit only 300 dinars per person per year, as opposed to the 90% of total income they had been able to send home in 1975. In fact, foreign workers in Libya were not permitted to make any financial transfers at all during the first half of 1985.

Egyptian President Hosni Mubarak challenged Gaddafi to admit that he had 'exhausted his country's wealth on adventurism and terrorist acts which he [took] pride in supporting and financing everywhere'. Libyan state radio, the Voice of the Great Arab Homeland, issued a sharp rejoinder: Egypt rejected the establishment of a united pan-Arab state. Its citizens, therefore, were foreigners, and the Libyan state was by no means responsible for finding them jobs. Gaddafi denounced as 'monkeys' the Arab heads of state who had 'sold themselves' to Washington. The deported Egyptian workers were complicit because they had refused to become Libyan citizens and

Table 6.1 Sectoral distribution of foreign labour in Libya, 1970–90

Sector	Number of workers (in thousands)					Percentage of total				
	1973	1978	1982	1985	1990	1973	1978	1982	1985	1990
Agriculture, Forestry and Fishing	14	29.0	29.2	25	10.3	11.8	11.5	8.8	12.8	7.4
Extraction of Oil and Natural Gas	3	2.0	2.7	2	2.5	2.5	0.8	0.8	1.1	1.7
Mining and Manufacturing	11	22	39.4	17	11.8	9.3	8.7	12	8.7	8.4
Electricity and Water	1	5.0	4.5	3.0	1.4	0.9	2	1.4	1.5	1
Construction	58	122	170.5	107	89.8	49.2	48.4	51.7	54.9	64.6
Wholesale and Retail Trade	4	5	1.5	1	0.5	3.4	2	0.5	0.5	0.4
Transport and Communication	2	8	11.6	4	2	1.7	3.2	3.5	2.1	1.4
Finance, Insurance and Banking	1	1	1.1	1	0.1	0.9	0.4	0.3	0.5	0.1
Administrative and Social Services	24	58	69.1	35	20.8	20.3	23	21	17.9	15
Total	118	252	329.6	195	139.2	100	100	100	100	100

Source: Aboulsayan, 2000, p. 143

transferred their savings out of Libya, thereby bolstering the Egyptian regime and the Camp David agreement (Fawat 1985). The expulsion of Egyptian workers was, again, part of a broader confrontation between the two regimes that included an Egyptian troop mobilisation along the border and the Libyan hijacking of an Egyptian airliner in 1985.

By 1989, Egypt had re-normalised its relations with the Arab world, and a new *rapprochement* emerged with Libya. In the spirit of cooperation, Libya agreed to reopen its labour market to Egyptian workers, and in August 1989 alone, about 70,000 Egyptians were reported to have crossed into Libya. By March 1990, Libya agreed to reimburse the previously deported Egyptians for financial losses, allotting $6 million to Egypt: $4 million was to be given immediately to 6,000 expelled workers, out of 18,000 complaints on file with the Egyptian Ministry of Labour. In the spirit of collaboration, Libya was happy to take in additional Egyptian labourers who had been forced to flee the Gulf amidst the turbulence of the 1990–1 Gulf War. This process culminated in the 4 December signing of ten *takamul* [integration] bilateral agreements on economic matters. The warming of relations, however, was only temporary, as by 1995, some 7,000 Egyptians were again expelled, this time in retaliation for the strengthening of Egyptian–Israeli relations (Feiler 1991).

But the use of Egyptian labour migrants as leverage survived the Gaddafi era. In early 2013, Libya also successfully employed restriction and displacement strategies in order to coerce Egypt into a specific policy shift: the ousting of the Gaddafi regime in 2011 had created tremendous political turmoil in Libya. Once the first phase of the civil war ended, the General National Congress emerged as the country's legislative authority and attempted to consolidate the transitional process in Libya. The Congress identified that, since 2011, a number of *ancien régime* members of the Gaddafi years had fled Libya seeking refuge in Egypt. Egypt in the immediate outbreak of the Libyan Civil War had become a safe haven for elites affiliated with the Gaddafi regime, who continued their economic and political activities from Cairo. The Congress believed that their extradition and trial in Libya was necessary for Libya's post-Gaddafi political transition. But Egyptian authorities resisted such extradition requests, citing a number of legal obstacles. For instance, Egyptian courts had forbidden the extradition of Gaddafi's cousin, Ahmed Gaddaf Alddam, because he claimed to have Egyptian citizenship. Similarly, other Libyan elites had already filed applications for Egyptian asylum, making a potential extradition to Libya legally difficult (see details in Reuters, 16 April 2013).

In contrast to Jordan, Libya had been a preferred destination for Egyptian workers seeking employment opportunities abroad since the early 1970s, as seen before (Feiler 2003, 101). The proximity to Egypt, the porous border between the countries, and the ample wealth that flowed into the resource-rich but labour-poor country, which contains the largest oil reserves of any African state, allowed the country to become a major destination of Egyptian migrant labour. In the later years of Gaddafi's rule, immigration controls for Egyptians became particularly relaxed (Tsourapas 2015a). Yet, Libya in 2012 contained only a small fraction of its earlier migrant labour force, mostly unskilled and low-skilled workers that had settled permanently in Libya: in the post-2011 era, most Egyptians fled due to the brutal Libyan civil war that, coupled with the NATO-led military intervention, had contributed to the collapse of the oil industry.

In the second half of 2012, Libya let it be known publicly that remaining Egyptian migrants would be employed as a strategy against Egypt in case of non-compliance with the extradition requests. 'A high-level source in [Egypt's] Ministry of Manpower and Migration has confirmed that Libya's threats to expel workers is not just a rumor' reported the *al-Zaman* daily in August 2012. '[The source] confirmed that there has been deafening silence on the part of officials, as concerns this issue and its being wrapped up with the critical and private political matter about the handover of senior members of the Gaddafi regime' (*al-Zaman*, 28 August 2012). Egypt downplayed the matter, while Farouk el Dessouky, Head of the Union of Egyptians Abroad, asserted that 'there is no abuse against Egyptians in Libya because of the crisis on the remnants of the Gaddafi regime' (*al-Watan*, 19 October 2012).

Similar strategies persisted after the fall of the Gaddafi regime. In early 2013, Libya sought to shift Egypt's extradition policy. The GNC initiated the implementation of tougher measures against Egyptians working in the country and identified that many Egyptians lacked proper immigration or health certificates, were holding expired residency permits, or had gained entrance into Libya via fraudulent documents. At the same time, members of the Egyptian Christian Coptic community in Libya were harassed and arrested on illegal emigration charges (*Daily News Egypt*, 2 March 2013). In mid-March, an Egyptian Coptic church in Benghazi was set on fire for the second time in 2013, while fifty-five Egyptian Copts were arrested on charges of proselytisation and reportedly tortured. One of them, Ezzat Attallah, eventually died while in custody in a Tripoli prison (see full coverage in MENA, 14 March 2013). The Egyptian government did not respond to the Libyan strategy of restriction, leading Libya to employ a strategy of displacement from late February onwards: Egyptians found without proper documentation were declared subject to immediate deportation, as the so-called bilateral 'visa crisis' escalated (*al-Ahram*, 25 February 2013). The assistant Egyptian foreign minister officially denied that Egyptians were facing any discrimination, although news broke that over a hundred Egyptians had been deported on 18 March, all of whom had reportedly paid 3,000 LE each (or $338 dollars, a sizeable sum) to purchase employment visas for Libya (*al-Gomhoriya*, 18 March 2013). Similar to the Jordanian case, Libya gradually intensified its displacement strategy: in late February, it formally closed the border to Egyptian migrants while, by late March, Libyan authorities were deporting over 400 workers daily on a variety of charges, even accusing some of being infected with hepatitis (MENA, 29 March 2013).

In late March, Egyptian authorities duly arrested the ex-Gaddafi Libyan officials, including Ali Maria, the former ambassador to Egypt, and Mohammed Ibrahim, the brother of senior Gaddafi-era official Ahmed Ibrahim. Ahmed Gaddaf Alddam himself was also arrested (Agence France-Presse, 24 March 2013). The latter 'handed himself in to the security forces after 10 vehicles surrounded his house in the Zamalek neighborhood of the Egyptian capital', effectively nullifying the Egyptian courts' decision of non-extradition (BBC, 19 March 2013). Twenty-three other Libyan citizens were immediately arrested and duly extradited. *Al-Ahram* cited officials employed in the Egyptian Interpol, who declared that these extraditions were conducted in return for Egyptian migrant workers jailed in Libya being released (*al-Ahram*, 28 March). The timing of these arrests strengthens the claim that Egypt complied with Libyan demands because of the latter's use of displacement: Prosecutor General Tala'at Abdallah issued the extradition decision two days after a Libyan delegation arrived in Egypt on 19 March, bearing an updated list of eighty-eight names of 'Gaddafi-era fugitives' (*al-Ahram*, 22 March 2013). They were returning a visit to Libya by a delegation representing the Egyptian prosecution, which had been dispatched to investigate the arrests of Egyptian migrants and the death of Ezzat Attalah (*Daily News Egypt*, 25 March 2013). According to *al-Hayat*: 'the Egyptian authorities wanted to send a positive message to their neighbours and this was the main reason behind their decision to act now'. The report continued: 'it must be noted that in the last few months, bilateral relations between the two neighbours had greatly deteriorated' (*al-Hayat*, 20 March 2013).

Egyptian compliance with Libyan demands led to the restoration of the *status quo ante*, as had occurred in Jordan a few months earlier. The arrest of the Gaddafi-era elites in Cairo led Libya to re-open the border between the two countries, after keeping it closed for over two months (*al-Ahram*, 26 April 2016). Providing further proof of the connection between Egyptian labour migration and the forced repatriation of Libyan elites, 'the Libyan authorities also promised to open their market to the Egyptian workers *in case all the figures taking refuge in Egypt are handed over* [emphasis added]' (*al-Hayat*, 20 March 2013). By June, the Egyptian Ministry of Manpower and Migration extolled the excellent bilateral relations between the two countries, going as far as to claim that Libya was now ready to receive 'millions of Egyptians' (*al-Ahram*, 7 June 2013). The Libyan Deputy Central Bank Governor Ali Salem Hibri summed up the relationship between Libya and Egypt: 'there are times when your upstairs neighbour has a leaking pipe and you need to help him fix it for your own peace of mind' (Reuters, 16 April 2013).

Overall, this section has highlighted the degree to which unskilled and low-skilled Egyptian workers abroad could become instruments of host-state coercion in its issue-linkage strategies. Drawing on Iraqi, Jordanian, and Libyan strategies, the empirical examples examined in this section point to the use of coercion in migration management as issue-linkage: Iraq tied the fate of its Egyptian migrant community to Egyptian foreign policy; Jordan aimed to coerce Egypt into a shift of its natural gas export policy; while Libya pursued a complex strategy under Gaddafi (seeking the destabilisation of the Egyptian regime) and post-Gaddafi, aiming to secure the extradition of *ancien régime* political elites from Egypt. The next section examines how similar strategies of issue-linkage become apparent in Middle East states' management of forced displacement.

Issue-linkage and post-2011 Syrian forced displacement

However, issue-linkage and strategies of leverage are not limited to the management of labour migration in the Middle East. Indeed, as has been seen earlier, forced migration often generates tensions in global politics and varied responses by host-states, most strikingly in the responses to the post-2011 displacement of Syrians across the Middle East and beyond. 'We can open the doors to Greece and Bulgaria anytime and we can put the refugees on buses', Turkish President Recep Tayyip Erdoğan declared to a group of European Union [EU] senior officials in February 2016. 'So how will you deal with refugees if you don't get a deal? Kill the refugees?' (Reuters 2016a). Arab host-states in the region – namely Lebanon and Jordan – have also repeatedly voiced their need for international economic support, albeit by promising to continue supporting refugee populations within their borders. This section aims to expand our understanding of the interplay between forced migration and power politics within the context of the Syrian refugee crisis, in order to address how refugee flows have featured in the foreign policy strategies of refugee rent-seeking behaviour across Jordan, Lebanon, and Turkey.

To what extent does Jordan constitute a refugee rentier state, and how has that influenced its foreign policy decision-making? With regard to the Syrian refugee crisis, the emergence of the Jordanian refugee rentier state occurred gradually, from 2013 onwards. This is primarily evident in the policymakers' attempt to render Syrian refugees as visible as possible to the international community, while also aiming to inflate their numbers. Despite a welcoming policy over the first two years, Jordan created the Directorate of Security Affairs for the Syrian Refugee Camps in March 2013 and, two months later, closed its border crossings with Syria, even to those carrying valid passports (Syrians do not need a visa for entry into Jordan). Palestinian Syrians, in particular, had been denied entry since April 2012, and officially since January 2013 (Human Rights Watch 2014). A number of security reasons have been identified for these border closures that highlight the potential risks for socio-political unrest that a large influx of Palestinian-Syrians into the country might entail. A state security rationale does not, however, adequately account for the fact that Jordanian border officers prompted Syrians to enter the country via informal crossings instead: at numerous times in the first three years of the Syrian Civil War, Jordan's formal borders were closed to Syrian passport-holders, who were encouraged to use informal border crossings along the eastern border instead.

While state security concerns were important for domestic policymakers, the shift in Jordan's policy on border crossings was primarily aimed at increasing the international visibility of the Syrian refugee issue. Those entering the country through informal crossing points are automatically recognised as *prima facie* refugees, according to the 1998 Memorandum of Understanding (MoU) signed between Jordan and United Nations High Commissioner for Refugees. As a result, with the contribution of aid workers, local authorities were able to classify all Syrians entering into Jordan as refugees, rather than visitors. Syrians entering through informal crossing points were directly sent to the Za'atari refugee camp, near Mafraq. Whereas, in November 2012 Za'atari hosted some 45,000 Syrians, by February 2013 it was home to over 76,000 Syrians, a number that reached 156,000 refugees by 11 March 2013. This strategy enabled the Jordanian state to highlight that it was facing a clearly enumerated influx of Syrian refugees, and to strengthen its appeals for international aid. The Jordanian security official in charge of the Azraq refugee camp, which was constructed in May 2014, noted that 'if we hadn't built the camps, then the world would not understand that we were going through a crisis' (Betts, Ali, and Memişoğlu 2017, 9). As Turner argues, 'part of the reason why Jordan built camps for Syrians is that it used encampment strategically to enable it to raise the profile of, and receive funds for, Syrian refugees on its territory' (Turner 2015, 393). In fact, Jordan insists that the number of Syrians inside its territory well exceeds the number of those formally registered: whereas the Office of the United Nations High Commissioner for Refugees (UNHCR) puts forth approximately 655,500 Syrians registered with the United Nations inside Jordan, the government argues that Jordan hosted 1.3 million Syrians in 2017.

A strong indication of Jordan's refugee rent-seeking behaviour lies in its treatment of earlier forced displacement, particularly Iraqi refugees that had entered its territory after 2003. By 2007, UNHCR estimated that Jordan hosted approximately 50,000 registered Iraqis, but officials would claim that the number was closer to one between 750,000 and 1 million. This would cost the Jordanian state $1bn annually. An independent report by Fafo, a Norwegian research institute commissioned by Jordan to establish an accurate estimate, produced a figure of 161,000 Iraqis, but the Jordanian government continued to inflate this figure. 'We used to exaggerate the numbers with the Iraqis, but we do not do that anymore', one high-ranking Jordanian official admitted, carefully noting that 'we are not exaggerating the Syrian numbers' (Arar 2017a, 14). At the same time, Jordan did not place Iraqis into camps, which has been identified as working 'strongly against Jordan's attempts to secure increased financial aid' (Turner 2015, 393). Camps can turn refugees into a visible and 'spatially legible population' (Peteet 2011, 18) and facilitate the counting of refugees, which in turn can facilitate fundraising (Harrell-Bond 1998); in Jordan's case, the Iraqis were less visible to the international community, a fact that Jordanian policymakers became quickly aware of.

A number of Jordanian domestic responses to Syrian refugees have been developed under a refugee rent-seeking rationale, particularly the July 2014 'bail out' process. According to this policy, Syrian refugees are permitted to exit their assigned camps only when they are able to secure a sponsorship from a Jordanian citizen, who has to be over 35 years of age, married, and employed in a stable position. The Jordanian sponsor should also be able to prove a family relationship with the applicant, and not have a criminal record (Amnesty International 2013). While reliable data on this is not available, the Jordanian state's adoption of a 'bail out' process has encouraged phenomena of corruption and greed in the dealings between Syrian refugees and the Jordanian social body: numerous instances have been recorded of well-off Syrians who have been able to 'buy' their way out of refugee camps in Jordan, for hefty prices. At the same time, the UNHCR has recorded instances of Syrians paying middlemen around $500 in order to be bailed out by unknown Jordanian citizens (United Nations High Commissioner for Refugees 2013, 8). The fact that Jordan cancelled this scheme in 2016, once camp-enclosed Syrians able to afford a Jordanian sponsor had concluded such transactions, speaks to the state's refugee rentier mentality.

With regard to foreign policy decision-making, the Jordanian refugee rentier state relies upon securing refugee rent from the international community. In the case of Jordan, negotiations with the international community culminated in the Jordan Compact, an agreement drafted in February 2016 within the context of a London Pledging Summit. The main objective during the London Summit was the creation of 200,000 employment opportunities for Syrians within Jordan over a three- to five-year period. Jordan also agreed to lift regulatory barriers in allowing refugees to work within the country, and to lower work permit charges for those seeking low-skilled work from 700 Jordanian dinars to 10 Jordanian dinars. The Compact put forth three broader aims:

1. Turning the Syrian refugee crisis into a development opportunity that attracts new investments and opens up the EU market with simplified rules of origin, creating jobs for Jordanians and Syrian refugees whilst supporting the post-conflict Syrian economy;
2. Rebuilding Jordanian host communities by adequately financing through grants to the Jordan Response Plan 2016–2018, in particular the resilience of host communities; and
3. Mobilizing sufficient grants and concessionary financing to support the macroeconomic framework and address Jordan's financing needs over the next three years, as part of Jordan entering into a new Extended Fund Facility program with the IMF. (Government of Jordan 2016)

The contribution to the Jordan Response Plan referred to a funding package that aimed to support Jordanian capacity to host refugees but that, by 2016, had only reached 30% of its target. In London, $700 millions of grants were raised with the expectation that additional pledges would provide an additional $700 million in 2017 and 2018. At the same time, the World Bank adopted the Concessional Financing Facility (CFF), which provided $147 million in low-interest loans, available only to middle-income, refugee-hosting countries. A drafted within the context of the donor conference on Syria, the Compact identified that 'a new paradigm is necessary, promoting economic development and opportunities in Jordan to the benefit of Jordanians and Syrian refugees' (Government of Jordan 2016). In particular, as Betts, Ali, and Memişoğlu (2017) argue, Jordan secured support for its wish to boost its manufacturing sector by integrating refugees into Special Economic Zones (SEZs): 'By allowing refugees to work in the SEZs, Jordan hopes to attract the additional support needed to make its own national development strategy work' (Betts et al. 2017, 10). This was made possible via tariff-free access to the European Union market for goods produced within SEZs with a certain degree of Syrian participation (15%) and provided Jordan issued 200,000 work permits to Syrians.

The provision of economic aid to the Jordanian government via the Jordan Compact in response to the Syrian refugee crisis is undisputed, with little doubt that the international community's support was due to Western states being 'keen to institute measures that might help to stem the flow of refugees to Europe', as the *Financial Times* put it (Reed 2017). While international aid to Jordan was linked to its treatment of the Syrian refugee population, Jordanian elites also perceived of this revenue as contributing to the country's economic development, within the broader aim of 'turning the crisis into an opportunity' – in other words, to function as a form of refugee rent. It is important to note that this discourse was espoused by World Bank policymakers, as well as the international community. Franck Bousquet, the World Bank Director for Regional Programs and Partnerships in the Middle East and North Africa, argued:

> It is critical that today we begin to finance projects to support vulnerable populations in Jordan and Lebanon ... these countries have made enormous sacrifices to meet the global responsibility of providing refuge from conflict, and it is vital that the international community unite to provide the long-term support that will help them both withstand shocks and continue to develop and prosper. (World Bank 2016)

This narrative was immediately picked up by local elites and policymakers. Jordan understands how 'the idea of turning the challenge of refugees into an economic opportunity is based on the protracted nature of the crisis', according to Imad Fakhoury, Jordanian minister of planning and international cooperation (*Financial Times* 2017) In mid-2016, as the EU relaxed trade rules with Jordan in order to create jobs for Syrian refugees, the Jordanian planning minister hailed this as 'an opportunity to transform the Syrian refugee crisis to an economic opportunity' (Reuters 2016b). As Saleh Kharabsheh, secretary general at the Jordanian Ministry of Planning and International Cooperation, argued: '[The CSS] will play a significant role in contributing to building the resilience of Jordan's host communities and boost economic growth so that we are able to provide basic services and economic opportunities to both Jordanians and Syrian refugees' (World Bank 2016). By February 2016, once Jordanian policymakers perceived international economic aid as serving the country's broader developmental goals rather than merely addressing the Syrian refugee crisis, Jordan embodied a refugee rentier state.

In its negotiations with the international community, Jordan adopted a backscratching strategy. For one, Jordanian elites highlighted the importance of multi-lateral action and cooperation in dealing with the effects of the Syrian refugee crisis in their country: 'in a country of 6.6 million Jordanians, we have opened our doors to 1.3 million Syrians fleeing violence in their homeland', Queen Rania declared at the 2016 United Nations Summit on Refugees and Migrants, providing an inflated estimate that is unsubstantiated by the UNHCR, 'just as we have opened our doors in the past to Palestinians, Iraqis, and others seeking a safe haven'. She concluded by arguing that, in view of Jordanian generosity, 'it cannot fall to the countries closest to the conflicts to shoulder this responsibility alone' ('Queen Rania's Speech at UN Summit for Refugees and Migrants' 2016). But there is little doubt that Jordanian elites aimed to reap economic benefits from hosting Syrian migrants – for one official, 2016 (the year of the Jordan Compact) was 'Jordan's golden year' (Arar 2017b, 308). In fact, as Jordan's 2015 appeal for international aid received less than a quarter of its £2.9bn goal (the *Guardian* 2015), the rhetoric intensified, but was always framed in a backscratching tone. King Abdullah would repeatedly state how cooperation would be a win-win strategy. In a February 2016 interview with the BBC, he asserted that:

> [the international community,] they realise that if they don't help Jordan it is going to make it more difficult for them to be able to deal with the refugee crisis. And, to be honest, all the leaders that we talk to know that by helping Jordan, they are actually helping themselves more. So it is in their vested interests ... I think the leaders of the international community have the spirit to help us (BBC 2016a).

At the same time, King Abdullah addressed his appeals towards the international community, and adopted cooperative language: 'the international community, we've always stood shoulder to shoulder by your side' he declared in February 2016. 'We're now asking for your help, you can't say no this time', he said (BBC 2016b). Abdullah aimed to highlight the plight of Jordan, rather than raise threats against other states: in a September 2016 television interview, Abdullah argued how 'unemployment is skyrocketing. Our health sector is saturated. Our schools are really going through difficult times. It's extremely, extremely difficult. And Jordanians are just have had it up to here. I mean we just can't take it anymore' (CBS 2016). Ahead of a donor conference on Syria in February 2016, King Abdullah became more blunt: 'I think it's gotten to a boiling point ... sooner or later, I think, the dam is going to burst', he warned; 'we can't do it anymore' (BBC 2016b).

Asked whether a more assertive foreign policy strategy would have been preferable, my respondents appeared reticent. Most frequently highlighted was the country's geographic location. One source in the Ministry of Planning and International Cooperation laughed it off – 'Send [the Syrian refugees] where? Israel?' While no one disputed that the Syrian refugee community in Jordan represented a sizeable force, the fact that Jordan is landlocked with no pathway to Europe was also frequently mentioned. As Arar also notes, quoting a Jordanian official she interviewed, 'we should have blackmailed the EU like Turkey did' (Arar 2017b, 25). In an official interview in the Ministry of Foreign Affairs and Expatriates he also doubted that a different policy would bring results: he argued that the influx of Iraqi refugees into Jordan following the 2003 invasion went largely unnoticed by the United States. In fact, back then, King Abdullah had famously declared that Jordan is stuck between 'Iraq and a hard place'.

Finally, the domestic repercussions of the Jordan Compact merit analysis: the negotiations leading to the Jordan Compact were based on the expectation that 200,000 employment opportunities would be provided for Syrian refugees, as a way of reducing their dependence on aid. In practice, this has been difficult given a slower-than-expected economic growth since 2016, high unemployment, as well as a lack of interest in investing in Jordan's business sector. By July 2017, only 60,000 work permits had been issued. This has resulted in significant tension between Jordan and the international donors, which was further fuelled by the Jordanian Ministry of Labour allowing each Syrian to carry more than one work permit. In an attempt to reach the 200,000-mark, the Jordanian government argued that work permits do not represent individuals: 'the permits are work opportunities', explained one Ministry official, 'it is possible for a Syrian to have more than one permit in a year if he has more than one job' (Betts et al. 2017, 11).

At the same time, in an effort to meet the requirements of the international community and to not jeopardise refugee rent inflows, Jordan has resorted to the tightening of restrictions on other migrant groups' employment within Jordan, namely the country's 500,000 to 1 million Egyptian workers. In June 2016, the Ministry of Labour ceased recruitment of foreign migrant labour, except domestic workers, citing 'the consequences of the Syrian refugee crisis and the entry of large numbers of Syrian refugees to the labor market' (Abaza 2016). While Jordanian migration diplomacy has attempted to leverage the status of Egyptian workers within the country against Egypt before (Tsourapas 2018), it is the first time that Egyptians have been discriminated against in the scramble to secure employment for Syrian refugees. For Linda al-Kalash, the director of Tamkeen, a legal aid and support centre for migrant workers, 'we are seeing a huge campaign to expel Egyptians' (Ellouk 2017). This has resulted in tight controls over Egyptians' paperwork by Jordanian authorities: according to Ahmed el-Sayed, an Egyptian construction worker in Amman, 'Three people were killed last week [August 2016] because they were running from the police ... they were working at a construction site when the police came, and in an attempt to escape they jumped from the third floor and eventually died' (Abaza 2016). For Ahmed Awad, the director of the Phenix Center for Economics & Informatics Studies in Amman:

> If Egyptian workers were already vulnerable and living in precarious situations, the Jordanian government's resolution at the international donors conference in London to issue work permits to 200,000 Syrians (at no cost to employers) within two years further exacerbated the situation. (Abaza 2016)

In contrast to Jordan, Lebanon did not develop a policy of placing Syrians into refugee camps, a decision that is linked to its long background of tacking socio-political issues arising from its construction of Palestinian refugee camps (Shami 1999). Yet, this does not imply that Lebanon did not adopt a refugee rentier state mentality, one that bears similarities to Jordan. In matters of enumeration, the two countries share the pattern of statistical inaccuracy in reporting Syrian refugee stocks estimates: UNHCR reported 1,001,051 registered Syrian refugees, but the organisation was ordered to suspend registrations as of May 2015. 'The government took a decision last October [2014] that included new border measures for all Syrians and also asked [UNHCR] to stop registering refugees unless in very exceptional humanitarian cases', an adviser to the Interior Minister Nohad Machnouk reported to *al-Jazeera*. 'Since the beginning of this year UNHCR has registered thousands of new Syrians, which is basically in contradiction with the Lebanese decision' (Al-Jazeera 2015). As a result, the Lebanese government has been able to put forth a wide range of estimates, going as high as 2.2 million refugees.

But evidence of refugee rent-seeking behaviour is ample: in January 2015, the government put forth legislation detailing a novel process regulating Syrians' residency in Lebanon. All Syrians that are over 15 years of age and registered with UNCHR were now expected to pay a $200 annual renewal fee to the Lebanese state, an amount that is exorbitant given that 70% of Syrian refugees in the country fall below the poverty line. Those who had not registered for the UNHCR were required to secure the 'sponsorship' of a Lebanese national, similar to the earlier process established in Jordan. In reality, UNHCR reported that Lebanese authorities requested evidence of sponsorship even of Syrians that had registered with them. This requirement has led to processes of exploitation and enrichment of Lebanese citizens, similar to the Jordanian case: 'sponsors are making a business out of it' one refugee reported. 'They sell sponsorships for up to $1,000 a person. Potential sponsors wait on the Syrian border or at the airport to sell sponsorships to new arrivals.' Another reported:

> My boss makes me work more than 12 hours a day at his shop. Sometimes I complain but then he threatens to cancel my sponsorship. What can I do? I have to do whatever he says. I feel like his slave. (Human Rights Watch, 2016)

According to a December 2014 directive by the General Security Directorate, Lebanese contractors would be forced to bear the cost of sponsoring each Syrian worker – estimated at $2,000 annually – which would include the 'cost of work and residence permits, health insurance, and notary contracts' (Shoufi 2015). As Lebanese officials aimed to extract rent in the form of permits by the private sector, this created a rift with the domestic construction industry, which was already able to profit from the influx of cheap Syrian labour. At the same time, there were frequent reports of Syrian refugees getting arrested on a regular basis (in most cases exclusively because of lack of legal residency, which is a criminal misdemeanour in Lebanese law). Exact data on this is unavailable; however, NGO representatives have confirmed that, in most instances, the actual criminal case neither reaches the courts nor results in a formal conviction by a judge; this suggests that the various fees that Syrians' families end up paying actually constitute unofficial bribes to the administrators of police detention facilities – or, in this chapter's argumentation, another dimension of refugee rent.

More prominently, Lebanon has not hesitated to deport Syrian refugees back to their home country. As early as 2012, Human Rights Watch identified processes of disrespecting the principle of non-refoulement in Lebanon with regard to 14 Syrian deportees (Human Rights Watch 2012). More frequently, Lebanese authorities grant temporary papers to unregistered Syrian refugees, with strict deadlines for producing legal documents, which would require they return to Syria. As Janmyr's research demonstrates, since mid-2014 Lebanon has been monitoring border crossings in order to 'de-register' Syrian refugees that cross into Syria – with 68,000 Syrians having their status revoked between June and October 2014 alone (Janmyr 2018). It should come as no surprise that the Lebanon Compact makes an explicit reference to 'ease the temporary stay of Syrian refugees, in particular regarding their residency status'. According to one refugee:

> Things are changing, and now the army is going in and arresting people in their homes, not waiting for them to come to checkpoints … When they came to take everyone, they took 27 people. They took every male above the age of 14 for four days. And they took all our documents and gave us one week to sort out our residency … It would have required going back to Syria … So none of us could do anything, [and] now we're all illegal in the country … My only hope is to get out of Lebanon, to get somewhere where I can educate my children. (Alabaster 2016)

The experience of Lebanon's attempts at attracting external economic aid is not dissimilar to that of Jordan. In December 2014, Lebanon launched the Lebanon Crisis Response Plan in Berlin, an agreement that formed part of the Regional Refugee and Resilience Plan. It stated that Lebanon has 'shown exceptional commitment and solidarity and has welcomed around 1.5 million refugees fleeing war-torn Syria [as] Lebanese communities have opened their schools, their clinics and even their homes to hundreds of thousands' of Syrian refugees. At the same time, however, the inflow of forcibly displaced Syrians created 'overwhelming pressures' on Lebanese institutional structures that were 'threatening its longer-term stability'. In response, the Plan aims to ensure the well-being of Syrians residing in Lebanon, but to also provide support for the Lebanese state:

1. Ensure the protection of vulnerable populations
2. Provide immediate assistance to vulnerable populations
3. Support service provision through national systems
4. Reinforce Lebanon's economic, social, and environmental stability.

The Plan initially sought a total of $2.48 billion for 2016, to implement programmes by the Lebanese government and the international community. In its 2017–20 planning, Lebanon proposed $2.8 billion in aid, in consultation with the United Nations. It also enjoyed access to CFF, as per World Bank decision. The discourse around Lebanon's access to low-interest loans was reminiscent of Jordan's. According to Philippe Lazzarini, United Nations resident and humanitarian coordinator in Lebanon:

> Dealing with long-term displacement crises requires innovative responses. Humanitarian support and development assistance need to be coordinated in order to increase the capacity of host communities and institutions from day one. Through close coordination and collaboration with the World Bank and other partners and donors, important concessional development assistance will be available for Lebanon to improve economic conditions, create jobs and transform the crisis into new opportunities. (World Bank 2016)

At the same time, in February 2016, Lebanon negotiated the Lebanon Compact, which enjoyed EU support and included a minimum of €400 million for 2016–17, over and above existing pledges. Again, the EU framed the Compact as aiming 'to turn the situation into an opportunity to improve the socio-economic prospects, security, stability and resilience of the whole Lebanon'. As in Jordan, the international aid that Lebanon received given its status as a host-state for Syrian refugees included significant amounts of rent. In particular, beyond funds targeted towards Syrian refugees, the Compact allocated:

> €15 million to boost Lebanon's productivity and competitiveness in the agribusiness and wood sectors … €13 million for the implementation of the National Plan to Safeguard Children and Women in Lebanon across the country … €1.5 million to reinforce the capacity of the Ministry of Youth and Sports to better address youth issues, including a €800,000 programme addressing drug abuse … €48 million for solid waste management programmes in addition to €5 million for the construction and equipment of 1 solid waste treatment facility and 1 sanitary landfill … €2 million to support the Lebanese Parliament, resulting in re-activation of the Legislative Tracking System in the Lebanese Parliament.

Much like Jordan, Lebanon relied on a backscratching strategy in negotiating the 2016 Compact agreement. This relied, as with Jordan, on appeals to multilateralism and cooperation on an international level, rather than threats. Echoing the Jordanian monarch's declaration, Prime Minister Hariri has repeatedly stated how he intends 'to make sure that the world understands that Lebanon is on the verge of a breaking point' (Reuters 2017a). At an April 2017 Brussels conference on Syria, Hariri argued for the international community to commit $10,000 to $12,000 per refugee in Lebanon over a span of five to seven years, while ensuring that this 'would equally benefit Lebanese citizens and displaced Syrians'. 'We have enough', Interior Minister Nohad Machnouk declared in January 2015. 'There's no capacity any more to host more displaced' (Associated Press 2015). According to Lebanon's Minister of Social Affairs Rashid Derbas, 'the glass cannot fit one more drop ... now we have 1.2 million [refugees]. I think this is a very exceptional proportion' (Human Rights Watch, 2016). Speaking to *Politico* in July 2017, Hariri expanded on how a small country of some 4 million Lebanese dealt with this:

> Yeah, 4 and a half million, so you can imagine the burden, and how much it is difficult. And we believe Lebanon is doing a public service for the entire world, and I believe Lebanon should be also compensated for that, because if those refugees didn't come to Lebanon, they would be everywhere in the world ... The international community needs to help Lebanon, especially the refugees because with 1 percent growth in Lebanon, we cannot manage to have jobs for the Lebanese and the Syrians. (Glasser 2017)

Officials approached for comment in Beirut highlighted the fact that Lebanon did not have a functioning government between March 2013 and December 2016, following the resignation of Prime Minister Mikati. With regard to the negotiating strategy concerning the Lebanon Compact and Lebanon's foreign policy, the general perception seemed to be the absence of strong international allies or bargaining chips. '*Ce n'est pas nous qui dictent les règles du jeu*' ('It is not us that call the shots'), according to an official in the Ministry of the Interior, which is tasked with responding to the Syrian refugee crisis. The point of whether Lebanon's proximity to Cyprus, an EU member-state, may be important was also dismissed. Despite hosting the most refugees per capita of any country, Lebanon is not considered a gateway to Europe: notwithstanding a waterway to an EU member-state (Cyprus), Syrian refugees have avoided the island because it offers neither an easy way into the rest of the continent (Reuters 2017b), nor a simple asylum process, with only 3% of asylum seekers granted refugee status: '[Cypriot officials] want to give refugees the message: Don't come to Cyprus because if you do, you won't get refugee status', according to Doros

Polykarpou, executive director of KISA, a Cypriot non-profit, 'and it works' (Karas 2015).

Turkey hosts the largest number of Syrian refugees, with over 3,567,000 registered as of October 2018, and exemplifies refugee rent-seeking behaviour. That said, Turkey differs in its treatment of them from Jordan and Lebanon in that it combines a number of refugee camps, primarily located across the border with Syria, while also allowing the vast majority of Syrians to reside across Turkey, particularly once the twenty-two camps, or Temporary Protection Centers in Şanlıurfa, Gaziantep, Hatay, and elsewhere in southern Turkey had been filled to capacity. The status of refugee rentier state is evident in the conclusion of long EU–Turkey negotiations, that culminated in the 2016 'deal'. This was preceded by an October 2015 Joint Plan of Action, and a €3 billion package that was negotiated with the EU in November 2015. This evolved into the 18 March 2016 deal, which added another €3 billion in aid, if Turkey agreed to a readmission of Syrians arriving in Greece and tighter border controls – a system resting on the (precarious) basis that Turkey constitutes a safe third country, which does not allow asylum-seekers in Turkey to move on to another state. For every Syrian returned to Turkey in the scheme, the EU pledged to resettle another in Europe, up to a cap of 72,000. In return, the EU made a number of concessions, including promises that:

> The fulfilment of the visa liberalisation roadmap will be accelerated with a view to lifting the visa requirements for Turkish citizens at the latest by the end of June 2016. Turkey will take all the necessary steps to fulfil the remaining requirements ... The EU will, in close cooperation with Turkey, further speed up the disbursement of the initially allocated €3 billion under the Facility for Refugees in Turkey. Once these resources are about to be used in full, the EU will mobilise additional funding for the Facility up to an additional €3 billion to the end of 2018 ... The EU and Turkey welcomed the ongoing work on the upgrading of the Customs Union. (European Council 2016b)

The European Commission agreed to provide €1 billion in funding, with €2 billion of additional funding from member-states (European Council 2016a). The administration of the €3 billion support was organised through the EU Facility for Refugees in Turkey, which focuses on six priority areas: humanitarian assistance; migration management; education; health; municipal infrastructure; and socio-economic support (European Commission 2017). As of June 2017, forty-eight projects have been contracted worth over €1.6 billion, out of which €811 million has been disbursed. As its one-year report states, 'projects will notably ensure that 500,000 Syrian children have access to formal education, 70 new schools are built; 2,081 teachers and other education personnel have received training and two million refugees will get access to primary healthcare services'. Similarly to Jordan and Lebanon, the concessions that Turkey gained involved issues that were not immediately linked to the Syrian refugee crisis – the most evident one being the visa liberalisation process. The promise to re-energise the accession process exclusively benefited the Turkish state and had no impact upon the country's non-Turkish population.

Unlike Jordan and Lebanon, Turkey developed a blackmailing strategy in its foreign policy decision-making with regard to its international management of the Syrian refugee crisis. This is evident in the threatening discourse that Ankara elite engaged in, targeting Brussels and EU member-states. Minutes of a February 2016 meeting between Erdoğan, Tusk, and Juncker (later confirmed by Erdoğan), have the Turkish prime minister openly threatening to flood Europe with displaced Syrians. The discussion included the amount of capital Turkey had spent on hosting displaced Syrian: in October 2015, for instance, the Turkish Interior Ministry announced that Turkey had spent over $8 billion supporting Syrians, 'surpassing the Turkish Interior Ministry's budget'. But Turkey's rationale was better served by a blackmailing strategy: 'we want this human strategy to end', Prime Minister Ahmet Davutoglu declared in 2016, detailing how Turkey wanted 'our citizens to travel visa free, and the customs union to be updated' (Associated Press 2016).

Interestingly, the outflow of refugees via the Aegean Sea into Greece and, subsequently, the rest of Europe effectively ceased in the aftermath of the signing of the EU–Turkey deal. Until early 2016, the large flows of irregular migrants from Syria into Europe via Turkey allowed the enrichment of a wide number of Turkish nationals associated with smuggling via the Aegean Sea, which immediately stopped in March 2016: in Istanbul, one of these smugglers, interviewed by *The New York Times*, boasted over $800,000 in profits, and having 'more than 80,000 missed calls from prospective customers' (*The New York Times* 2017). In Izmir, *al-Jazeera* identified how $1,000 would allow a smuggler to 'launch boats unmolested by police or gendarmes for a day' (Reidy 2016). Following the EU–Turkey deal, all smuggling business stopped; the smuggler identified by *The New York Times* is now considering opening a seaside café, instead.

Turkey's blackmailing strategy continued following the signing of the 2016 deal. One day after the European Parliament called for a pause in the country's EU accession talks over the Turkish government's repressive response to a July 2016 coup attempt, Erdoğan declared that 'we are the ones who feed 3–3.5 million refugees in this country … You have betrayed your promises. If you go any further those border gates will be opened' (Pitel and Beesley 2016). This raises an important point with regard to the domestic political repercussions of refugee rent-seeking, particularly with regard to refugee host-states' governments' attempts at consolidating authoritarian rule. The European Parliament's decisions are not binding for EU member-states; however, observers were keen to note that Erdoğan's warnings had come a few days in advance of the second round of the Austrian 2016 Presidential elections. The EU response was rather lacklustre: 'rhetorical threats are absolutely unhelpful and should not be the standard tone between partners', one senior EU official noted on the record. 'This will not help Turkey's credibility in the eyes of European citizens. Europe will not be blackmailed' (Pitel and Beesley 2016).

All three states examined above fall under the category of refugee rentier states, given the fact that they received external economic aid that was dependent on their status as hosting forcibly displaced populations, and that they came to rely on substantial external rent linked to their continuous hosting of these refugee populations. This refugee rent is encapsulated in the three agreements negotiated between these refugee rentier states and the international community – the February 2016 Jordan Compact, the February 2016 Lebanon Compact, and the March 2016 EU–Turkey deal, respectively. At the same time, as per this chapter's theoretical framework, their foreign policy with regard to the refugee issue falls under the broad strategies of backscratching and blackmailing. Jordan and Lebanon broadly employed a backscratching strategy – although domestic elites made urgent pleas for help, they highlighted multi-lateralism, tended to approach the matter with reference to the responsibility of the international community to help, and praised the positive sum value of inter-state cooperation. Turkey, on the other hand, employed a different strategy that came closer to black-mailing: elites made little reference to cooperation or multi-lateralism, and put forth distinct threats that aimed to coerce their target audience, rather than ensure cooperation.

What accounts for this variation in policymaking? The data collected suggests that Lebanon and Jordan were not able to employ a blackmail-ing strategy, even though there was a desire to follow Turkey's example. While the sizeable community of Syrian refugees was deemed important, the two countries' location and elites' doubts on their countries' strategic importance appeared to rule out a more forceful or aggressive policy. In the Turkish case, however, elites' perception of the country's geopolitical importance – particularly with regard to its proximity to Greece – appeared to have enabled the government's blackmailing strategy. The geopolitical importance of the host-state appears to matter with regard to Jordanian and Turkish strategy historically: back in the late 1960s, King Hussein did not hesitate to use Jordan's hosting of thousands of Palestinian refugees in order to blackmail the United States for a solution to their status. This can be explained by the significant geopolitical importance of Jordan in the late 1960s as the major United States ally in the region, a status that the country has since lost. Similarly, Turkey's behaviour post-Gulf War – when, in 1991, it successfully blackmailed the United States on the fate of Kurdish refugees within its borders – was also predicated on its strategic importance for Washington at the time (details on both cases: Greenhill 2010, 296–97, 316–17).

A number of alternative explanations for the three refugee rentier states' behaviour are unconvincing. What of the argument that Jordan genuinely sought a cooperative solution to the Syrian refugee crisis or that it would not consider the deportation of Syrians for humanitarian reasons? This is discounted by two policies that Jordan developed domestically: firstly, the 'bail out' process strongly suggests that Jordan aimed to employ the Syrian refugee issue for economic gain. Furthermore, Jordan did engage in the marginalisation and deportation of migrant populations – that of Egyptians, which undermines the argument that Jordanian policy was driven by a humanitarian rationale. With regard to Lebanon, a number of policies discount the potential counterargument that Lebanese backscratching policy resulted from its human rights protection record or, put differently, that Lebanon would not consider deporting Syrian refugees for humanitarian reasons. For one, not only did Lebanon order UNHCR to stop registering new refugees but, in January 2015, the government put forth legislation detailing a novel process regulating Syrians' residency in Lebanon. More importantly, however, Lebanon has not hesitated to deport Syrian refugees back to their home country. Could the Turkish policy of blackmailing be accounted for via alternative explanations? One such explanation could be that Turkey was unable to control its European borders and, therefore, was forced into a policy of confrontation rather than accommodation with the EU. Yet, empirical facts discount this argument, particularly given the impressive decrease in crossings across the Aegean Sea since the signing of the EU–Turkey deal. Turkish state officials, in other words, were more than able to secure its European borders when they had the incentive to do so.

Overall, this section has examined how forced displacement features in the foreign policy decision-making of refugee host-states, and how it is linked to their issue-linkage migration diplomacy. In doing so, it has attempted to move beyond discussion of coercion, and to highlight the full range of strategies available to host-states by drawing on the literature on rentier states and issue-linkage strategies. As per the book's theorisation, it has demonstrated how host-states may pursue strategies of *blackmailing* and *backscratching* in these states' foreign policy. Through a within-case analysis of Jordanian, Lebanese, and Turkish responses to the post-2011 Syrian refugee crisis, it has demonstrated how international aid to refugee host-states constitutes a form of rent. In response, refugee host-states' refugee rent-seeking behaviour appears to result in a blackmailing strategy when it contains a large number of refugees and when states' elites perceive of their country as having geopolitical importance vis-à-vis the target-state(s) – as in Turkey. Alternatively, state elites are more likely to opt for a backscratching strategy – as in the case of Lebanon and Jordan.

Conclusion

This chapter aimed to enrich the discussion on migration diplomacy strategies across the Middle East by identifying how labour and forced migration may feature in host-states' issue-linkage strategies. The turbulent relationship between Egypt and two key Arab migrant host-states (Iraq and Libya) allows us to identify the importance of long-term unskilled or low-skilled migration as an instrument of leverage. The short-term migration of Egyptian workers into Libya carried distinct short-term socio-economic advantages for the Libyan and Iraqi states, but there was little hesitation in employing them against Egypt. In this example of issue-linkage migration diplomacy, coercion is dependent upon the personalistic relationship between sending- and host-states' regimes. Beyond this, issue-linkage strategies may also be linked to specific policy concessions that the host-state demands from the sending-state. This becomes evident in Arab states' migration diplomacy in the aftermath of the 2011 Arab Uprisings, particularly in the relations between Libya, Jordan, and Egypt. At the same time, if we were to broaden the scope of analysis, similar patterns would be evident elsewhere in the Middle East: the breakdown of Yemeni-Saudi relations in 1990 led to the decision to expel the entire Yemeni migrant community from the Kingdom, as approximately one million Yemeni workers were forced to leave Saudi Arabia (Okruhlik and Conge 1997). More recently, the hostility between Qatar and the remaining GCC states has also led to the imposition of travel restriction as well as expulsions of Qataris across the rest of the Gulf.

The chapter's second part shifts focus to forced migration, and examines how Jordan, Lebanon, and Turkey sought to employ migration diplomacy in order to secure international funding for their management of Syrian refugees within their borders. While all three engaged in post-2011 *refugee rent-seeking behaviour*, Jordan and Lebanon deployed a backscratching strategy based on bargains, while Turkey deployed a blackmailing strategy based on threats. To what extent do refugee rent-seeking strategies apply beyond the three cases outlined in this chapter? The main findings appear to apply to both current and historical cases. One could argue that states which find themselves in a geostrategically important position and face an influx of refugee populations are historically prone to strategies of blackmailing. One main example of this is Libya under Gaddafi: Libya's proximity to Europe and its status as a host-state for sub-Saharan African refugees led Gaddafi to demand an annual payment of €5 billion by the EU in order to prevent it from 'turning black' with refugees back in 2009 (Paoletti 2010; Tsourapas 2017a). Beyond blackmailing, refugee rentier states are also engaging with backscratching strategies. In the Middle East context, the EU concluded a number of 'Mobility Partnerships' with Morocco in June 2013, Tunisia in March 2014, and Jordan in October 2014 that offer certain perks to these states in return for their management of irregular migration and refugee flows (Collyer 2012). While these countries may be considered geostrategically important for Europe, they lack the large numbers of Syrian refugees that would allow them to pursue a blackmailing policy. Historically, Pakistan relied on extensive American economic support for hosting over a million displaced Afghans in the aftermath of the 1979 Soviet invasion of Afghanistan. While Pakistan contained a large number of refugees, relations with the United States were tense and it had yet to become the geopolitically important state it is today.

Note

1 Earlier versions of this chapter have been published in Tsourapas (2018, 2019).

Conclusion

'Anyone who says anything about our country, what happens to them?'
Nabila Makram, Egypt's minister for immigration, asked in July 2019,
during a private party for Egyptian expatriates in Toronto. 'We cut', she
said, while making a throat-slitting gesture with her hand (BBC 2019). This
chilling statement coincided with an increased attention to the management
of migration and diasporas by numerous Arab and non-Arab states in the
Middle East. This book has argued that a fruitful approach to understanding
the international relations of migration and diaspora politics in the Middle
East is the examination of cross-border mobility via a *migration diplomacy*
framework, including both the strategic use of migration flows as a means
to obtain other aims, and the use of diplomatic methods to achieve goals
related to migration. As highlighted in the first part of the book, such an
approach enables a shift towards the study of migration outside the Global
North – or, more particularly, emphasises the South–South dimension of
cross-border mobility. At the same time, it provides an inter-disciplinary
framework that allows the introduction of insights from migration and
refugee studies, Middle East studies, as well as comparative politics and
international relations.

Following a theoretical and historical introduction to the study of migration
politics in the broader Middle East, the book examined distinct dimensions
of migration diplomacy in the region. Firstly, a focus on Egyptian emigration
policymaking in the 1952–2011 era highlighted how emigration-related
processes become embedded in governmental practices of establishing and
maintaining power: under Gamal Abdel Nasser, high-skilled emigration
became an instrument of cultural diplomacy while, under Anwar Sadat and
Hosni Mubarak, it served as an instrument of inter-state relations and, at
times, closer cooperation with Arab states. Secondly, Middle East states'
vacillating approach towards their citizens abroad was examined via a focus

on five North African states (Algeria, Libya, Morocco, Tunisia, and Egypt). All five states sought to profit materially from these communities while minimising any political threat they may pose. Thirdly, the book examined how the oil-rich Arab monarchies have extended their support for a number of sending-states' ruling regimes – notably Egypt and Jordan – via cooperation on labour migration. And, finally, it shifted attention to the use of labour and forced migrants as political leverage by host-states, both in North Africa as well as the Middle East.

Do these processes of migration diplomacy extend beyond the case studies studied here? One unexplored dimension of authoritarian states' migration diplomacy practices refers to the use of emigration as an instrument of cultural diplomacy; the Soviet Union during the Cold War dispatched hundreds of high-skilled Russian scientists and bureaucrats across the Eastern bloc as a way of contributing to host-states' development and instilling communist ideals. The rationale behind Moscow's policy is arguably best understood through a foreign policy, rather than a developmental or comparative politics, lens. Castro's rise to power in Cuba spearheaded the policy of 'medical internationalism', through which Cuba would financially support the emigration of thousands of medical staff – doctors, nurses, and so on – across Latin America and Africa for cultural diplomacy purposes. Egyptian and Israeli use of emigration as a foreign aid component within the context of the Arab–Israeli rivalry is reminiscent of the Cold-War-era competition between the two superpowers over the Third World. Similarly, there exist a number of parallels between intra-Arab rivalry and the competition between China and the USSR over the leadership of the communist world during the Cold War. In all these cases, cross-border mobility has been an important aspect of authoritarian emigration states' foreign policy agendas.

More broadly, the normative use of emigration (or its rejection) as an instrument of authoritarian regimes is also frequent: in the context of the Cold War, Soviet dissidents would duly have their citizenship removed – such as Aleksandr Solzhenitsyn, the Russian author of the 1973 classic *The Gulag Archipelago*. Members of the Egyptian Muslim Brotherhood that managed to flee Egypt in the 1950s and 1960s would also be denationalised and forbidden from returning to the homeland (Mitchell 1969). As seen earlier, Moroccan expatriates who did not take part in social activities organised by the state-sponsored *Fédération des Amicales des Marocains* (modelled after Algeria's AAF), either expressed fear about returning to the Kingdom, or met with a number of difficulties from border officials (Brand 2002, 9). Hirt and Mohammad identify how those Eritreans leaving the state are seen as traitors: they are made to sign 'letters of regret' and promise to repay their loyalty via a 2% diaspora tax, incurred for any consular transaction (Hirt and Mohammad 2017). In sub-Saharan Africa, over the last decade, many returnees from the Democratic Republic of the Congo face suspicion by police officers upon arrival and, at times, arbitrary arrest and detention, particularly with regard to 'unpatriotic' activities they allegedly engaged in while abroad (Alpes 2019).

Beyond the management of emigration, authoritarian states' use of repressive tactics against their migrant and diaspora communities is not limited to the Middle East. While the Khashoggi case may constitute the most gruesome recent example of Saudi violence, the Kingdom has been implicated in a number of disappearances of political dissenters, including the 2003 kidnapping of Prince Sultan bin Turki in Geneva and the 2015 disappearance of Prince Turki bin Bandar al-Saud, who had applied for asylum in France (Hearst 2018). In the context of the Cold War, the Bulgarian Secret Service was implicated in the assassination of Bulgarian émigré Georgi Markov in London via a micro-engineered pellet that contained ricin and was fired into his leg from an umbrella. The Pinochet regime ordered the killing of former diplomat Orlando Letelier, who used his post in the Institute for Policy Studies to become a key voice of Chilean resistance abroad; he died by a car bomb explosion in September 1976 in Washington, DC. More recently, prominent Chinese critics have reportedly been subjected to illicit renditions: such as journalist and activist Li Xin who disappeared while seeking refuge in Thailand in January 2016, only to reportedly re-appear in China a few days later (Buckley 2016). Similarly, the disappearance of five people associated with the Causeway Bay Books independent bookstore in Hong Kong (specialising in books on Chinese politics that are not available in the People's Republic), have sparked concern for state-led renditions and contributed to the rise of Hong Kong's Anti-Extradition Law Amendment Bill Movement.

But, as Chapter 4 on North African practices suggested, repression extends well beyond violence: a number of countries, including Syria and Iran, have employed digital surveillance of expatriate activities while also threatening their well-being or the safety of their relatives and friends back home (Moss 2016b; Michaelsen 2018). Malek Jandali, a well-known German-born Syrian-American pianist, reported that, following the performance of *Watani Ana* (I Am My Homeland), Syrian security forces beat up his parents in Homs, telling them 'this is what happens when your son mocks the government' (Kelemen 2011). In 2017, members of China's Uighur community who were studying abroad were ordered to return home, with family members being held hostage by Chinese authorities until they did so (Radio Free Asia 2017). Central Asian states have also not hesitated to threaten residents who are relatives or friends of émigré activists (Cooley and Heathershaw 2017), while Turkey and other Middle Eastern states tend to rely on their consular and embassy services in order to control and intimidate overseas citizens and diaspora members (Østergaard-Nielsen 2003b). Israeli spy software is used by Saudi Arabia (which purchased the Pegasus spyware for $55 million in 2017), as well as by other Gulf monarchies to target diaspora dissidents, including Yahya Assiri, Ghanem al-Dosari, and, reportedly, Khashoggi himself. Human Rights Watch has investigated how the Ethiopian government has sent emails to citizens abroad containing attachments infected with FinFisher, a German spyware program that allows unfettered access to citizens' computers (Horne 2014).

Autocratic countries of origin have also developed varying degrees of cooperation with countries of transit and destination, from regional migration regimes or sharing information to extradition treaties. Jiang Yefei and Dong Guanping, two Chinese citizens who had been designated refugees by UNHCR and relocated to Thailand, were deported to China in November 2015 – in what Amnesty International called 'a worrying new pattern of China putting pressure on third-party countries to repatriate dissidents and others who have left China for economic and social reasons' that includes a rising number of ethnic Uighurs (Buckley 2015). In 2014, Azeri journalist Rauf Mirgadirov was deported from Turkey, where he had been living there since 2010, and arrested upon arrival at Baku airport. The deportation of Mirgadirov to Azerbaijan was made a few days after Erdoğan's visit to Baku. Similarly, Georgian authorities have been suspected of aiding the May 2017 disappearance of Azeri opposition journalist Afgan Mukhtarli in Tbilisi, where he had been living in self-imposed exile since 2015. At the time of his disappearance, Mukhtarli had been investigating the business holdings of the family of Azeri President Ilham Aliyev in Georgia for the Organized Crime and Corruption Reporting Project (BBC 2017). Two months later, Mukhtarli re-surfaced in Azerbaijan, and was sentenced to a six-year prison term.

In the Middle East, Turkey relies on such processes, even attempting to implicate Western liberal states in this scheme: the creation of a distinct Kurdish diaspora identity and nationalist movement in Europe following the 1980 military coup in Turkey has led to Turkish government attempts to cooperate with host-states in monitoring and restricting political dissidents' behaviour abroad (Østergaard-Nielsen 2003b, 94), culminating in the 1999 arrest of PKK leader Abdullah Öcalan, in Greece. More recently, Turkish President Recep Tayyip Erdoğan has repeatedly pressured the US government for the extradition of Gülen, who has lived in Pennsylvania since 1999 (Gall 2019). Egypt under the el-Sisi military regime has cooperated with a number of Middle Eastern host-states in its ongoing fight against the Egyptian Muslim Brotherhood. Saudi Arabia and the United Arab Emirates have been key allies in that regard. In early 2014, Egyptian nationals Ahmed Mossad Elmaadawi Mohamed and his father-in-law, Mr Abdul Rahim Mohamed

Yousef Nour Al Din were arrested in Abu Dhabi, and have disappeared since (Alkarama 2014). In early 2019, twelve Egyptians were deported to Egypt from Turkey and at least four from Malaysia, at least five of whom are currently missing (Human Rights Watch 2019). In July 2019, Kuwait extradited seven Egyptian migrants, suspected of being members of the Muslim Brotherhood, 'in accordance with joint agreements between the two countries', as Deputy Kuwaiti Foreign Minister stated (Gomaa 2019), '… this cooperation is ongoing and will continue because we know the security of Egypt is the security of Kuwait'.

Finally, the use of migrants and refugees as instruments of political leverage is not limited to the cases studies examined in this book. In Afghanistan, authorities have not hesitated to use both restriction and displacement against Pakistani labour migrants entering the country since mid-2016. Afghanistan recently adopted a law that requires passports, rather than mere identity cards, and frequently deports Pakistani labour migrants in an effort to force Pakistan to reverse its decision to unilaterally close the Chaman border crossing (*Times of India* 2016); in response, in March 2017, Pakistan's prime minister decided to open the crossing 'as a gesture of goodwill' (BBC News 2017). Elsewhere, bilateral disputes between Egypt and Sudan, including the contested border of the Halayeb Triangle, led Khartoum to adopt a strategy of restriction in April 2017, by barring entry to Egyptian men aged between sixteen and fifty without visas (Atef 2017).

Similarly, with regard to states' management of forced migration, in May 2019, Iran's deputy foreign minister stated that, if crude exports continue to decrease in light of American sanctions, 'it is possible that we ask our Afghan brothers and sisters to leave Iran'. In September 2019, Turkey threatened to open the border with Syria and allow internally displaced Syrians into its territory, if the Assad regime launches its 'massive offensive against Idlib'. Ethiopia negotiated a $500 million aid packet in 2019 in light of its status as a host-state of almost 1 million refugees. Manus Island and Nauru received over $5 billion from Australia between 2012 and 2018 in order to continue serving as offshore processing centres for asylum seekers – an astronomical sum, considering Nauru's annual GDP is $114 million. A few weeks after the 2016 EU–Turkey Deal, Kenya's national security head threatened to close down the Dadaab refugee camp, one of the largest in the world, because the West had been getting away with it 'on the cheap'. Looking back at how they dealt with the Syrian refugee crisis, Jordanian officials said, 'we should have blackmailed the EU like Turkey did'. But refugee rent-seeking strategies are no longer limited to the Global South: in 2015, Greek Foreign Minister Nikos Kotzias said that, if Greece was forced out of the Eurozone, 'there will be tens of millions of immigrants and thousands of jihadists' flooding Western Europe.

Overall, this book aims to contribute to an evolving research agenda on the international politics of migration in the Global South. In doing so, it is able to shed additional light on key debates on the rising trend towards authoritarianism across world politics: for instance, the rise of China as a global power cannot be disassociated from '*wenhua ruan shili*', or the cultural soft power it pursues in a number of ways, including the dispatch of Chinese teachers to over 500 Confucius Institutes across the world. In the Middle East, the Iranian–Saudi competition also includes a transnational dimension of efforts aimed at exerting religious influence beyond the two states' borders. Similarly, Turkish foreign policy includes a soft power dimension in its emigration diplomacy, as the Diyanet – the Directorate of Religious Affairs – trains, funds, and dispatches thousands of imams annually to over 2000 mosques abroad. At the same time, Western states' traditional reluctance against hosting migrants and refugees has grown exponentially across both sides of the Atlantic. It feeds into 'out of sight, out of mind' policies that reward host-states of first asylum for serving as buffer zones against asylum-seekers – from the Middle East and North Africa to Mexico. Through the prism of migration diplomacy, this book suggests that analyses of power politics in the Middle East, as well as in the broader Global South, are incomplete if they do not take migrants, refugees, and diasporas into account – not necessarily as weapons in terms of 'new wars', but as instruments of diplomatic practice, as well as subjects and objects of inter-state negotiations and leverage – in other words, as part and parcel of the international system.

References

Abaza, Jihad. 2016. "Egyptian Workers Face Clampdown in Jordan as Syrians Join Labour Market." *Middle East Eye*, 29 August 2016. www.middleeasteye. net/in-depth/features/jordans-crackdown-egyptian-migrant-workers-stirs-anger-confusion-1239563644. Accessed on 31 January 2021.

Abou-El-Fadl, Reem. 2015. "Neutralism Made Positive: Egyptian Anti-Colonialism on the Road to Bandung." *British Journal of Middle Eastern Studies* 42 (2): 219–40.

Aboulsayan, Ahmed. 2000. Oil, Economic Growth and Structural Change in the Libyan Economy, 1960-1990. PhD thesis. SOAS, University of London.

Abu-Odeh, Adnan. 1999. *Jordanians, Palestinians & the Hashemite Kingdom in the Middle East Peace Process*. Washington, DC: United States Institute of Peace.

Adamson, Fiona B. 2006. "Crossing Borders: International Migration and National Security." *International Security* 31 (1): 165–99.

Adamson, Fiona B. 2015. "Blurring the Lines: Diaspora Politics and Globalized Constituencies." *WPR: World Politics Review*, 14 July 2015. www.worldpoliticsreview.com/articles/16224/blurring-the-lines-diaspora-politics-and-globalized-constituencies. Accessed on 31 January 2021.

Adamson, Fiona B. 2016. "The Growing Importance of Diaspora Politics." *Current History* 115 (784): 291–97.

Adamson, Fiona B., and Madeleine Demetriou. 2007. "Remapping the Boundaries of 'State' and 'National Identity': Incorporating Diasporas into IR Theorizing." *European Journal of International Relations* 13 (4): 489–526.

Adamson, Fiona B., and Gerasimos Tsourapas. 2019. "Migration Diplomacy in World Politics." *International Studies Perspectives* 20 (2): 113–28.

Adamson, Fiona B., and Gerasimos Tsourapas. 2020. "The Migration State in the Global South: Nationalizing, Developmental, and Neoliberal Models of Migration Management." *International Migration Review* 54 (3): 853–82.

Adida, Claire L., and Desha M. Girod. 2011. "Do Migrants Improve Their Hometowns? Remittances and Access to Public Services in Mexico, 1995–2000." *Comparative Political Studies* 44 (3): 3–27.

Ahmadov, Anar K., and Gwendolyn Sasse. 2016. "A Voice Despite Exit: The Role of Assimilation, Emigrant Networks, and Destination in Emigrants' Transnational Political Engagement." *Comparative Political Studies* 49 (1): 78–114.

Akgündüz, Ahmet. 2008. *Labour Migration from Turkey to Western Europe, 1960-1974: A Multidisciplinary Analysis.* Farnham: Ashgate Publishing.

Al-Jazeera. 2015. "Syrians in Lebanon: 'Glass Cannot Fit One More Drop.'" www.aljazeera.com/news/2015/05/syrians-lebanon-glass-fit-drop-150529082240227.html. Accessed on 31 January 2021.

Al-Mamlakah al-Urdunniyyah al-Hashimiyyah, Al-Majlis al-Qawmi l-il-Takhtit, Khittat al-Tanmiyah al-Thulathiyyah, 1973–75 (n.p., n.d.), p. 271.

Al-Najjar, Zaynab. 1972. Enrolment in the Division of Public Service and Emigration: Is There a Conflict of Organisational Objectives? Unpublished PhD dissertation. American University of Cairo.

Al-Rasheed, Madawi. 2010. *A History of Saudi Arabia.* Second Edition. New York, NY: Cambridge University Press.

Alabaster, Olivia. 2016. "Syrian Refugees in Lebanon Live in Fear of Deportation." *Al-Jazeera*, 22 January 2016. www.aljazeera.com/news/2016/01/syrian-refugees-lebanon-live-fear-deportation-160117102350730.html. Accessed on 31 January 2021.

Aldoukalee, Salmah Alzarog. 2013. An Investigation into the Challenges Faced by Libyan PhD Students in Britain. Unpublished PhD Dissertation. University of Salford.

Alemán, José, and Dwayne Woods. 2014. "No Way Out: Travel Restrictions and Authoritarian Regimes." *Migration and Development* 3 (2): 285–305.

Alkarama. 2014. "United Arab Emirates: Two Egyptians Disappeared in Abu Dhabi." Alkarama. www.alkarama.org/en/articles/united-arab-emirates-two-egyptians-disappeared-abu-dhabi. Accessed on 31 January 2021.

Alpes, Jill. 2019. "After Deportation, Some Congolese Returnees Face Detention and Extortion." Washington, DC: Migration Policy Institute. www.migrationpolicy.org/article/after-deportation-some-congolese-returnees-face-detention-and-extortion. Accessed on 31 January 2021.

Ambrosio, Thomas. 2010. "Constructing a Framework of Authoritarian Diffusion: Concepts, Dynamics, and Future Research." *International Studies Perspectives* 11 (4): 375–92.

Amin, Galal A. 1995. *Egypt's Economic Predicament: A Study in the Interaction of External Pressure, Political Folly, and Social Tension in Egypt, 1960–1990.* New York, NY: E.J. Brill.

Amin, Galal A., and Elizabeth Taylor Awni. 1986. *Hijrat Al-amālah Al-Misrīyah: Dirāsah Naqdīyah Lil-Buhuth Wa-Al-Dirāsāt Al-Khāssah Bi-Hijrat Al-amālah Al-Misrīyah Ilá Al-Khārij [Egyptian Labor Migration: A Critical Study of Research and Studies on the Migration of Egyptian Workers Abroad].* Ottawa: Markaz al-Buhuth lil-Tanmiyah al-Dawlīyah.

Amman Center for Human Rights Studies. 2012. "Amman Center Welcomes the Decision to Stop Deportation of Egyptian Workers." www.achrs.org/english/index.php/center-news-mainmenu-79/others-mainmenu-38/324-amman-center-welcomes-the-decision-to-stop-deportation-of-egyptian-workers.html. Accessed on 31 January 2021.

Amnesty International. 2013. "Growing Restrictions, Tough Conditions: The Plight of Those Fleeing Syria to Jordan." www.amnestyusa.org/reports/growing-restrictions-tough-conditions-the-plight-of-those-fleeing-syria-to-jordan/. Accessed on 31 January 2021.

Andreas, P., and T. Snyder. 2000. *The Wall Around the West: State Borders and Immigration Controls in North America and Europe.* New York, NY: Rowman and Littlefield.

Appleyard, Reginald. (ed.) 1999. *"Emigration Dynamics in Developing Countries: Vol. IV: The Arab Region.* Aldershot: Ashgate.

Arar, Rawan. 2017a. "Leveraging Sovereignty: The Case of Jordan and the International Refugee Regime." Refugees and Migration Movements in the Middle East. Washington, DC: The Project on Middle East Political Science (POMEPS).

Arar, Rawan. 2017b. "The New Grand Compromise: How Syrian Refugees Changed the Stakes in the Global Refugee Assistance Regime." *Middle East Law and Governance 9* (3): 298–312.

Arreguin-Toft, Ivan. 2005. *How the Weak Win Wars: A Theory of Asymmetric Conflict.* Cambridge: Cambridge University Press.

Askari, Hossein G., and John Thomas Cummings. 1977. "The Middle East and the United States: A Problem of 'Brain Drain.'" *International Journal of Middle East Studies 8* (1): 65–90.

Associated Press. 2015. "Lebanon Restricts Free Entry of Syrian Refugees to Limit Sunni Inflow." *The Guardian,* 5 January 2015, sec. World news. www.theguardian.com/world/2015/jan/05/lebanon-syrian-refugees-sunni-visa-rules. Accessed on 31 January 2021.

Associated Press. 2016. "Turkey Threatens to Back out of EU Migrant Deal over Visas." *France 24,* 19 April 2016. www.france24.com/en/20160419-turkey-migrant-deal-eu-visa-free-travel Accessed on 31 January 2021.

Aswani, Alaa. 2011. *On the State of Egypt: A Novelist's Provocative Reflections.* Translated by Jonathan Wright. Cairo: American University in Cairo Press.

Atef, Maged. 2017. "Egypt and Sudan's Escalating Border Dispute". *Foreign Affairs,* 15 May 2017. www.foreignaffairs.com/articles/egypt/2017-05-15/egypt-and-sudans-escalating-border-dispute. Accessed on 31 January 2021.

Ayubi, Nazih N. M. 1983. "The Egyptian 'Brain Drain': A Multidimensional Problem." *International Journal of Middle East Studies 15* (4): 431–50.

Ayubi, Nazih N. M. 1991. *The State and Public Policies in Egypt Since Sadat.* Political Studies of the Middle East Series, no. 29. Reading: Ithaca Press.

Ayubi, Nazih N. M. 1995. *Over-Stating the Arab State: Politics and Society in the Middle East.* London: I.B. Tauris.

Babiracki, Patryk. 2015. *Soviet Soft Power in Poland Culture and the Making of Stalin's New Empire, 1943–1957.* Chapel Hill, NC: The University of North Carolina Press.

Barnett, Michael N. 1998. *Dialogues in Arab Politics: Negotiations in Regional Order.* New York, NY: Columbia University Press.

Barsalou, Judith Marie. 1985. Foreign Labor in Saudi Arabia: The Creation of a Plural Society. Unpublished PhD dissertation. Columbia University, New York.

Basch, Linda G., Nina Glick Schiller, and Cristina Szanton Blanc. 1994. *Nations Unbound: Transnational Projects, Postcolonial Predicaments, and Deterritorialized Nation-States.* Langhorne, PA: Gordon and Breach.

Baster, James. 1955. "The Economic Problems of Jordan." *International Affairs 31* (1): 26–35.

BBC. 2016a. "Interview with His Majesty King Abdullah II | King Abdullah II Official Website." 2016. https://kingabdullah.jo/en/interviews/interview-his-majesty-king-abdullah-ii-2. Accessed on 31 January 2021.

BBC. 2016b. "Syria Conflict: Jordanians 'at Boiling Point' Over Refugees." *BBC News,* 2 February 2016. www.bbc.co.uk/news/world-middle-east-35462698. Accessed on 31 January 2021.

BBC. 2017. "Afgan Mukhtarli: Did Georgia Help Abduct an Azeri Journalist?," 2017. www.bbc.com/news/world-europe-40606599. Accessed on 31 January 2021.

BBC. 2019. "Egypt Minister Downplays Threat to 'Cut' Critics Abroad," 2019. www.bbc.com/news/world-middle-east-49101954. Accessed on 31 January 2021.

BBC. 2017. "Pakistan PM Orders Afghan Border Crossings to Reopen". 20 March 2017, sec. Asia. www.bbc.co.uk/news/world-asia-39328784. Accessed on 31 January 2021.

Beattie, Kirk J. 2000. *Egypt During the Sadat Years*. New York, NY: Palgrave.

Beau, Nicolas. 1995. *Paris, Capitale Arabe*. Paris: Éditions du Seuil.

Beblawi, Hazem. 1987. "The Rentier State in the Arab World." *Arab Studies Quarterly* 9 (4): 383–98.

Bel-Air, Françoise De. 2016. *Migration Profile: Tunisia. Migration Policy Centre Policy Brief No. 8*. Florence: European University Institute. http://cadmus.eui.eu/bitstream/handle/1814/45144/MPC_PB_2016_08.pdf. Accessed 31 January 2021.

Beling, Willard A., ed. 1968. *The Role of Labor in African Nation-Building*. New York, NY: Praeger.

Berenskoetter, Felix, and Michael J. Williams. 2007. *Power in World Politics*. New York, NY: Routledge.

Betts, Alexander. 2011. "International Cooperation in the Refugee Regime." In: Alexander Betts and Gil Loescher (eds) *Refugees in International Relations*, 53–85. Oxford: Oxford University Press.

Betts, Alexander. 2017. *Protection by Persuasion: International Cooperation in the Refugee Regime*. Ithaca, NY: Cornell University Press.

Betts, Alexander, Ali Ali, and Fulya Memişoğlu. 2017. "Local Politics and the Syrian Refugee Crisis: Exploring Responses in Turkey, Lebanon, and Jordan." Oxford: University of Oxford, Refugee Studies Institute www.rsc.ox.ac.uk/publications/local-politics-and-the-syrian-refugee-crisis-exploring-responses-in-turkey-lebanon-and-jordan. Accessed on 31 January 2021.

Betts, Alexander, and Will Jones. 2016. *Mobilising the Diaspora – How Refugees Challenge Authoritarianism*. Cambridge: Cambridge University Press.

Betts, Alexander, and Gil Loescher (eds). 2011. *Refugees in International Relations*. Oxford: Oxford University Press.

Binder, Leonard. 1958. "The Middle East as a Subordinate International System." *World Politics* 10 (3): 408–29.

Birks, J. S., and C. A. Sinclair. 1980. *International Migration and Development in the Arab Region*. Geneva: International Labour Office.

Black, Ian. 2011. "Gaddafi's Libyan Rule Exposed in Lost Picture Archive." *The Guardian*. www.theguardian.com/world/2011/jul/18/gaddafi-brutal-regime-exposed-lost-archive. Accessed on 31 January 2021.

Boucher, Anna, and Justin Gest. 2014. "Migration Studies at a Crossroads: A Critique of Immigration Regime Typologies." *Migration Studies* 3 (2): 182–98.

Bouras, Nadia. 2013. "Shifting Perspectives on Transnationalism: Analysing Dutch Political Discourse on Moroccan Migrants' Transnational Ties, 1960–2010." *Ethnic and Racial Studies* 36 (7): 1219–31.

Brand, Laurie A. 2002. "States and Their Expatriates: Explaining the Development of Tunisian and Moroccan Emigration-Related Institutions." Working Paper No. 52. La Jolla, CA: University of California, San Diego.

Brand, Laurie A. 2006. *Citizens Abroad: Emigration and the State in the Middle East and North Africa*. Cambridge: Cambridge University Press.

Brand, Laurie A. 2010. "National Narratives and Migration: Discursive Strategies of Inclusion and Exclusion in Jordan and Lebanon." *International Migration Review* 44 (1): 78–110.

Brand, Laurie A. 2011. "Migrants and Sending States: Reflections on the Relationship." CARIM Analytic and Synthetic Notes 2011/32. Florence: European University Institute. http://cadmus.eui.eu/bitstream/handle/1814/16205/CARIM_ASN_2011_32.pdf?sequence=1. Accessed on 31 January 2021.

Brand, Laurie A. 2013. *Jordan's Inter-Arab Relations: The Political Economy of Alliance-Making*. New York, NY: Columbia University Press.

Brand, Laurie A. 2014a. *Official Stories: Politics and National Narratives in Egypt and Algeria*. Stanford, CA: Stanford University Press.

Brand, Laurie A. 2014b. "Arab Uprisings and the Changing Frontiers of Transnational Citizenship: Voting from Abroad in Political Transitions." *Political Geography* 41 (July): 54–63.

Bredeloup, Sylvie, and Olivier Pliez. 2011. "The Libyan Migration Corridor." San Domenico di Fiesole, Italy: European University Institute; Migration Policy Institute. https://cadmus.eui.eu/bitstream/handle/1814/16213/EU-US%20Immigration%20Systems%202011%20-%2003.pdf?sequence=1. Accessed on 10 February 2021.

Brinkerhoff, Jennifer M. 2005. "Digital Diasporas and Governance in Semi-authoritarian States: The Case of the Egyptian Copts." *Public Administration and Development* 25 (3): 193–204.

Brinkerhoff, Jennifer M. 2009. *Digital Diasporas: Identity and Transnational Engagement*. Cambridge: Cambridge University Press.

Brownlee, Jason. 2012. *Democracy Prevention: The Politics of the U.S.-Egyptian Alliance*. New York, NY: Cambridge University Press.

Brubaker, Rogers. 1990. "Frontier Theses: Exit, Voice, and Loyalty in East Germany." *Migration World* 18 (3/4): 12–17.

Brubaker, Rogers. 2005. "The 'Diaspora' Diaspora." *Ethnic and Racial Studies* 28 (1): 1–19.

Buckley, Chris. 2015. "Thailand Deports 2 Dissidents to China, Rights Groups Say." *The New York Times*. www.nytimes.com/2015/11/19/world/asia/thailand-deports-2-dissidents-to-china-rights-groups-say.html?module=inline. Accessed on 31 January 2021.

Buckley, Chris. 2016. "Journalist Who Sought Refuge in Thailand is Said to Return to China." *The New York Times* www.nytimes.com/2016/02/04/world/asia/china-thailand-li-xin.html. Accessed on 31 January 2021.

Byman, Daniel, and Jennifer Lind. 2010. "Pyongyang's Survival Strategy: Tools of Authoritarian Control in North Korea." *International Security* 35 (1): 44–74.

Cammett, Melani Claire, Ishac Diwan, Alan Richards, and John Waterbury. 2015. *A Political Economy of the Middle East*. Fourth Edition. Boulder, CO: Westview Press.

Carothers, Thomas. 2009. "Democracy Assistance: Political vs. Developmental?" *Journal of Democracy* 20 (1): 5–19.

Carroll, Raymond. 1982. *Anwar Sadat*. New York, NY: Franklin Watts.

Castles, Stephen, Mark J. Miller, and Hein De Haas. 2014. *The Age of Migration*. Fifth Edition. New York, NY: Guilford Press.

CBS. 2016. "Jordan in 'Dire Straits' Says King Abdullah." 2016. http://vista.sahafi.jo/art.php?id=8580fd17b4f8f643a7b9500fdb9dc166cf15c687. Accessed on 31 January 2021.

Chalcraft, John. 2010. "Monarchy, Migration and Hegemony in the Arabian Peninsula. Kuwait Programme on Development, Governance and Globalisation in the Gulf

States." LSE Global Governance October 2010 Number 12. https://core.ac.uk/download/pdf/17357.pdf. Accessed on 8 February 2021.

Chami, Ralph, Adolfo Barajas, Thomas Cosimano, Connel Fullenkamp, Michael Gapen, and Peter Montiel. 2008. *Macroeconomic Consequences of Remittances.* Washington, DC: International Monetary Fund.

Choucri, Nazli. 1977. "The New Migration in the Middle East: A Problem for Whom?" *International Migration Review* 11 (4): 421–43.

Choucri, Nazli. 1997. "Demography, Migration, and Security in the Middle East." In Guazzone Laura (ed). *The Middle East in Global Change: The Politics and Economics of Interdependence versus Fragmentation.* London: Palgrave Macmillan.

Choucri, Nazli. 2002. "Migration and Security: Some Key Linkages." *Journal of International Affairs* 56 (1): 97–122.

Cockburn, Harry. 2016. "Turkey Coup: Erdogan bans All Academics from Leaving Country as Government Crackdown Intensifies." *Independent.* www.independent.co.uk/news/world/europe/turkey-coup-erdogan-academics-ban-leaving-country-government-crackdown-latest-a7146591.html. Accessed on 31 January 2021.

Collyer, Michael. 2006. "Transnational Political Participation of Algerians in France. Extra-Territorial Civil Society Versus Transnational Governmentality." *Political Geography* 25 (7): 836–49.

Collyer, Michael. 2012. "Migrants as Strategic Actors in the European Union's Global Approach to Migration and Mobility." *Global Networks* 12 (4): 505–24.

Collyer, Michael. (ed.) 2013. *Emigration Nations: Policies and Ideologies of Emigrant Engagement.* New York, NY: Palgrave Macmillan.

Collyer, Michael. 2016. "Geopolitics as a Migration Governance Strategy: European Union Bilateral Relations with Southern Mediterranean Countries." *Journal of Ethnic and Migration Studies* 42 (4): 606–24.

Cooley, Alexander A., and John Heathershaw. 2017. *Dictators Without Borders: Power and Money in Central Asia.* New Haven, CT: Yale University Press.

Cooley, John K. 1982. *Libyan Sandstorm.* New York, NY: Holt, Rinehart, and Winston.

Cooper, Mark N. 1982. *The Transformation of Egypt.* London: Croom Helm.

Coutin, Susan Bibler. 2007. *Nations of Emigrants - Shifting Boundaries of Citizenship in El Salvador and the United States.* Ithaca, NY: Cornell University Press.

Cremeans, Charles Davis. 1963. *The Arabs and the World; Nasser's Arab Nationalist Policy.* New York, NY: Praeger.

Dalmasso, Emanuela, Adele Del Sordi, Marlies Glasius, et al. 2017. "Intervention: Extraterritorial Authoritarian Power." *Political Geography* 64 (May) 95–104.

Davidson, Christopher M. 2008. *Dubai: The Vulnerability of Success.* New York, NY: Columbia University Press.

Davis, Christina L. 2009. "Linkage Diplomacy: Economic and Security Bargaining in the Anglo-Japanese Alliance, 1902–23." *International Security* 33 (3): 143–79.

Dawisha, A. I. 1975. "Intervention in the Yemen: An Analysis of Egyptian Perceptions and Policies." *Middle East Journal* 29 (1): 47–63.

De Bel-Air, Francoise. 2016. "Migration Profile: Jordan." Florence, Italy: European University Institute. https://cadmus.eui.eu/bitstream/handle/1814/44065/MPC_PB_201606.pdf?sequence=1&isAllowed=y. Accessed on 31 January 2021.

De Genova, Nicholas, and Nathalie Peutz (eds) 2010. *The Deportation Regime: Sovereignty, Space, and the Freedom of Movement.* Durham, NC: Duke University Press.

De Haas, Hein. 2007. *Between Courting and Controlling, the Moroccan State and 'Its' Emigrants*. Oxford: Centre on Migration, Policy and Society, Oxford University.

Dekmejian, R. Hrair. 1971. *Egypt Under Nasir; A Study in Political Dynamics*. Albany, NY: State University of New York Press.

Délano, Alexandra. 2011. *Mexico and Its Diaspora in the United States: Policies of Emigration Since 1848*. New York, NY: Cambridge University Press.

Department of Labor. 1973. *Annual Report of the Immigration & Naturalization Service*. Washington, DC: US Immigration & Naturalisation Service. http://catalog.hathitrust.org/Record/000546059. Accessed on 31 January 2021.

Dessouki, Ali E. Hillal. 1982. "The Shift in Egypt's Migration Policy: 1952–1978". *Middle Eastern Studies* 18 (1): 53–68.

Dib, George. 1978. "Migration and Naturalization Laws in Egypt, Lebanon, Syria, Jordan, Kuwait, and the United Arab Emirates. Part I: Migration Laws." *Population Bulletin of the Economic Commission for Western Asia* 15: 33–62.

Dowding, Keith, Peter John, Thanos Mergoupis, and Mark Vugt. 2000. "Exit, Voice and Loyalty: Analytic and Empirical Developments." *European Journal of Political Research* 37 (4): 469–95.

Dowty, Alan. 1989. *Closed Borders: The Contemporary Assault on Freedom of Movement*. New Haven, CT: Yale University Press.

Doyle, David. 2015. "Remittances and Social Spending." *American Political Science Review* 109 (4): 785–802.

Ehteshami, Anoushiravan. 2003. "Reform from Above: The Politics of Participation in the Oil Monarchies." *International Affairs* 79 (1): 53–75.

El-Solh, Camillia F. 1985. Egyptian Migrant Peasants in Iraq. A Case-Study of the Settlement Community in Khalsa. Unpublished PhD dissertation. University of Oxford.

Ellermann, A. (2009). *States Against Migrants: Deportation in Germany and the United States*. Cambridge: Cambridge University Press.

Ellouk, Bernard. 2017. "One Man's Curse Is Another Man's Blessing: How Egyptian Guest Labour Suffers from Syria Crisis." *The Jordan Times*, 23 August 2017. www.jordantimes.com/news/local/one-man%E2%80%99s-curse-another-man%E2%80%99s-blessing-how-egyptian-guest-labour-suffers-syria-crisis. Accessed on 31 January 2021.

Erdmann, Gero, André Bank, Bert Hoffmann, and Thomas Richter. 2013. "International Cooperation of Authoritarian Regimes: Toward a Conceptual Framework." GIGA Working Paper Series 229. GIGA German Institute of Global and Area Studies.

Escribà-Folch, Abel, Covadonga Meseguer, and Joseph Wright. 2015. "Remittances and Democratization." *International Studies Quarterly* 59 (3): 571–86.

Escribà-Folch, Abel, Covadonga Meseguer, and Joseph Wright. 2018. "Remittances and Protest in Dictatorships." *American Journal of Political Science* 62 (4): 889–904.

European Commission. 2017. "Communication from the Commission to the European Parliament and the Council First Annual Report on the Facility for Refugees in Turkey." https://ec.europa.eu/neighbourhood-enlargement/sites/near/files/170302_facility_for_refugees_in_turkey_first_annual_report.pdf. Accessed on 31 January 2021.

European Council. 2016a. "Refugee Facility for Turkey: Member States Agree on Details of Financing – Consilium." www.consilium.europa.eu/en/press/press-releases/2016/02/03/refugee-facility-for-turkey/#. Accessed on 31 January 2021.

European Council. 2016b. "EU-Turkey Statement." March 18, 2016. www.consilium. europa.eu/en/press/press-releases/2016/03/18-eu-turkey-statement/.

Fargues, Philippe. 2004. "Arab Migration to Europe: Trends and Policies." *The International Migration Review* 38 (4): 1348–71.

Fargues, Philippe. 2014. "The Fuzzy Lines of International Migration. A Critical Assessment of Definitions and Estimates in the Arab Countries. A Critical Assessment of Definitions and Estimates in the Arab Countries (June 1, 2014)." Florence, Italy: European University Institute, Robert Schuman Centre for Advanced Studies Research Paper No. RSCAS 71.

Farouk-Sluglett, M., and P. Sluglett. 2001. *Iraq Since 1958: From Revolution to Dictatorship*. London: I.B. Tauris.

Fawat, Ibrahim. 1985. "Libya: Economic Crisis, Political Expulsions." *AfricAsia* 22 (1985): 32–43

Feiler, Gil. 1986. "The Number of Egyptian Workers in the Arab Oil Countries, 1974–1983: A Critical Discussion." Tel Aviv: The Dayan Center.

Feiler, Gil. 1991. "Migration and Recession: Arab Labor Mobility in the Middle East, 1982–89." *Population and Development Review* 17 (1): 134–55.

Feiler, Gil. 2003. *Economic Relations Between Egypt and the Gulf Oil States, 1967–2000: Petro-Wealth and Patterns of Influence*. Brighton: Sussex Academic Press.

Fernández-Molina, Irene, and Miguel Hernando De Larramendi. 2020. "Migration diplomacy in a de facto destination country: Morocco's new intermestic migration policy and international socialization by/with the EU." *Mediterranean Politics*. DOI: 10.1080/13629395.2020.1758449

Ferris, Jesse. 2013. *Nasser's Gamble: How Intervention in Yemen Caused the Six-Day War and the Decline of Egyptian Power*. Princeton, NJ: Princeton University Press.

Fillieule, Olivier, and Isabelle Sommier. 2018. *Marseille Années 68*. Paris: Presses de Sciences Po.

Financial Times. 2017. "EU Accord Opens Door for Jordan," May 30, 2017. www.ft.com/content/ccd2ee20-bad1–11e6–8b45-b8b81dd5d080. Accessed on 31 January 2021.

Fitzgerald, David. 2006. "Inside the Sending State: The Politics of Mexican Emigration Control." *International Migration Review* 40 (2): 259–93.

Fitzgerald, David. 2009. *A Nation of Emigrants: How Mexico Manages Its Migration*. Berkeley, CA: University of California Press.

Frank, Andre Gunder. 1966. "The Development of Underdevelopment." *Monthly Review* 18 (4): 17–31.

Frowd, Philippe M. 2020. "Producing the 'Transit' Migration State: International Security Intervention in Niger." *Third World Quarterly* 41 (2): 340–58.

Gall, Carlotta. 2019. "Erdoğan Goes His Own Way as Turkish Distrust with U.S. Grows." *The New York Times*, 16 July 2019. www.nytimes.com/2019/07/16/ world/asia/turkey-Erdoğan-missile-trump.html. Accessed on 31 January 2021.

Gamlen, Alan. 2008. "The Emigration State and the Modern Geopolitical Imagination." *Political Geography* 27 (8): 840–56.

Gamlen, Alan. 2014. "Diaspora Institutions and Diaspora Governance." *International Migration Review* 48 (September): S180–217.

Gause, F. Gregory. 1999. "Systemic Approaches to Middle East International Relations." *International Studies Review* 1 (1): 11–31.

Geddes, Andrew, and Mehari Taddele Maru. 2020. "Localising Migration Diplomacy in Africa? Ethiopia in its Regional and International Setting." EUI Working

Papers 2020/50. https://cadmus.eui.eu/bitstream/handle/1814/68384/RSCAS%20 2020_50.pdf?sequence=1&isAllowed=y. Accessed on 31 January 2021.

Geisser, Vincent. 2012. "Quelle Révolution Pour Les Binationaux? Le Rôle des FrancoTunisiens dans La Chute de la Dictature et dans la Transition Politique." *Migrations Société* 24 (143): 155–78.

Gerges, Fawaz A. 1994. *The Superpowers and the Middle East: Regional and International Politics, 1955–1967*. Boulder, CO: Westview Press.

Gerges, Fawaz A. 2012. *Obama and the Middle East: The End of America's Moment?* New York, NY: Palgrave Macmillan.

Gilbar, Gad G. 1997. *Population Dilemmas in the Middle East: Essays in Political Demography and Economy*. London: Frank Cass.

Gillette, Alain, and Abdelmalek Sayad. 1984. *L'immigration Algérienne en France*. Paris: Éditions entente.

Glasser, Susan B. 2017. "Saad Hariri: The Full Transcript." *Politico*, 31 July 2017. www.politico.com/magazine/story/2017/07/31/saad-hariri-the-full-transcript-215439. Accessed on 31 January 2021.

Goddard, Stacie E., and Daniel H. Nexon. 2016. "The Dynamics of Global Power Politics: A Framework for Analysis." *Journal of Global Security Studies* 1 (1): 4–18.

Gomaa, Ahmed. 2019. "Kuwait Extradites Accused Muslim Brotherhood Cell to Egypt." *Al Monitor*, 4 August 2019. www.al-monitor.com/pulse/originals/2019/07/ kuwait-deportation-wanted-brotherhood-by-egypt-judiciary.html. Accessed on 31 January 2021.

Gordenker, Leon. 1987. *Refugees in International Politics*. London: Croom Helm.

Government of Jordan. 2016. "The Jordan Compact: A New Holistic Approach between the Hashemite Kingdom of Jordan and the International Community to Deal with the Syrian Refugee Crisis." http://reliefweb.int/report/jordan/jordan-compact-new-holistic-approach-between-hashemite-kingdom-jordan-and. Accessed on 31 January 2021.

Greenhill, Kelly M. 2002. "Engineered Migration and the Use of Refugees as Political Weapons: A Case Study of the 1994 Cuban Balseros Crisis." *International Migration* 40 (4): 39–74.

Greenhill, Kelly M. 2003. "The Use of Refugees as Political and Military Weapons in the Kosovo Conflict." In: Raju GC Thomas (ed.) *Yugoslavia Unraveled: Sovereignty, Self-Determination, Intervention*. Lanham, MD: Lexington Books.

Greenhill, Kelly M. 2010. *Weapons of Mass Migration – Forced Displacement, Coercion, and Foreign Policy*. Ithaca, NY: Cornell University Press.

Greenhill, Kelly M. 2016. "Open Arms Behind Barred Doors: Fear, Hypocrisy and Policy Schizophrenia in the European Migration Crisis." *European Law Journal* 22 (3): 317–32.

Grillo, R. D. 2006. *Ideologies and Institutions in Urban France: The Representation of Immigrants*. Cambridge: Cambridge University Press.

Guevarra, Anna Romina. 2009. *Marketing Dreams, Manufacturing Heroes: The Transnational Labor Brokering of Filipino Workers*. New Brunswick, NJ: Rutgers University Press.

Haas, Ernst B. 1980. "Why Collaborate? Issue-Linkage and International Regimes." *World Politics* 32 (03): 357–405.

Haddad, Yvonne Y. 1987. "Islamic 'Awakening' in Egypt". *Arab Studies Quarterly* 9 (3): 234–59.

Hahn, Peter L. 1991. *The United States, Great Britain, and Egypt, 1945–1956: Strategy and Diplomacy in the Early Cold War*. Chapel Hill, NC: University of North Carolina Press.

Hanna, Michael Wahid. 2013. "Hanna, 2013 – With Friends Like These, Coptic Activism in the Diaspora." *Middle East Report* 43 (Summer 2013): 28–31.

Hansen, R., J. Koehler, and J. Money. (eds). 2011. *Migration, Nation States, and International Cooperation*. New York, NY: Routledge.

Harrell-Bond, Barbara. "Camps: Literature Review." *Forced Migration Review* 2 (August 1998): 22–23.

Hashemite Kingdom of Jordan, National Planning Council. n.d. *Five Year Plan for Economic and Social Development 1981–1985*. Amman: Royal Scientific Society Press

Hawley, Donald. 2007. *The Emirates: Witness to a Metamorphosis*. Norwich: Michael Russell.

Haykal, Mohammed Hasaneyn. 1956. "An African Policy for Egypt." *The Egyptian Economic & Political Review* August: 21–24.

Haykal, Mohammed Hasaneyn. 1973. *The Cairo Documents; the Inside Story of Nasser and His Relationship with World Leaders, Rebels, and Statesmen*. Garden City, NY: Doubleday.

Haykal, Mohammed Hasaneyn. 1978. *Sphinx and Commissar: The Rise and Fall of Soviet Influence in the Arab World*. London: Collins.

Haykal, Mohammed Hasaneyn. 1983. *Kharīf Al-Ghaḍab: Qiṣṣat Bidāyat Wa-Nihāyat ʿaṣr Anwar Al-Sādāt*. Al-Ṭabʿah 9. Beirut: Sharikat al-Maṭbūʿāt.

Hear, Nicholas Van. 1998. *New Diasporas: The Mass Exodus, Dispersal and Regrouping of Migrant Communities*. London: University College London Press.

Hearst, David. 2018. "Saudi Journalist Jamal Khashoggi Criticised the Regime – and Paid with His Life." *The Guardian*, 8 October 2018. www.theguardian.com/commentisfree/2018/oct/08/saudi-journalist-jamal-khashoggi-istanbul. Accessed on 31 January 2021.

Heisler, Barbara Schmitter. 1985. "Sending Countries and The Politics of Emigration and Destination." *International Migration Review* 19 (3): 469–84.

Henderson, Simon. 2015. *Jordan's Energy Supply Options: The Prospect of Gas Imports from Israel*. Washington, DC: The German Marshall Fund of the United States. file:///C:/Users/Noel%20McPherson/Downloads/Henderson_JordansEnergySupply_Oct15_web.pdf. Accessed on 11 February 2021.

Heydemann, Steven, and Reinoud Leenders. 2011. "Authoritarian Learning and Authoritarian Resilience: Regime Responses to the 'Arab Awakening.'" *Globalizations* 8 (5): 647–53.

Hinnebusch, Raymond A. 1985. *Egyptian Politics Under Sadat: The Post-Populist Development of the Authoritarian-Modernizing State*. Cambridge: Cambridge University Press.

Hinnebusch, Raymond A. 2003. *The International Politics of the Middle East*. Manchester: Manchester University Press.

Hirschman, Albert O. 1970. *Exit, Voice, and Loyalty: Responses to Decline in Firms, Organizations, and States*. Cambridge, MA: Harvard University Press.

Hirschman, Albert O. 1993. "Exit, Voice, and the Fate of the German Democratic Republic: An Essay in Conceptual History." *World Politics* 45 (2): 173–202.

Hirst, David, and Irene Beeson. 1981. *Sadat*. London: Faber and Faber.

Hirt, Nicole, and Abdulkader Saleh Mohammad. 2017. "By Way of Patriotism, Coercion, or Instrumentalization: How the Eritrean Regime Makes Use of the Diaspora to Stabilize Its Rule." *Globalizations* 15 (2): 232–47.

Hollifield, James Frank. 1992. *Immigrants, Markets, and States: The Political Economy of Postwar Europe*. Cambridge, MA: Harvard University Press.

Hollifield, James Frank. 2004. "The Emerging Migration State." *International Migration Review* 38 (3): 885–912.

Hollifield, James Frank. 2012. "Migration and International Relations." In: Marc R. Rosenblum and Daniel J. Tichenor (eds) *The Oxford Handbook of The Politics of International Migration*, 345–82. Oxford: Oxford University Press.

Hollifield, James F., Philip Martin, and Pia Orrenius (eds). 2014. *Controlling Immigration: A Global Perspective*. Stanford, CA: Stanford University Press.

Hopwood, Derek. 1991. *Egypt, Politics and Society, 1945–1990*. Third Edition. London: HarperCollins Academic.

Horne, Felix. 2014. "How Ethiopia Spies on Its Diaspora in Europe." Human Rights Watch. www.hrw.org/news/2014/04/01/how-ethiopia-spies-its-diaspora-europe. Accessed on 31 January 2021.

Hourani, Albert Habib C N – DS37.7 .H67 1991. 2013. *A History of the Arab Peoples*. London: Faber & Faber.

Hufbauer, Gary Clyde, Jeffrey J. Schott, and Kimberly Ann Elliott. 1990. *Economic Sanctions Reconsidered: History and Current Policy*. Washington, DC: Peterson Institute.

Human Rights Watch. 2012. "Letter to Lebanese Officials Regarding Deportation of Syrians." www.hrw.org/news/2012/08/04/letter-lebanese-officials-regarding-deportation-syrians. Accessed on 31 January 2021.

Human Rights Watch. 2014. "Not Welcome: Jordan's Treatment of Palestinians Escaping Syria." www.hrw.org/report/2014/08/07/not-welcome/jordans-treatment-palestinians-escaping-syria. Accessed on 31 January 2021.

Human Rights Watch. 2016. "Lebanon: Residency Rules Put Syrians at Risk." www.hrw.org/news/2016/01/12/lebanon-residency-rules-put-syrians-risk. Accessed on 31 January 2021.

Human Rights Watch. 2019. Egypt: Deported Dissidents Missing. www.hrw.org/news/2019/04/04/egypt-deported-dissidents-missing. Accessed on 31 January 2021.

Huysmans, Jef. 2000. "The European Union and the Securitization of Migration." *JCMS: Journal of Common Market Studies* 38 (5): 751–77.

Ibrahim, Saad Eddin. 1982. *The New Arab Social Order: A Study of the Social Impact of Oil Wealth*. Westview's Special Studies on the Middle East. Boulder, CO: Westview Press.

Ibrahim, Sunallah. 2001. *Zaat*. Cairo: The American University in Cairo Press.

İçduygu, Ahmet, and Damla B. Aksel. 2014. "Two-to-Tango in Migration Diplomacy: Negotiating Readmission Agreement between the Eu and Turkey." *European Journal of Migration and Law* 16 (3): 337–63.

Iskander, Natasha. 2010. *Creative State: Forty Years of Migration and Development Policy in Morocco and Mexico*. Ithaca, NY: Cornell University Press.

Ippolito, Francesca, and Seline Trevisanut. 2015. *Migration in the Mediterranean, Mechanisms of International Cooperation*. Cambridge: Cambridge University Press.

James, Laura M. 2006. *Nasser at War: Arab Images of the Enemy*. Basingstoke: Palgrave Macmillan.

Jankowski, James P. 2002. *Nasser's Egypt, Arab Nationalism, and the United Arab Republic*. Boulder: Lynne Rienner Publishers.

Janmyr, Maja. 2018. "UNHCR and the Syrian Refugee Response: Negotiating Status and Registration in Lebanon." *The International Journal of Human Rights* 22 (3): 393–419.

Kaldor, Mary. 2013. *New and Old Wars: Organised Violence in a Global Era*. New York, NY: John Wiley & Sons.

Kamel, Mohamed Ibrahim. 1986. *The Camp David Accords: A Testimony*. London: KPI Limited.

Kandil, Hazem. 2015. *Inside the Brotherhood*. Cambridge: Polity Press.

Kapiszewski, Andrzej. 2001. *Nationals and Expatriates: Population and Labour Dilemmas of the Gulf Cooperation Council States*. Reading: Ithaca Press.

Kapiszewski, Andrzej. 2006a. "Arab Versus Asian Migrant Workers in the GCC Countries." RPRT. *United Nations Expert Group Meeting on International Migration and Development in the Arab Region*. Beirut.

Kapiszewski, D., L. MacLean, and B. Read. 2015. *Field Research in Political Science: Practices and Principles* (Strategies for Social Inquiry). Cambridge: Cambridge University Press.

Kapur, Devesh. 2010. *Diaspora, Development, and Democracy: The Domestic Impact of International Migration from India*. Princeton, NJ: Princeton University Press.

Karas, Tania. 2015. "Why Migrants Are Going to Great Lengths to Avoid Cyprus." *Kathimerini*, September 28, 2015. www.ekathimerini.com/201968/article/ekathimerini/news/why-migrants-are-going-to-great-lengths-to-avoid-cyprus. Accessed on 31 January 2021.

Kays, Doreen. 1984. *Frogs and Scorpions: Egypt, Sadat and the Media*. London: Frederick Muller.

Keely, Charles B., and Bassam Saket. 1984. "Jordanian Migrant Workers in the Arab Region: A Case Study of Consequences for Labor Supplying Countries." *The Middle East Journal* 38 (4): 685–98.

Kelemen, Michele. 2011. "Syrian Exiles Fear Long Reach of Secret Police." National Public Radio. www.npr.org/2011/10/03/141014954/syrian-exiles-fear-long-reach-of-secret-police.

Keohane, Robert O. 1984. *After Hegemony: Cooperation and Discord in the World Political Economy*. Princeton, NJ: Princeton University Press.

Keohane, Robert Owen, and Joseph S. Nye. 1987. "Power and Interdependence Revisited." *International Organization* 41 (4): 725–53.

Kerr, Malcolm H. 1978. *The Arab Cold War: Gamal 'abd Al-Nasir and His Rivals, 1958–1970*. Third Edition. London: Oxford University Press.

Kerr, Malcolm H., and al-Sayyid Yasin (eds). 1982. *Rich and Poor States in the Middle East: Egypt and the New Arab Order*. Boulder, CO: Westview Press.

Khater, Akram Fouad. 2001. *Inventing Home: Emigration, Gender, and the Middle Class in Lebanon, 1870–1920*. Berkeley, CA: University of California Press.

King, Charles, and Neil J Melvin. 2006. "Diaspora Politics: Ethnic Linkages, Foreign Policy, and Security in Eurasia." *International Security* 24 (3): 108–38.

Kissinger, Henry. 1982. *Years of Upheaval*. Boston, MA: Little, Brown.

Koinova, Maria. 2009. "Diasporas and Democratization in the Post-Communist World." *Communist and Post-Communist Studies* 42 (1): 41–64.

Koinova, Maria. 2012. "Autonomy and Positionality in Diaspora Politics." *International Political Sociology* 6 (1): 99–103.

Koinova, Maria. 2014. "Why Do Conflict-Generated Diasporas Pursue Sovereignty-Based Claims Through State-Based or Transnational Channels? Armenian, Albanian and Palestinian Diasporas in the UK Compared." *European Journal of International Relations* 20 (4): 1043–71.

Koinova, Maria, and Gerasimos Tsourapas. 2018. "How do countries of origin engage migrants and diasporas? Multiple actors and comparative perspectives." *International Political Science Review* 39 (3): 311–21.

Korany, Bahgat. 1986. "Political Petrolism and Contemporary Arab Politics, 1967–1983". *Journal of Asian and African Studies* 21 (1–2): 66–80.

Korany, Bahgat, and Ali E. Hillal Dessouki (eds). 2008. *The Foreign Policies of Arab States: The Challenge of Globalization.* Third Edition. Cairo: American University in Cairo Press.

Kosinski, Leszek A. 1978. "Yugoslavia and International Migration." *Canadian Slavonic Papers/Revue Canadienne Des Slavistes* 20 (3): 314–38.

Krasner, Stephen D. 1999. *Sovereignty: Organized Hypocrisy.* Princeton, NJ: Princeton University Press.

Kreinin, Mordechai E. 1964. *Israel and Africa; a Study in Technical Cooperation.* New York, NY: Praeger.

Laurence, Jonathan. 2012. *The Emancipation of Europe's Muslims: The State's Role in Minority Integration.* Princeton, NJ: Princeton University Press.

Lesch, Ann Mosely. 1986. "Egyptian Labor Migration: Economic Trends and Government Policies." *American Universities Field Staff Report*, Africa, No. 38.

Levitsky, Steven R., and Lucan A. Way. 2011. *Competitive Authoritarianism: Hybrid Regimes After the Cold War.* New York, NY: Cambridge University Press.

Levitt, Peggy. 1998. "Social Remittances: Migration Driven Local-Level Forms of Cultural Diffusion." *International Migration Review* 32 (4): 926–48.

Levitt, Peggy, and Rafael De la Dehesa. 2003. "Transnational Migration and the Redefinition of the State: Variations and Explanations." *Ethnic and Racial Studies* 26 (4): 587–611.

Lindsay, James M. 1986. "Trade Sanctions as Policy Instruments: A Re-Examination." *International Studies Quarterly* 30 (2): 153–73.

Lippman, Thomas W. 1989. *Egypt After Nasser: Sadat, Peace, and the Mirage of Prosperity.* New York, NY: Paragon House.

Lischer, Sarah Kenyon. 2003. "Collateral Damage: Humanitarian Assistance as a Cause of Conflict." *International Security* 28 (1): 79–109.

Lischer, Sarah Kenyon. 2015. *Dangerous Sanctuaries: Refugee Camps, Civil War, and the Dilemmas of Humanitarian Aid.* Ithaca, NY: Cornell University Press.

Loescher, Gil. 1992. *Refugee Movements and International Security.* London: Brassey's for the International Institute for Strategic Studies.

Loescher, Gil. 1996. *Beyond Charity: International Cooperation and the Global Refugee Crisis: A Twentieth Century Fund Book.* New York, NY and Oxford: Oxford University Press.

Loescher, Gil, and John A. Scanlan. 1986. *Calculated Kindness.* New York, NY: The Free Press.

Mack, Andrew. 1975. "Why Big Nations Lose Small Wars: The Politics of Asymmetric Conflict." *World Politics* 27 (2): 175–200.

Maghur, Azza. 2010. "Highly-Skilled Migration (Libya) - Legal Aspects." CARIM Analytic and Synthetic Notes 2010/31. Florence, Italy: European University Institute. http://cadmus.eui.eu/bitstream/handle/1814/13685/CARIM_ASN_2010_31.pdf?sequence=1&isAllowed=y. Accessed 31 January 2021.

Mahdavy, Hussein. 1970. "The Patterns and Problems of Economic Development in Rentier States: The Case of Iran." In: M. A. Cook (ed.) *Studies in the Economic History of the Middle East*, 428–67. Oxford: Oxford University Press.

Malit, Froilan T. Jr., and Gerasimos Tsourapas. 2021. "Migration Diplomacy in the Gulf – Non-State Actors, Cross-Border Mobility, and the United Arab Emirates." *Journal of Ethnic and Migration Studies.* DOI: 10.1080/1369183X.2021.1878875.

Mann, Michael. 2004. *Fascists.* Cambridge: Cambridge University Press.

Margheritis, Ana. 2015. *Migration Governance Across Regions: State-Diaspora Relations in the Latin America-Southern Europe Corridor.* New York, NY: Taylor & Francis Limited.

Markowitz, Fran, and Anders H. Stefansson (eds). 2004. "Homecomings to the Future: From Diasporic Mythographies to Social Projects of Return." In: *Homecomings: Unsettling Paths of Return,* 2–20. Lanham: Lexington Books.

Martin, Lisa L. 1992. "Interests, Power, and Multilateralism." *International Organization* 46 (4): 765–92.

Martin, Lisa L. 1993. *Coercive Cooperation: Explaining Multilateral Economic Sanctions.* Princeton, NJ: Princeton University Press.

Martin, Philip L. 1991. *The Unfinished Story: Turkish Labour Migration to Western Europe: With Special Reference to the Federal Republic of Germany.* Geneva: International Labour Organization.

Massey, Douglas S. 1999. "International Migration at the Dawn of the Twenty-First Century: The Role of the State." *Population and Development Review* 25 (2): 303–22.

Matthews, Roderic D., and Matta Akrawi. 1949. *Education in Arab Countries of the Near East: Egypt, Iraq, Palestine, Transjordan, Syria, Lebanon.* Washington, DC: American Council on Education.

McDermott, Anthony. 1988. *Egypt from Nasser to Mubarak: A Flawed Revolution.* London: Routledge.

McDougall, James. 2017. *A History of Algeria.* Cambridge: Cambridge University Press.

Mearsheimer, John J., and Stephen M. Walt. 2008. *The Israel Lobby and US Foreign Policy.* London: Penguin.

Merkel, Wolfgang. 2010. "Are Dictatorships Returning? Revisiting the 'Democratic Rollback' Hypothesis." *Contemporary Politics* 16 (1): 17–31.

Meseguer, Covadonga, and Katrina Burgess. 2014. "International Migration and Home Country Politics." *Studies in Comparative International Development* 49 (1): 1–12.

Messiha, Suzanne A. 1980. *Export of Egyptian School Teachers to Saudi Arabia and Kuwait: A Cost-Benefit Analysis.* Cairo Papers in Social Science, Vol. 3. Cairo: American University in Cairo.

Messina, Anthony M., and Gallya Lahav. 2006. *The Migration Reader: Exploring Politics and Policies.* London: Lynne Rienner Publishers.

Messina, Claire. 1994. "From Migrants to Refugees: Russian, Soviet and Post-Soviet Migration." *International Journal of Refugee Law* 6 (4): 620–35.

Michaelsen, Marcus. 2018. "Exit and Voice in a Digital Age: Iran's Exiled Activists and the Authoritarian State." *Globalizations* 15 (2): 248–64.

Michaelson, Ruth. 2016. "Arrest of leading Egyptian feminist Azza Soliman sparks anger." *The Guardian.* www.theguardian.com/world/2016/dec/07/womens-rights-activist-azza-soliman-arrested-in-egypt. Accessed on 31 January 2021.

Miller, Michael K., and Margaret E. Peters. 2018. "Restraining the Huddled Masses: Migration Policy and Autocratic Survival." *British Journal of Political Science* 50 (2): 403–33.

Misnad, Sheikha. 1985. *The Development of Modern Education in the Gulf*. London: Ithaca Press.

Mitchell, Richard P. 1969. *The Society of the Muslim Brothers*. London: Oxford University Press.

Miyashita, Akitoshi. 2003. *Limits to Power: Asymmetric Dependence and Japanese Foreign Aid Policy*. Oxford: Lexington Books.

Moravcsik, Andrew. 1998. *The Choice for Europe: Social Purpose and State Power from Messina to Maastricht*. Ithaca, NY: Cornell University Press.

Morawska, Ewa. 2003. "Disciplinary Agendas and Analytic Strategies of Research on Immigrant Transnationalism: Challenges of Interdisciplinary Knowledge." *International Migration Review* 37 (3): 611–40.

Mosley, Layna, and David A. Singer. 2015. "Migration, Labor, and the International Political Economy." *Annual Review of Political Science* 18 (1): 283–301. https://doi.org/10.1146/annurev-polisci-020614-094809.

Moss, Dana M. 2016a. "Diaspora Mobilization for Western Military Intervention During the Arab Spring." *Journal of Immigrant & Refugee Studies* 14 (3): 277–97.

Moss, Dana M. 2016b. "Transnational Repression, Diaspora Mobilization, and the Case of the Arab Spring." *Social Problems* 63 (4): 480–98.

Mufti, Malik. 2012. "The United States and Nasserist Pan-Arabism." In: David W. Lesch and Mark L. Haas (eds) *The Middle East and the United States: History, Politics, and Ideologies*, Fifth Edition. Boulder CO: Westview Press.

Müller-Funk, Lea. 2016. "Diaspora Mobilizations in the Egyptian (Post)Revolutionary Process: Comparing Transnational Political Participation in Paris and Vienna." *Journal of Immigrant & Refugee Studies* 14 (3): 353–70.

Munz, Rainer, and Myron Weiner, eds. 1997. *Migrants, Refugees, and Foreign Policy – U.S. and German Policies towards Countries of Origin*. Oxford: Berghahn Books.

Nasser, Gamal Abdel. 1966. *On Africa*. Cairo: Ministry of National Guidance, Information Administration.

National Science Foundation. 1973. *Immigrant Scientists and Engineers in the United States; A Study of Characteristics and Attitudes*. Survey of Science Resources Series. Washington, DC: National Science Foundation.

Natter, Katharina. 2014. "Fifty Years of Maghreb Emigration." International Migration Institute Working Papers. Oxford.

Natter, Katharina. 2015. "Revolution and Political Transition in Tunisia: A Migration Game Changer?" Washington, DC: Migration Policy Institute. www.migrationpolicy.org/article/revolution-and-political-transition-tunisia-migration-game-changer. Accessed on 31 January 2021.

Natter, Katharina. 2018. "Rethinking Immigration Policy Theory Beyond 'Western Liberal Democracies.'" *Comparative Migration Studies* 6 (1): 4.

Naujoks, Daniel. 2013. *Migration, Citizenship, and Development: Diasporic Membership Policies and Overseas Indians in the United States*. New Delhi: Oxford University Press.

Norman, Kelsey P. 2018. "Inclusion, Exclusion or Indifference? Redefining Migrant and Refugee Host State Engagement Options in Mediterranean 'Transit' Countries." *Journal of Ethnic and Migration Studies* 45 (1): 42–60.

Norman, Kelsey P. 2020. "Migration Diplomacy and Policy Liberalization in Morocco and Turkey." *International Migration Review* 54 (4): 1158–83.

Nyíri, Pál. 2013. "Chinese migration, 1949 to present". In: I. Ness (ed.) *The Encyclopedia of Global Human Migration*. Oxford and New York, NY: Wiley-Blackwell. https://doi.org/10.1002/9781444351071.wbeghm133.

O'Ballance, Edgar. 1971. *The War in the Yemen*. London: Faber.

Obdeijn, Herman, Paolo De Mas, and Phillip Hermans. 2012. *Geschiedenis van Marokko*. Amsterdam: Bulaaq.

Obeidi, Amal. 1999. *Political Culture in Libya*. Richmond: Curzon Press.

Okruhlik, Gwenn, and Patrick Conge. 1997. "National Autonomy, Labor Migration and Political Crisis: Yemen and Saudi Arabia." *Middle East Journal* 51 (4): 554–65.

Ong, Aihwa. 1996. "Cultural Citizenship as Subject-Making: Immigrants Negotiate Racial and Cultural Boundaries in the United States [and Comments and Reply]". *Current Anthropology* 37 (5): 737–62.

Orrenius, Pia, and Madeline Zavodny. 2012. "Economic Effects of Migration: Receiving States", In: Marc R. Rosenblum and Daniel J. Tichenor (eds) *The Oxford Handbook of The Politics of International Migration*. Oxford: Oxford University Press.

Østergaard-Nielsen, Eva (ed.) 2003a. *International Migration and Sending Countries: Perceptions, Policies and Transnational Relations*. Basingstoke: Palgrave Macmillan.

Østergaard-Nielsen, Eva. 2003b. *Transnational Politics: Turks and Kurds in Germany*. London and New York: Routledge.

Østergaard-Nielsen, Eva. 2003c. "Turkey and the 'Euro Turks': Overseas Nationals as an Ambiguous Asset." In: Eva Østergaard-Nielsen (ed.) *International Migration and Sending Countries: Perceptions, Policies and Transnational Relations*, 77–98. Basingstoke: Palgrave Macmillan.

Oweiss, I. M. 1980. "Migration of Egyptians". *L'Egypte Contemporaine* 71 (381): 201–12.

Oxfam. 2002. "Adrift in the Pacific: The Implications of Australia's Pacific Refugee Solution." www.oxfam.org.au:80/campaigns/refugees/pacificsolution/adriftinthepacific_OCAA.pdf. Accessed on 31 January 2021.

Oye, Kenneth A. 1979. *Eagle Entangled: US Foreign Policy in a Complex World*. Boston, MA and Harlow: Addison-Wesley Longman Ltd.

Oyen, Meredith. 2015. *The Diplomacy of Migration: Transnational Lives and the Making of U.S.-Chinese Relations in the Cold War*. The United States in the World. Ithaca, NY: Cornell University Press.

Paoletti, Emanuela. 2010. *The Migration of Power and North-South Inequalities: The Case of Italy and Libya*. London: Springer.

Paoletti, Emanuela. 2011. "Migration and Foreign Policy: The Case of Libya." *The Journal of North African Studies* 16 (2): 215–31.

Pargeter, Alison. 2012. *Libya: The Rise and Fall of Qaddafi*. New Haven, CT: Yale University Press.

Paul, Thazha Varkey. 1994. *Asymmetric Conflicts: War Initiation by Weaker Powers*. Cambridge: Cambridge University Press.

Pearlman, Wendy. 2013. "Emigration and Power – A Study of Sects in Lebanon, 1860–2010." *Politics & Society* 41 (1): 103–33.

Peretz, Pauline. 2015. *Let My People Go: The Transnational Politics of Soviet Jewish Emigration During the Cold War*. Vol. 1. London: Routledge.

Peteet, Julie. 2011. "Cartographic Violence, Displacement and Refugee Camps: Palestine and Iraq." In: Are Knudsen and Sari Hanafi (eds) *Palestinian Refugees: Identity, Space and Place in the Levant*, 13–28. Abingdon: Routledge.

Pitel, Laura, and Arthur Beesley. 2016. "Erdogan threatens to let 3m Refugees into Europe." *Financial Times*, 25 November. www.ft.com/content/c5197e60-b2fc11e6-9c37-5787335499a0. Accessed on 31 January 2021.

Pfaff, Steven. 2006. *Exit-Voice Dynamics and the Collapse of East Germany: The Crisis of Leninism and the Revolution of 1989.* Durham, NC: Duke University Press.

Queen Rania. 2016. "Queen Rania's Speech at UN Summit for Refugees and Migrants." Queen Rania Official Website (blog). 19 September 2016. www.queenrania.jo/en/media/speeches/queen-ranias-speech-un-summit-refugees-and-migrants-ny-usa. Accessed on 31 January 2021.

Radio Free Asia. 2017. "Uyghurs Studying Abroad Ordered Back to Xinjiang Under Threat to Families." www.rfa.org/english/news/uyghur/ordered-05092017155554.html. Accessed on 31 January 2021.

Rahmy, Ali Abdel Rahman. 1981. *The Egyptian Policy in the Arab World: Intervention in Yemen, 1962–1967: Case Study.* Geneva: University of Geneva.

Reed, John. 2017. "EU Accord Opens Door for Jordan." *Financial Times*, 30 May. www.ft.com/content/ccd2ee20bad1-11e6-8b45-b8b81dd5d080. Accessed on 31 January 2021.

Reidy, Eric. 2016. "EU-Turkey Refugee Deal Puts Smuggling on Pause," *Al-Jazeera*, 29 April. www.aljazeera.com/news/2016/04/eu-turkey-refugee-deal-puts-smuggling-pause-160424074234523.html. Accessed on 31 January 2021.

Reuters. 2016a. "Turkey's Erdoğan Threatened to Flood Europe with Migrants." *Reuters*, 8 February. www.reuters.com/article/us-europe-migrants-eu-turkey-idUSKCN0VH1R0. Accessed on 31 January 2021.

Reuters. 2016b. "EU Relaxes Trade Rules with Jordan to Create Jobs for Syrian Refugees." *Reuters*, 21 July. www.reuters.com/article/us-mideast-crisis-syria-jordan-refugees-idUSKCN1012M4. Accessed on 31 January 2021.

Reuters. 2017a. "Lebanon Near 'Breaking Point' Over Syrian Refugee Crisis: Pm Hariri." 31 March. www.reuters.com/article/us-mideast-crisis-syria-lebanon/lebanon-near-breaking-point-over-syrian-refugee-crisis-pm-hariri-idUSKBN1722JM. Accessed on 31 January 2021.

Reuters. 2017b. "More Than 300 Syrian Refugees Rescued, Arrive in Cyprus." *Reuters*, 10 September. www.reuters.com/article/us-cyprus-migrants/more-than-300-syrian-refugees-rescued-arrive-in-cyprus-idUSKCN1BL0DE. Accessed on 31 January 2021.

Rodriguez, Robyn Magalit. 2010. *Migrants for Export: How the Philippine State Brokers Labor to the World.* Minneapolis, MN: University of Minnesota Press.

Rodriguez, Robyn Magalit, and Helen Schwenken. 2013. "Becoming a Migrant at Home: Subjectivation Processes in Migrant-Sending Countries Prior to Departure." *Population, Space and Place* 19 (4): 375–88.

Roy, Delwin A. 1991. "Egyptian Emigrant Labor: Domestic Consequences." *Middle Eastern Studies* 27 (4): 551–82.

Ryan, Curtis R. 2009. *Inter-Arab Alliances: Regime Security and Jordanian Foreign Policy.* Gainesville, FL: University Press of Florida.

Sadat, Anwar. 1974. The October Working Paper. Cairo: Ministry of Information, State Information Service.

Sadat, Anwar. 1978. *Al-Bahth 'an Al-Dhat.* Cairo: Modern Egyptian Library.

Sadat, Anwar. 1978. *In Search of Identity: An Autobiography.* New York, NY: Harper & Row.

Sadiq, Kamal. 2009. *Paper Citizens: How Illegal Immigrants Acquire Citizenship in Developing Countries.* New York: Oxford University Press.

Sahraoui, Nina. 2015. "Acquiring 'Voice' Through 'Exit': How Moroccan Emigrants Became a Driving Force of Political and Socio-Economic Change." *The Journal of North African Studies* 20 (4): 522–39.

Saleh, Saniyah 'Abd al-Wahhab. 1979. "Attitudinal and Social Structural Aspects of the Brain Drain: The Egyptian Case." *Cairo Papers in Social Science* 5 (2): 1–132.

Sassen, Saskia. 1988. *The Mobility of Labor and Capital: A Study in International Investment and Labor Flow.* Cambridge: Cambridge University Press.

Sayigh, Yezid. 1991. "The Gulf Crisis: Why the Arab Regional Order Failed." *International Affairs* 67 (3): 487–507.

Sayyid-Marsot, Afaf Lutfi. 2007. *A History of Egypt: From the Arab Conquest to the Present.* Second Edition. Cambridge: Cambridge University Press.

Schenk, Caress. 2016. "Assessing Foreign Policy Commitment Through Migration Policy in Russia." *Demokratizatsiya: The Journal of Post-Soviet Democratization* 24 (4): 475–499.

Schiller, Nina Glick, Linda Basch, and Cristina Szanton Blanc. 1995. "From Immigrant to Transmigrant: Theorizing Transnational Migration." *Anthropological Quarterly* 68 (1): 48–63.

Schmidt, Dana Adams. 1968. *Yemen: The Unknown War.* London: Bodley Head.

Seccombe, Ian J. 1985. "International Labor Migration in the Middle East: A Review of Literature and Research, 1974–84." *International Migration Review* 19 (2): 335–52.

Seeberg, Peter, and Jan Claudius Völkel. 2020. "Introduction: Arab responses to EU foreign and security policy incentives: Perspectives on migration diplomacy and institutionalized flexibility in the Arab Mediterranean turned upside down." *Mediterranean Politics.* DOI: 10.1080/13629395.2020.1758451

Sell, Ralph R. 1988. "Egyptian International Labor Migration and Social Processes: Toward Regional Integration." *International Migration Review* 22 (3): 87–108.

Shaheen, Kareem. 2017. "US-Turkey Row Escalates with Tit-for-Tat Travel and Visa Restrictions." *The Guardian.* www.theguardian.com/world/2017/oct/09/us-suspends-handling-of-visas-in-turkey-after-arrest-of-consulate-staffer. Accessed on 31 January 2021.

Shain, Yossi. 2007. *Kinship & Diasporas in International Affairs.* Ann Arbor, MI: University of Michigan Press.

Shain, Yossi, and Aharon Barth. 2003. "Diasporas and International Relations Theory." *International Organization* 57 (3): 449–79.

Shami, Seteney. 1999. "Emigration Dynamics in Jordan, Palestine and Lebanon." In: R. Appleyard (ed.), *Emigration Dynamics in Developing Countries: Vol. IV: The Arab Region,* 128–201. Aldershot: Ashgate.

Shin, Adrian J. 2017. "Tyrants and Migrants Authoritarian Immigration Policy." *Comparative Political Studies* 50 (1): 14–40.

Shoufi, Eva. 2015. "A New Face for the Exploitation of Syrian Workers in Lebanon?" *Al-Akhbar,* 20 February. https://english.al-akhbar.com/node/23883. Accessed on 31 January 2021.

Simmons, Beth, and Zachery Elkins. 2005. "On Waves, Clusters and Diffusion: A Conceptual Framework." *Annals of the American Academy of Political and Social Science* 598 (1): 33–51.

Simon, Gildas. 1979. *L'espace Des Travailleurs Tunisiens En France: Structures Et Fonctionnement D'un Champ Migratoire International.* Poitiers: G. Simon.

Soliman, Samer. 2011. *The Autumn of Dictatorship: Fiscal Crisis and Political Change in Egypt under Mubarak.* Stanford, CA: Stanford University Press.

Stahl, Charles W., and Reginald Thomas Appleyard. 2007. *Migration and Development in the Pacific Islands: Lessons from the New Zealand Experience.* Canberra: Australian Agency for International Development.

Stedman, Stephen John, and Fred Tanner. 2004. *Refugee Manipulation: War, Politics, and the Abuse of Human Suffering.* Washington, DC: Brookings Institution Press.

Tadros, Mariz. 2013. *Copts at the Crossroads: The Challenges of Building Inclusive Democracy in Contemporary Egypt.* Cairo: The American University in Cairo Press.

Talani, Leila Simona. 2010. *From Egypt to Europe: Globalisation and Migration Across the Mediterranean.* London: Tauris Academic Studies.

Tarrow, Sidney G. 2005. *The New Transnational Activism.* Cambridge Studies in Contentious Politics. New York, NY: Cambridge University Press.

Tasney, Oisín. 2016. *International Politics of Authoritarian Rule.* Oxford: Oxford University Press.

Teitelbaum, Michael S. 1984. "Immigration, Refugees, and Foreign Policy." *International Organization* 38 (3): 429–50.

Teitelbaum, Michael S. 2001. "International Migration: Predicting the Unknowable." In: Myron Weiner and Sharon Stanton Russell (eds) *Demography and National Security,* 21–37. New York, NY: Berghahn Books.

The Economist. 2016. "To Silence Dissidents, Gulf States Are Revoking Their Citizenship." *The Economist,* 26 November. www.economist.com/news/middle-east-and-africa/21710679-many-are-left-stateless-result-silence-dissidents-gulf-states-are. Accessed on 31 January 2021.

The Guardian. 2015. "WFP to Cut Food Vouchers for Syrian Refugees in Jordan and Lebanon," 1 July. www.theguardian.com/global-development/2015/jul/01/syria-refugees-food-vouchers-cut-lebanon-jordan-wfp-un. Accessed on 31 January 2021.

The Times of India. 2016. "Afghanistan Deports 250 Pakistanis Due to Border Tension". *The Times of India.* 28 August. http://timesofindia.indiatimes.com/world/south-asia/Afghanistan-deports-250-Pakistanis-due-to-border-tension/articleshow/53896729.cms. Accessed on 31 January 2021.

Thiollet, Hélène. 2011. "Migration as Diplomacy: Labor Migrants, Refugees, and Arab Regional Politics in the Oil-Rich Countries." *International Labor and Working-Class History* 79 (1): 103–21.

Tibi, Bassam. 1998. *Conflict and War in the Middle East: From Interstate War to New Security.* Second Edition. London: Palgrave Macmillan.

Torpey, John. 1998. "Coming and Going: On the State Monopolization of the Legitimate 'Means of Movement.'" *Sociological Theory* 16 (3): 239–59.

Trebous, Madeleine. 1970. *Migration and Development - The Case of Algeria.* Paris: Development Center of the Organization for Economic Cooperation and Development.

Tsourapas, Gerasimos. 2013. "The Other Side of a Neoliberal Miracle: Economic Reform and Political De-Liberalization in Ben Ali's Tunisia." *Mediterranean Politics* 18 (1): 23–41.

Tsourapas, Gerasimos. 2014. "Notes from the Field: Researching emigration in post-2011 Egypt." *American Political Science Association Migration & Citizenship Newsletter* 2 (2): 58–63.

Tsourapas, Gerasimos. 2015a. "The Politics of Egyptian Migration to Libya." *Middle East Research and Information Project*. www.merip.org/mero/mero031715. Accessed on 31 January 2021.

Tsourapas, Gerasimos. 2015b. "Why Do States Develop Multi-Tier Emigrant Policies? Evidence from Egypt." *Journal of Ethnic and Migration Studies* 41 (13): 2192–2214.

Tsourapas, Gerasimos. 2016. "Nasser's Educators & Agitators across al-Watan al-'Arabi: Tracing the Foreign Policy Importance of Egyptian Regional Migration, 1952–1967." *British Journal of Middle Eastern Studies* 43 (3): 324–41.

Tsourapas, Gerasimos. 2017a. "Migration Diplomacy in the Global South: Cooperation, Coercion & Issue-Linkage in Gaddafi's Libya." *Third World Quarterly* 38 (10): 2367–85.

Tsourapas, Gerasimos. 2017b. "The Politics of 'Exit': Emigration & Subject-Making Processes in Modern Egypt." *Journal of Middle East and North African Migration Studies* 4 (1): 29–49.

Tsourapas, Gerasimos. 2018. "Labor Migrants as Political Leverage: Migration Interdependence and Coercion in the Mediterranean." *International Studies Quarterly* 62 (2): 383–95.

Tsourapas, Gerasimos. 2019a. "The Syrian Refugee Crisis and Foreign Policy Decision-Making in Jordan, Lebanon, and Turkey." *Journal of Global Security Studies* 4 (4): 464–81.

Tsourapas, Gerasimos. 2019b. *The Politics of Migration in Modern Egypt: Strategies for Regime Survival in Autocracies*. Cambridge: Cambridge University Press.

Tsourapas, Gerasimos. 2020a. "The Long Arm of the Arab State." *Ethnic and Racial Studies* 43 (2): 351–70.

Tsourapas, Gerasimos. 2020b. "Global Autocracies: Strategies of Transnational Repression, Legitimation, and Co-Optation in World Politics." *International Studies Review*. DOI: 10.1093/isr/viaa061.

Tsuda, Takeyuki (ed.) 2009. *Diasporic Homecomings: Ethnic Return Migration in Comparative Perspective*. Stanford, CA: Stanford University Press.

Turner, Frederick Jackson. 1920. *The Frontier in American History*. New York, NY: H. Holt and Company.

Turner, Lewis. 2015. "Explaining the (Non-) Encampment of Syrian Refugees: Security, Class and the Labour Market in Lebanon and Jordan." *Mediterranean Politics* 20 (3): 386–404.

United Arab Republic. 1958. *Nasser's Speeches and Press Interviews*. Cairo: UAR Information Department, 246–47.

United Arab Republic. 1959. *Nasser's Speeches and Press Interviews*. Cairo: UAR Information Department.

United Nations. 1949. *Final Report of the United Nations Economic Survey Mission for the Middle East: The technical supplement*. New York, NY: United Nations.

United Nations High Commissioner for Refugees. 2013. "From Slow Boil to Breaking Point: A Real-Time Evaluation of UNHCR's Response to the Syrian Refugee Emergency." www.unhcr.org/52b83e539.pdf. Accessed on 31 January 2021.

US Department of State. 1994. "1993 Human Rights Report: Libya." www.refworld.org/docid/3ae6aa184c.html. Accessed on 31 January 2021.

Van Hear, Nicholas. 1998. *New Diasporas: The Mass Exodus, Dispersal and Regrouping of Migrant Communities*. London: University College London Press.

Van Heelsum, Anja. 2002. *Explaining Trends, Developments and Activities of Moroccan Organisations in the Netherlands*. Paper for the Sociaal Wetenschappelijke

Studiedagen. Amsterdam: Institute for Migration and Ethnic Studies (IMES), University of Amsterdam.

Vanderbush, Walt, and Patrick Jude Haney. 2005. *The Cuban Embargo: The Domestic Politics of an American Foreign Policy*. Pittsburgh, PA: University of Pittsburgh Press.

Vandewalle, Dirk. 2012. *A History of Modern Libya*. Second Edition. Cambridge: Cambridge University Press.

Varadarajan, Latha. 2010. *The Domestic Abroad: Diasporas in International Relations*. New York, NY: Oxford University Press.

Vatikiotis, P. J. 1991. *The History of Modern Egypt: From Muhammad Ali to Mubarak*. Fourth Edition. Baltimore, MD: Johns Hopkins University Press.

von Soest, Christian. 2015. "Democracy Prevention: The International Collaboration of Authoritarian Regimes." *European Journal of Political Research* 54 (4): 623–38.

Waterbury, John. 1975. "The Opening, Part III: De-Nasserisation." *American Universities Field Staff*, Northeast Africa Series, 20 (4).

Waterbury, John. 1983. *The Egypt of Nasser and Sadat: The Political Economy of Two Regimes*. Princeton NJ: Princeton University Press.

Weiner, Myron. 1985. "On International Migration and International Relations". *Population and Development Review* 11 (3) 441–55.

Weiner, Myron. 1992. "Security, Stability, and International Migration." *International Security* 17 (3): 91–126.

Weiner, Myron, and Michael S. Teitlebaum. 2001. *Political Demography, Demographic Engineering*. New York, NY: Berghahn Books.

Weyland, Kurt. 2010. "The Diffusion of Regime Contention in European Democratization, 1830-1940." *Comparative Political Studies* 43 (8–9): 1148–76.

Whitaker, Beth Elise. 2002. "Refugees in Western Tanzania: The Distribution of Burdens and Benefits Among Local Hosts." *Journal of Refugee Studies* 15 (4) 339–58.

Whitehead, Laurence (ed.) 1996. *The International Dimensions of Democratization: Europe and the Americas*. Oxford: Oxford University Press.

Wickham, Carrie Rosefsky. 2005. *Mobilizing Islam: Religion, Activism and Political Change in Egypt*. New York, NY: Columbia University Press.

Wickramasekara, Piyasiri. 2015. Bilateral Agreements and Memoranda of Understanding on Migration of Low Skilled Workers: A Review. Geneva: International Labour Organization. www.ilo.org/wcmsp5/groups/public/—ed_protect/—protrav/—migrant/documents/publication/wcms_385582.pdf. Accessed on 9 February 2021.

Wilson, Rodney. 1994. "The Economic Relations of the Middle East: Toward Europe or within the Region?" *Middle East Journal* 48 (2): 268–87.

World Bank. 2016. Concessional Financing Facility Funds Projects to Support Refugees and Host Communities Impacted by the Syrian Crisis. Press Release. Washington, DC: The World Bank. www.worldbank.org/en/news/press-release/2016/07/28/concessional-financing-facility-funds-projects-to-support-refugees. Accessed on 31 January 2021.

Wynn, Wilton. 1959. *Nasser of Egypt: The Search for Dignity*. Clinton, MA: Colonial Press.

Yom, Sean L. 2015. "The New Landscape of Jordanian Politics: Social Opposition, Fiscal Crisis, and the Arab Spring." *British Journal of Middle Eastern Studies* 42 (3): 284–300.

Zohry, Ayman, and Priyanka Debnath. 2015. *A Study on the Dynamics of the Egyptian Diaspora: Strengthening Development Linkages*. Cairo: International Organization for Migration.

Zohry, Ayman, and Barbara Harrell-Bond. 2003. *Contemporary Egyptian Migration: An Overview of Voluntary and Forced Migration.* Brighton: University of Sussex Development Research Centre on Migration, Globalisation and Poverty. www.hic-mena.org/img/documents/DRC%20working%20paper%203-Egypt.pdf. Accessed on 9 February 2021.

Zolberg, Aristide R. 1988. "The Roots of American Refugee Policy." *Social Research*, 55 (4) 649–78.

Zolberg, Aristide R. 1989. "The Next Waves: Migration Theory for a Changing World." *The International Migration Review* 23 (3): 403–30.

Zolberg, Aristide R., Astri Suhrke, and Sergio Aguayo. 1989. *Escape from Violence: Conflict and the Refugee Crisis in the Developing World.* New York, NY: Oxford University Press.

Index

EU authorised representative for GPSR:
Easy Access System Europe, Mustamäe tee 50,
10621 Tallinn, Estonia
gpsr.requests@easproject.com

www.ingramcontent.com/pod-product-compliance
Lightning Source LLC
Chambersburg PA
CBHW071534300326
41935CB00049B/1474